NEIGHBOURS AND THE LAW

AUSTRALIA AND NEW ZEALAND
The Law Book Company Ltd.
Sydney : Melbourne : Perth

CANADA AND U.S.A.
The Carswell Company Ltd.
Agincourt, Ontario

INDIA
N. M. Tripathi Private Ltd.
Bombay
and
Eastern Law House Private Ltd.
Calcutta and Delhi
M.P.P. House
Bangalore

ISRAEL
Steimatzky's Agency Ltd.
Jerusalem : Tel Aviv : Haifa

MALAYSIA : SINGAPORE : BRUNEI
Malayan Law Journal (Pte.) Ltd.
Singapore and Kuala Lumpur

NEIGHBOURS
AND THE LAW

JOHN PUGH-SMITH M.A. (OXON)
of Gray's Inn, Barrister, and of the Western Circuit

LONDON   SWEET & MAXWELL   1988

Published in 1988 by
Sweet & Maxwell Limited
11 New Fetter Lane, London
Computerset by Promenade Graphics Ltd.,
Cheltenham
Printed and bound in Great Britain by
Butler and Tanner Limited, Frome, Somerset

British Library Cataloguing in Publication Data
Pugh-Smith, John
  Neighbours and the law.
  1. England. Real property. Disputes. Law
  I. Title
  344.2064'3

  ISBN 0–421–36570–6

PREFACE

"Neighbours' disputes" tend to be regarded by practitioners as the pariah of litigation. They frequently lead to complex, emotionally charged and protracted proceedings which often call upon the furthest reaches of legal knowledge and law libraries. To help ease these painful experiences, with which I remain all too familiar, I have attempted to bring the various divergent areas of law under this heading beneath one cover.

The aim of this book is to provide a concise statement of the main areas of law with which the lawyer in general practice is likely to be faced, together with a few more esoteric areas as a matter of interest. The reader should, of course, refer to the relevant specialist works where more detailed information is required on a particular subject. Of necessity, I have had to summarise much basic law. I apologise, in advance, for re-stating the obvious on occasions and for requiring the reader to refer extensively to the footnotes for the less obvious. The legal perspective is taken principally from the position of the residential freeholder. Wherever applicable, I have also included references to the position of the lessee, the provisions of whose lease are likely to be highly relevant in addition to the general legal considerations adumbrated in the text. For ease of reference I have tended to use the general term "landowner" to describe the person whose rights are to be upheld. However, there are certain topics where particular terminology has had to be adopted; but I hope that the reader's understanding will not be swept away by a sudden flood of upper and lower riparian owners, dominant and servient tenements and the like.

I have attempted to state the law, so far as the constraints of legal research and publishing allow, as at April 1, 1988.

Despite the hopes expressed in Chapter 7 (Planning Control) the final form of the 1988 General Development Order, the Planning (Applications) Regulations and the Inquiries Procedure Rules is still not known. The Department of the Environment expect to publish this material during the course of Summer 1988, and no doubt frustratingly just before or just after this book is published.

On the other hand, in *Porter* v. *Honey, The Times*, April 7, 1988, the Divisional Court has, at last, determined that deemed planning consent for the display of estate agents' "for sale" boards outside a residential property is limited to a total of one advertisement per sale or letting under the present Class III(a) of regulation 14 of the Town and Country Planning (Control of Advertisements) Regulations 1984 (S.I. 1984 No. 421). With effect from October 28, 1988, a new Class III(a) (introduced by the Town and Country Planning (Control of Advertisements) (Amendment No. 2) Regulations 1987 (S.I. 1987 No. 2227)) will limit "for sale" boards on residential properties to a single board not exceeding 0.5 square metres in area (or two joined boards not exceeding 0.6 square metres in area) and to one board not exceeding 2 square metres in area (or two joined boards not exceeding 2.3 square metres) on commercial, industrial and agricultural premises. In all instances if the board is displayed on a building it must not project more than one metre from the face of that building.

As a matter for further debate readers should also note that there may now, in law, be no right to inspect plans deposited under the Building Act 1984 for the purposes of Building Regulations approval (see [1988] J.P.L. 246).

Finally, this Preface would be incomplete without an expression of my gratitude to the editorial staff at Sweet & Maxwell for their perseverance with this project (and especially with my handwriting), to my family for their support and encouragement and to all those "neighbours" without whom the reasons for writing this book would never have arisen.

John Pugh-Smith
Inner Temple,
April 15, 1988.

CONTENTS

TABLE OF CASES

TABLE OF STATUTES

TABLE OF STATUTORY INSTRUMENTS

TABLE OF RULES OF THE SUPREME COURT

1 BOUNDARIES

Description

Documents of title

The best description and evidence of ownership of the landowner's boundaries will be in his documents of title.

The part of a deed which describes the property which has been conveyed or leased is known as "the parcels" or "parcels clause." In order to avoid disputes, the parcels clause should describe the property with reasonable certainty to make it identifiable, *e.g.* by giving a name or some denoting mark or by identifying it by measurements or abuttals[1] or by reference to a plan. Help will invariably be gained from the choice of

Descriptive words   descriptive words:

"Land"   This is the most concise word that can be used. It is defined by statute[2] as including

> "land of any tenure, and mines and minerals, whether or not held apart from the surface, buildings or parts of buildings (whether the division is horizontal, vertical or made in any other way) and other corporeal hereditaments . . . "

If there is nothing to restrict its technical meaning by express reference (*e.g.* to a marsh or meadow) the word "land" includes all kinds, whether arable, meadow or otherwise,[3] all buildings erected on it,[4] including not only the site but also the structure,[5] everything on or under the soil including, subject to the rights of British Coal (formerly the National Coal Board) and the Crown, all mines and minerals beneath it and the air space above it.[6]

The rights impliedly ganted by section 62 of the Law of Property Act 1925 into a conveyance should also be borne in mind. The material parts of the section state as follows:

> "(1) *A conveyance of land* shall be deemed to include and shall by virtue of this Act operate to convey, with the land, all buildings, erections, fixtures, commons, hedges, ditches, fences, ways, waters, watercourses, liberties, privileges, easements, rights, and advantages whatsoever, appertaining or reputed to appertain to the land, or any part thereof, or at the time of conveyance, demised, occupied, or enjoyed with, or reputed or known as part or parcel of or appurtenant to the land or any part thereof.

---

[1] *i.e.* the boundaries.
[2] L.P.A. 1925, s.205, (*i*), (*ix*).
[3] *e.g. Cooke* v. *Yates* (1827) 4 Bing.90.
[4] *Newcomen* v. *Coulsen* (1877) 5 Ch.D. 133 at 142; but the "building" should be affixed to the land. See *e.g. Dean* v. *Andrews* (1986) 52 P. & C.R. 17 (freestanding greenhouse only a chattel); and also *Holland* v. *Hodgson* (1872) L.R. 7 C.P. 328 and *H. E. Dibble* v. *Moore* [1970] 2 Q.B. 181.
[5] *Bisney* v. *Swanston* (1972) 225 F.G. 2299.
[6] *Ibid.* See pp. 94–96, 106–108.

(2) *A conveyance of land, having houses or other buildings thereon*, shall be deemed to include and shall by virtue of this Act operate to convey, with the land, houses, or other buildings, all outhouses, erections, fixtures, cellars, areas, courts, courtyards, cisterns, sewers, gutters, drains, ways, passages, lights, watercourses, liberties, privileges, easements, rights, and advantages whatsoever, appertaining or reputed to appertain to the land, houses, or other buildings conveyed, or any of them, or any part thereof, or, at the time of conveyance, demised, occupied, or enjoyed with, or reputed or known as part or parcel of or appurtenant to, the land, houses, or other buildings conveyed, or any of them, or any part thereof."

"Appurtenances"   Frequently, this term is found in the expression "land and appurtenances." Primarily, the word means (and conveys) what strictly belongs to the land as a feature or right.[7] However, in certain contexts it can mean "usually held or enjoyed with the land."[8] Accordingly, the phrase "with the appurtenances" does not include a feature of the land or buildings which although used for the benefit of the demised property does not form part of it (*e.g.* a staircase to the upper floors of an adjoining building), nor does it include a part of the building which has been separated from the demised property and has not been occupied with it for many years prior to the demise.[9] On the other hand the "general words" of section 62 of the Law of Property Act 1925 may well pass more rights than are implied by the word "appurtenances."[10]

"Premises"   In its strict and original sense, this word used to be an alternative expression for the word "parcels" in the context "the said premises" meaning "that which had gone before."[11] However, it has been taken to mean "appurtenances" as in the phrase "mansion house gardens and premises"[12] and has also been used as an informal meaning for the word building.[13] It should be regarded as meaning, generally, real property of one sort or another, including a cave.[14]

In addition, certain other words and phrases have now acquired technical meanings. The more usual expressions are set out below:

"Abut"   This denotes touching or bordering the land in question. Thus, where a hoarding was separated from a road by a narrow strip of land, it was held not to abut onto the street.[15]

---

[7] *Bolton* v. *Bolton* (1879) 11 Ch.D. 968.
[8] *Westwood* v. *Heywood* [1921] 2. Ch. 130; *Trim* v. *Sturminster R.D.C.* [1938] 2 K.B. 508.
[9] *Kerslake* v. *White* (1819) 2 Stark. 508.
[10] See further p. 35.
[11] *Gardiner* v. *Sevenoaks R.D.C.* [1950] 2 All E.R. 84 at 85.
[12] *Lethbridge* v. *Lethbridge* (1862) 31 L.J. Ch. 737.
[13] *County Hotel Co.* v. *L.N.W. Railway Co.* [1918] 2 K.B. 251.
[14] *Gardiner* v. *Sevenoaks R.D.C.* [1950] 2 All E.R. 84.
[15] *Mayor, Aldermen and Councillors of Hackney* v. *Lee Conservancy Board* [1904] 2 K.B. 541 at 554.

"Adjacent, adjoining and contiguous"   These denote proximity (or "neighbouring") without the necessity of physical contact.[16] However, when used in conjunction with the word "land," the word "adjoining" in its primary sense means that which was near so as to touch, in some part, the land which it is said to adjoin.[17]

"Appertaining" or "belonging to"   These expressions originally referred to (and included) such rights as were attached to the land by reason of the fact that the land had at one time been part of a manor over which the rights had existed. The expressions now mean "land normally occupied with," *e.g.* demised premises.[18]

"Bounded by"   The use of this expression will depend upon the particular circumstances of the case. Where adjoining properties are bounded by a hedge or a ditch, such features can be wholly included or excluded.[19] However, where the feature is the potential subject matter of an independent title (*e.g.* a house or land) then that feature will normally be excluded from the subject matter of the grant.[20] Where a building is bounded by an external wall, both sides of that wall will normally be included.[21]

"Bungalow"   This has been defined as a building of which the walls, with the exception of any gables, are no higher than the ground floor and of which the roof starts at a point not substantially higher than the top of the wall of the ground floor.[22]

"Curtilage"   This means land, in the physical sense, which belongs to a house or church[23] and will include "a garden, yard, field or place of void ground lying near and belonging to the messuage."[24] It has, however, been held not to include an orchard behind a house and its outbuildings.[25]

"Dwellinghouse"   This refers to that part of the building in which occupant has dwelt but can also include a cellar, even though it has been used for storage in connection with the adjoining property.[26]

"Excepting" and "reserving"   An "exception" is something in existence at the time of the grant (*e.g.* minerals) which is left out of it. As a matter of construction, it will be construed in favour of the grantor, having been inserted for the benefit of the grantor.[27] A "reservation" concerns some benefit which is to be created.

---

[16] *Cave* v. *Horsell* [1912] 3 K.B. 533 at 544.
[17] *Re Ecclesiastical Commissioners for England's Conveyance* [1936] Ch. 430.
[18] *Evans* v. *Angell* (1858) 26 Beav. 202 at 205.
[19] *Re Belfast Dock Act 1854, ex p. Earl of Ranfurly* (1867) 1 I.R. Eq. 128 at 140.
[20] *Lord* v. *Sydney City Commissioners* (1859) 12 Moo.P.C.C. 473.
[21] See, *e.g. Goldfoot* v. *Welch* [1914] 1 Ch. 213; *Sturge* v. *Hackett* [1962] 1 W.L.R. 1257.
[22] *Ward* v. *Paterson* [1929] 2 Ch. 396.
[23] *Re St. John's Church, Bishop's Hatfield* [1967] P. 113.
[24] *Termes De La Ley* (1671 ed.), as cited in *Re St. John's Church*, above.
[25] *Asquith* v. *Griffin* (1884) 48 J.P. 724; *Brass* v. *London County Council* [1904] 2 K.B. 336.
[26] *Grigsby* v. *Melville* [1974] 1 W.L.R. 80.
[27] *Savill Bros. Ltd.* v. *Bethell* [1902] 2 Ch. 523.

Originally, the term only applied to the reservation of services to be provided by a tenant (*e.g.* the payment of rent) but is now applied, for example, to a re-grant of a right of way or a *profit à prendre*.[28] In cases of doubt, a reservation will be construed against the purchaser of a property, as the re-grantor, rather than the vendor.[29]

"Farm"   This includes not only the principal dwelling-house but also all arable land, meadow, pasture, wood and the like belonging to or occupied within it.[30]

"Farmbuilding"   This expression includes farmhouses.[31]

"House," "messuage" and "cottage"   These include such land commonly occupied therewith as is reasonably necessary (*e.g.* outbuildings, orchard, garden and courtyard[32]) as distinguished from being a matter of pleasure.[33]

"House and premises"   In this context the word "premises" only refers to that question intimately connected with the house and will not include an adjoining meadow.[34]

"Land covered by water" and "pool"   These expressions pass the water and the soil forming the bed.[35]

"Water"   This word passes only the right to the water itself and any fishing rights.[36]

"Woods" and "trees"   The former term, both in the singular and in the plural, includes the soil as well as all the foliage,[37] whereas the word "trees" simply covers trees.[38]

Principles of construction

Where possible, full effect should be given to all terms of description, whether they have a general or a specific meaning.[38a] However, if different parts of the description are inconsistent, then that part which defines the property clearly and definitely will be accepted and the remainder may be disregarded, following the maxim *falsa demonstratio non nocet cum de corpore constat, i.e.* a false description does not vitiate (the deed) where there is no doubt as to who the person is meant.[39] For example, if

[28] *e.g. Lady Dunsany* v. *Bedworth* (1979) 38 P. & C.R. 546.
[29] *St. Edmunsbury & Ipswich Diocesan Board of Finance* v. *Clark (No. 2)* [1975] 1 W.L.R. 468.
[30] *Whitfield* v. *Langdale* (1875) 1 Ch.D. 61.
[31] *Cooke* v. *Cholmondeley* (1858) 4 Drew. 326.
[32] *e.g. Re Willis* [1911] 2 Ch. 563.
[33] *Pulling* v. *London, Chatham & Dover Railway Co.* (1864) 10 L.T. 741.
[34] *Minton* v. *Geiger* (1873) 28 L.T. 449.
[35] *Broadbent* v. *Ramsbotham* (1856) 11 Exch. 602.
[36] *e.g. Bradford Corpn.* v. *Ferrand* [1902] 2 Ch. 655; *Ecroyd* v. *Goulthard* [1898] 2 Ch. 358 at 366.
[37] *Whistler* v. *Paslow* (1618) Cro. Jac. 487; 79 E.R. 416.
[38] *Stanley* v. *White* (1811) 14 Fast. 332; 104 E.R. 630.
[38a] The Court of Appeal has recently stated that a question of construction is a question of law in respect of which no burden of proof lay on either side, although the onus was on a party relying on surrounding circumstances as an aid to construction to prove those circumstances (see *Scott* v. *Martin* [1987] 2 All E.R. 813 at 817).
[39] *Llewellyn* v. *Earl of Jersey* (1843) 11 M. & W. 183; *Eastwood* v. *Ashton* [1915] A.C. 900 at 914.

the premises are sufficiently described in specific terms (*e.g.* by naming the street or giving measurements) any additional erroneous description will be rejected as a *falsa demonstratio*. In applying this maxim, it is immaterial in what part of the description the error occurs.[40] However, this rule is subject to the rule *non accipi debent verba in demonstrationem falsam quae competunt in limitationem veram*, namely, that additional words are not rejected as importing a false description if they can be read as words of restriction. Therefore, if there is any doubt as to whether words are a *falsa demonstratio* or words of restriction, the latter must be assumed since the law will not assume that a description is erroneous or false.[41] It will then be a matter of construction to see which are the leading words of description and which are subordinate.[42]

Extrinsic evidence   It is only when no definite conclusion can be reached from the various parts of the deed that extrinsic evidence can be used in certain limited circumstances. For example, it may be used to show to what property the description applies[43] or what is included in the strict words of the deed.[44] However, such evidence will not be admissible if it tends to vary or contradict the deed.[45] Moreover, if an express agreement is made that the parties will be bound by a particular marking out of the land, such a marking will prevail, even though it may be incorrect.[46]

Rectification   Generally, a court will only rectify an instrument if it fails to record the intention of both parties.[47] "It presupposes a prior contract and it requires proof that, by common mistake, the final completed instrument as executed fails to give proper effect to the prior contract. For this purpose, evidence of what took place prior to the execution of the completed document is admissible and essential."[48] Rectification can also be ordered on the ground of unilateral mistake but only in the rare instance where the applicant can prove that he believed a particular term to be included in the contract and the other party concluded the contract with the omission or variation of that term in the knowledge that the first party believed the term to be included.[49] **Burden of proof**   In all cases involving rectification, the burden of proof on the applicant is a heavy one; and he must establish his case by evidence which leaves no fair and reasonable doubt that the deed does not embody the final intention of the parties.[50] Moreover, since rectification is an equitable remedy, the applicant may

[40] *Cowan* v. *Truefitt* [1899] 2 Ch. 309.
[41] *Eastwood* v. *Ashton* [1915] A.C. 900.
[42] *Cowen* v. *Truefitt Ltd.* [1899] 2 Ch. 309.
[43] *e.g. Fox* v. *Clarke* [1874] 9 Q.B. 565; *Spall* v. *Owen* (1981) 44 P. & C.R. 36.
[44] *Williams* v. *Morgan* (1850) 15 Q.B. 782.
[45] *Scarfe* v. *Adams* [1981] 1 All E.R. 843.
[46] *Willson* v. *Greene, Moss* [1971] 1 W.L.R. 635, following the otherwise unreported decision of the Court of Appeal in *Webb* v. *Nightingale* (1956–57) 107 L.J. 359.
[47] *Craddock Bros.* v. *Hunt* [1923] 2 Ch. 136.
[48] *Lovell & Christmas Ltd.* v. *Wall* (1911) 104 L.T. 85, *per* Cozens-Hardy M.R.; see also *Joscelyne* v. *Nissen* [1970] 2 Q.B. 86.
[49] *A. Roberts & Co. Ltd.* v. *Leicestershire C.C.* [1961] Ch. 555.
[50] *Fowler* v. *Fowler* (1859) 4 De G. & J. 250 at 265.

disentitle himself to relief as a result of delay. The effect of rectification is that the deed is to be read as if it had been originally drawn in its rectified form.[51] However, the deed does not have to be executed afresh but can be endorsed with a copy of the court order and read accordingly.

Plans

Construction   It is common conveyancing practice for the verbal description of land to be supplemented by reference to a plan.[52] Indeed, if the wording is ambiguous, even a plan annexed to the conveyance to which no direct reference is made may be considered.[53] The function of such a plan is usually to show where the land is located, not to define its boundaries.[54] Mere attachment of a plan to a conveyance does not warrant its accuracy.[55] Should the verbal description and the plan disagree, it is, once again, a question of construction as to which will prevail.

The following are examples of common conveyancing phraseology where wording is linked to a plan:

(1) "More particularly described"—The plan will prevail.[56]
(2) "More particularly delineated"—These words have the same effect.[57]
(3) "For identification only"—This phrase cannot over-rule a description in words.[58]
(4) "For the purposes of delineation only"—The same comment applies. In addition, the plan is to be regarded as not being true to scale.[59]

Ambiguity   The maxim *falsa demonstratio non nocet* can also apply here. For example, where the description stated that the boundary ran along the centre line of a hedge but added "which said piece of land is delineated on the plan drawn hereon" and the plan showed the boundary lines at the foot of the hedge, the plan was ignored.[60] Equally, a verbal description can prevail over an inaccurate plan[61] since, as a matter of construction, the description is to be read as a whole.[62]

Format   If the plan is to be of help, it follows that it must be sufficiently clear and detailed to be self-explanatory. Usually, the plan in question will either have formed part of another deed or be independent of the title (*e.g.* a tithe map or Ordnance Survey extract). In the latter instance, the edition copied should be

---

[51] *Cradock Bros.* v. *Hunt* [1923] 2 Ch. 136 at 151.
[52] *Wiggington & Milner Ltd.* v. *Winster Engineering Ltd.* [1978] 1 W.L.R. 1462.
[53] *Leachman* v. *L. & K. Richardson* [1969] 1 W.L.R. 1129; see also *Scott* v. *Martin* [1987] 2 All E.R. 813 (reference also made to a planning permission).
[54] *Moreton C. Cullimore (Gravels) Ltd.* v. *Routledge* (1977) 121 S.J. 202.
[55] *Re Sparrow and James' Contract* [1910] 2 Ch. 60.
[56] *Eastwood* v. *Ashton* [1915] A.C. 900.
[57] *Wallington* v. *Townsend* [1939] Ch. 588.
[58] *Hopgood* v. *Brown* [1955] 1 All E.R. 550 at 557–558. See also *Neilson* v. *Poole* (1969) 20 P. & C.R. 909 and *Wigginton Milner Ltd.* v. *Winster Engineering Ltd.* [1978] 1 W.L.R. 1462.
[59] *Re Freeman and Taylors Contract* (1907) 97 L.T. 39.
[60] *Maxted* v. *Plymouth Corporation* [1957] C.L.Y. 243.
[61] *Boyd Gibbins Ltd.* v. *Hockham* (1966) 199 E.G. 229.
[62] See also pp. 17–20 for the position where title is registered.

stated. Equally, although it may not be expressly mentioned that the plan is based upon or extracted from this source, such an assumption may be drawn from, for example, the presence of parcel numbers or "T" marks.

Tithe maps Although section 64 of the Tithe Act 1836 provided that the map or plan annexed to the instrument of tithe apportionment should be deemed satisfactory evidence of its accuracy, it was subsequently held that tithe commutation maps were never intended by the legislature to be the evidence of title to the land and therefore could not be conclusive evidence of the boundaries between two adjoining owners[63] or as evidence of the extent or existence of a footpath.[64]

Ordnance Survey maps It is the practice of the Ordnance Survey to draw the boundary line down the middle of features (*e.g.* hedges and fences) and general presumption should be ignored in such circumstances.[65]

"T" marks "T" marks either define ownership or the responsibility for the maintenance of the boundary feature. The convention is that the "T" is written with its cross-stroke parallel to the boundary and its down stroke touching the boundary on the side of the boundary of the property in whose ownership the fence lies or to whom its maintenance falls. Where no reference is made to "T" marks in the deed it can be no more than persuasive evidence of ownership. The same comment applies to the filed plan with a registered title in certain circumstances.[66]

"H" marks "H" marks are now used infrequently. They are intended to indicate a party wall. The "H" is written so that its vertical strokes are parallel to the boundary, one on each side of it. Without a verbal explanation, they cannot be regarded as of any evidential value.

Physical features

Where boundaries either follow or are defined by reference to certain physical features, advantage may be taken of certain legal presumptions which will apply unless or until rebutted by contrary evidence.[67] The following considerations apply:

Basements Where these premises extend under the street, they may be taken to extend up to the horizontal boundary between the highway and the sub-soil[67a] although no formal presumption yet exists to this effect.

Beach As a definition of a boundary the term "beach" may, prima facie, have the same meaning as seashore[68] but can extend

[63] *Wilberforce* v. *Hearfield* (1877) 5 Ch.D. 709.
[64] *Stoney* v. *Eastbourne R.D.C.* [1927] 1 Ch. 367; *Copestake* v. *West Sussex C.C.* [1911] 2 Ch. 331.
[65] See further pp. 8, 13.
[66] See further p. 19.
[67] *Beaufort (Duke of)* v. *Swansea Corporation* (1849) 3 Exch. 413 and see also pp. 19–20 where title is registered.
[67a] See "*Highways*" below. See also *Walker U.D.C.* v. *Wigham, Richardson and Co. Ltd., Wigham, Richardson and Co. Ltd.* v. *Walker U.D.C.* (1901) 85 L.T. 579 and Highways Act 1980, s.179 (control of construction of cellars, etc., under a street).
[68] *Government of State of Penang* v. *Beng Hong Oon* [1972] A.C. 425.

further to include land in apparent continuity with the beach at the high water mark until there is a change of vegetation or physical barrier or a road.[69]

Canals   No presumptions apply to canals or other artificial watercourses since they would have been dug originally by a person either on his own land or on land acquired from an adjoining owner for such a purpose.[70]

Commons   As a result of the Commons Registration Act 1965, all such land and rights must now have been registered.[71] Such information will be conclusive evidence of all matters so registered.[72] Accordingly, a determination of the boundaries of such land and those of any adjoining properties will have already been made as a result of such procedure.[73] Any unclaimed land will be vested in, for instance, the local authority.

Flats and maisonettes   There are no settled presumptions in respect of flats and maisonettes. Where part of a house is leased, the demise will normally include the external walls enclosing the holding, unless provision is made to the contrary in the lease.[74] The upper boundary is no lower than the underside of the floor-joists to which the ceiling is fixed.[75] The lower boundary will include at least some part of the floor.[76] The demise of a top floor flat may include the roof above it.[77]

Foreshore   See *Seashore* (below).

Forests   The boundaries of the royal forests were fixed by the Delimitation of Forests Act 1640. Reference should be made to special Acts of Parliament and letters patent as to disafforestation or transfer into private ownership.

Hedges and ditches   Where a bank or hedge[78] (or both) adjoin an artificial ditch, the presumption is that the boundary is on the edge of the ditch which is furthest from the features.[79] If more than one bank or hedge adjoin such a ditch, or there is one such feature without the other, then the presumption will not arise. Equally, where the ditch is a natural watercourse, it is unlikely that the presumption will be held to apply[80]; for the rationale behind it is that nobody constructing a ditch would intentionally commit a trespass by placing spoil on the adjoining land. It should also be noted that whilst it is Ordnance Survey practice to draw the boundary line down the middle of these features this

[69] *Tito* v. *Waddell (No. 2)* [1977] Ch. 106.
[70] *Chamber Colliery Co.* v. *Rochdale Canal Co.* [1895] A.C. 564.
[71] The closing date was August 1, 1970.
[72] See s.10. See also *Corpus Christi College* v. *Gloucestershire County Council* [1983] Q.B. 360.
[73] All plans and documents are open to public inspection.
[74] *Campden Hill Towers Ltd.* v. *Gardner* [1977] Q.B. 823.
[75] *Sturge* v. *Hackett* [1962] 1 W.L.R. 1257 at 1266.
[76] *Phelps* v. *City of London Corporation* [1916] 2 Ch. 255 at 264.
[77] *Cockburn* v. *Smith* [1924] 2 K.B. 119; *Fisher* v. *Winch* [1939] 1 K.B. 666.
[78] See also p. 9.
[79] *Noye* v. *Reed* (1827) 1 Man. & Ry. K.B. 63 at 65.
[80] *Marshall* v. *Taylor* [1895] 1 Ch. 641 at 647.

practice does not follow any presumption in law, although judicial notice has been taken of it.[81] However, where the limits and acreage of land conveyed were described by reference to the Ordnance Survey map, the boundary was taken as the centre line of the hedge.[82] Local customs may also be of relevance in this instance. For example, in North Norfolk, it is presumed that the hedge on the northern side of the land is owned by the adjoining owner in the absence of any specific statement to the contrary.

Highways If the highway is fenced or hedged on both sides, its area will be presumed to extend to such features but only if it can be shown that they were erected (or planted) to separate the adjoining land from the highway.[83] It may also be presumed that the boundary of any land adjoining the highway runs down the middle of that highway, but only where the conveyancing history of the land adjoining the highway is unknown. This presumption applies to streets in both town and country[84] and to private roads.[85] It extends to the subsoil but rarely to the surface because, in most instances, this will have been adopted by the highway authority in whom the legal estates vests.[86] The thickness of the surface depends on how much is required for "highway purposes."[87] The presumption is rebutted if the conveyance of the land refers to the road as an "intended road"[88] or where it has already been dedicated[89] or, in all probability, where the land conveyed forms part of a building estate.[90]

Houses It is presumed that a house is conveyed or demised in its entirety. Accordingly, foundations and projecting eaves will be included, although not shown on any plan, but not the air space between them.[91] Equally, in the absence of contrary evidence, there is a presumption that the boundary line runs down the middle of any shared wall.[92]

Lakes There is no settled presumption about the position of the boundary where properties in different ownership are separated by a lake.[93]

Railways No special presumptions apply since at the time of the construction of the railways the land had to be acquired, invariably, from the adjoining owner as a separate plot.[94] The

---

[81] *Davey* v. *Harrow Corporation* [1958] 1 Q.B. 60.
[82] *Fisher* v. *Winch* [1939] 1 K.B. 666.
[83] *Hinds and Diplock* v. *Brecon C.C.* [1938] 4 All E.R. 24; *Att.-Gen.* v. *Beynon* [1970] Ch. 1.
[84] *London & N.W. Railway Co.* v. *Westminster Corpn.* [1902] 1 Ch. 269.
[85] *Smith* v. *Howden* (1863) 14 C.B. (N.S.) 398.
[86] Highways Act 1980, s.263; L.P.A. 1925, s.7(1) and *Tithe Redemption Commission* v. *Runcorn U.D.C.* [1954] Ch. 383.
[87] *e.g. Baird* v. *Tunbridge Wells Corporation* [1894] 2 Q.B. 867.
[88] *Leigh* v. *Jack* (1879) L.R. 5 Ex. 264.
[89] *Re Whites' Charities* [1898] 1 Ch. 659.
[90] *e.g. Giles* v. *County Building Constructors (Hertford) Ltd.* (1971) 22 P. & C.R. 978.
[91] *Truckell* v. *Stock* [1957] 1 W.L.R. 161.
[92] L.P.A. 1925, s.38(1).
[93] *Marshall* v. *Ullswater Steam Navigation Co. Ltd.* (1863) 3 B. & S. 732.
[94] *Thompson* v. *Hickman* [1907] 1 Ch. 550.

boundary of a railway will usually include the boundary fence by reason of fencing obligations imposed by statute in the last century.[95]

Rivers   The bed of a *tidal* river at any point at which the water flows and reflows regularly belongs to the Crown, the boundary being medium high water mark unless it can be proved that a specific grant has been made by the Crown to a particular person.[96] So far as *non-tidal* rivers are concerned, the natural presumption is that the owner of the land abutting the river owns the bed up to the middle of the stream[97] but not islands.[98] Great accretions to either bank belong to that riparian owner, the midline boundary being automatically adjusted. However, if the river changes its course suddenly, the boundary will remain as before.[99]

Rooms   The precise boundaries of a room will vary according to whether its walls constitute outside walls or partitions. In the former instance, the whole of the outside wall will be included but only an undefined part of the partition wall.[1]

Seashore or foreshore   These words are synonymous. It may be presumed that the boundary between the seashore and any adjoining land follows the line reached by a medium high tide between ordinary spring and neap tides.[2] The lower boundary is taken as the medium low water mark. If the line of the medium high tide moves, then the boundary is taken from its new position; and it is a question of construction of the deed at which point the boundary shown be fixed.[3] Land reclaimed from the sea belongs to the Crown and not to the owner.[4]

Streams   The bed will be the joint property of the riparian owners. As with a non-tidal river each will own it to the middle of the stream.[5] There is, however, no usual presumption as to the ownership of the running water above.

Wires and pipes   Unless otherwise stated, these will become the property of the grantee, who may also have exclusive rights of use. Any easement will automatically carry ancillary rights of entry to the land for inspection, cleaning, repair and replacement.[6]

---

[95] Railways Clauses Consolidation Act 1845, s.68.
[96] *Att.-Gen.* v. *Lonsdale* (1868) L.R. 7 Eq. 377; *Govt. of Penang* v. *Beng Hong Oon* [1972] A.C. 425.
[97] *Blount* v. *Layard* [1891] 2 Ch. 681.
[98] *Great Torrington Commons Conservators* v. *Moore Stevens* [1904] 1 Ch. 347.
[99] *Southern Centre of Theosophy Inc.* v. *State of South Australia* [1982] A.C. 706.
[1] *Phelps* v. *City of London Corporation* [1916] 2 Ch. 255 at 263.
[2] *Mellor* v. *Walmesley* [1905] 2 Ch. 164.
[3] *Baxendale* v. *Instow Parish Council* [1981] 2 W.L.R. 1055.
[4] *Att.-Gen. of S. Nigeria* v. *John Holt & Co. (Liverpool) Ltd.* [1915] A.C. 599.
[5] See *Blount* v. *Layard* [1891] 2 Ch. 681.
[6] *Jones* v. *Pritchard* [1908] 1 Ch. 630.

Evidence of boundaries

Documents of record

Title deeds Discovery of the title deeds of the adjoining property may be obtained in the usual way since such documents are material to the conduct of the action. Previously, a third party called as a witness could refuse to produce his title deeds. However, this rule of evidence is now abolished for civil cases by section 16(1)(*b*) of the Civil Evidence Act 1968. Where the original title deeds relating to the land in question are in the possession of a third party (*e.g.* the mortgagee) then a *subpoena duces tecum* must be issued.

Public documents To constitute a public document[7] it must be proved[8]:

(1) that it was made with the intention that it should be retained or made available for public inspection; and
(2) that the person who undertook the survey was a public officer acting in a quasi-judicial capacity to the extent of satisfying himself as to the truth of the facts recorded.

The documents should also be produced from proper custody (*e.g.* local authority archives).

Examples that have been admitted have been admiralty charts and deposited plans,[9] the Domesday Book,[10] a tithe map and tithe apportionment survey,[11] maps drawn by authority of a Royal Commission,[12] surveys of Crown Lands[13] and surveyor's reports made by statutory authority.[14]

Surprisingly, an Ordnance Survey map is not generally admissible[15] as evidence of private boundaries. However, in practice reference can usually be made to it as a result of its being utilised as a plan to a private deed.

Verdicts, decrees and judgments[16] are also admissible in evidence as documents of public record but not the award of an arbitrator except in a subsequent action between the same parties.[17]

Ancient documents Ancient documents may be admitted as evidence of boundaries. However, they must be more than 20 years old and must, once again, be produced from proper custody.[18] They will be presumed to have been validly executed including any

---

[7] As to what is a public document, see *R.* v. *Sealby* [1965] 1 All E.R. 701.

[8] See Evidence Act 1845, s.1; Evidence Act 1851, s.14. Public documents are also an exception to the hearsay rule.

[9] *Att.-Gen.* v. *Antrobus* [1905] 2 Ch. 188 but not private Admiralty maps and so on.

[10] *Duke of Beaufort* v. *John Aird & Co.* (1904) 20 T.L.R. 602.

[11] *Knight* v. *David* [1971] 3 All E.R. 1066.

[12] *New Romney Corpn.* v. *New Romney Commissioners of Sewers* [1892] 1 Q.B. 840.

[13] *Doe d. William IV* v. *Roberts* (1844) 12 M. & W. 520.

[14] *Evans* v. *Merthyr Tydfil Urban Council* [1899] 1 Ch. 241.

[15] Ordnance Survey Act 1841, s.12.

[16] *Neill* v. *Duke of Devonshire* (1882) 8 App.Cas. 135.

[17] See *Russell on Arbitration* (12th ed.) pp. 352–356; and see *Doe d. Morris* v. *Rosser* (1802) 3 East. 15 (as to title to land); *Evans* v. *Rees* (1839) 10 Ad. & El. 151 at 155 (not evidence against strangers).

[18] This depends on the facts of the case. In the case of a cancelled lease, it means from the custody of the lessor or lessee (*Plaxton* v. *Dare* (1829) 10 B. & C. 17).

alterations to them.[19] Examples include cancelled leases[20] and other deeds.

Ecclesiastical terriers

Ecclesiastical terriers list the temporal possessions of parish churches. They are drawn up under canon law and must be signed by a competent official[21] and produced from proper custody.[22] Such documents are helpful if the dispute concerns glebe land and adjoining boundaries.

Private maps and surveys

Private maps and surveys are not generally admissible in evidence.[23] However, they become admissible when annexed to a deed or to a declaration by a deceased person.[24] Tithe commutation maps are not admissible as evidence of private boundaries.[25] So far as Land Registry plans are concerned, it is unlikely that they would be helpful, except where the entries upon them are in issue, since the delineation of boundaries is not, in normal circumstances, sufficiently precise. An office copy of any plan filed in the Registry is admissible to the same extent as the original.[26]

General maps and atlases

General maps and atlases may be produced as evidence of facts within public knowledge[27] (*e.g.* county boundaries) but not as regards private rights.[28]

Declarations by deceased persons

Three types of declaration may be admitted:

(1) A declaration by a deceased person from his personal knowledge of the facts which were against his pecuniary or proprietary interests at the time when the declaration was made, *e.g.* the boundaries of a manor[29] but not the statement of a deceased tenant as to the boundaries of a demised property.[30]

(2) A declaration made by a deceased person in the course of duty recorded contemporaneously and from personal knowledge[31] *e.g.* entries made by a land surveyor in a field book during the course of a drainage survey.[32]

(3) A declaration made by a deceased person concerning public or general rights and interests and, thereby, affecting a particular class or group of people[33] *e.g.* a

[19] Evidence Act 1938, s.4—any alterations are presumed to have been made before execution.

[20] *Plaxton* v. *Dare* (1829) 10 B. & C. 17.

[21] *e.g.* the incumbent and churchwardens.

[22] *e.g.* the diocesan record office, the episcopal or archdeacon's registry or the charter chest of the parish church itself (*Atkins* v. *Hatton* (1794) 2 Anst. 386).

[23] See *e.g. Wakeman* v. *West* (1836) 7 C. & P. 479.

[24] s.10(1) of the Civil Evidence Act 1968 includes plans within the definition of "documents."

[25] *Wilberforce* v. *Hearfield* (1877) 5 Ch.D. 709.

[26] L.R.A. 1925, s.113.

[27] *Deybell's Case* (1821) 4 B. & Ald. 243.

[28] *Read* v. *Bishop of Lincoln* [1892] A.C. 644.

[29] *Doe d. Molesworth* v. *Sleeman* (1846) 9 Q.B. 298.

[30] *Papendick* v. *Bridgwater* (1855) 5 E. & B. 166, following the principle that a tenant may not derogate from his landlord's title.

[31] *Mercer* v. *Denne* [1905] 2 Ch. 538; such declarations are also now admissible under the Civil Evidence Act 1968, s.4.

[32] *Mellor* v. *Walmesley* [1905] 2 Ch. 164.

[33] *i.e.* the whole community (*e.g.* public rights of way) or a substantial part of the community (*e.g.* a right in common) *and* such declarations must directly assert or deny the existence of the right. See *Evans* v. *Merthyr Tydfil Urban Council* [1899] 1 Ch. 241.

declaration by a deceased tenant as to the rights of all the tenants of the manor.[34]

Other documents

Civil Evidence Acts

The Civil Evidence Acts 1968 and 1972 can make "first hand" documentary (and oral) hearsay admissible, subject to the service of the appropriate notices under rules of court.[35] A relevant example may be the particulars of sale when the land in question was sold at auction.[36]

Oral evidence

Experts

Section 3 of the Civil Evidence Act 1972 provides that an expert's opinion on a matter on which he is qualified to give an opinion will be admissible in any civil proceedings. Normal practice[37] requires that such evidence is adduced, initially, in the form of a report, a copy of which is served prior to trial.[38] Unless the contents of the report are agreed, the expert must attend the hearing for the purposes of cross-examination.

Other witnesses

The general rule is that any fact required to be proved at trial must be proved by the examination of the witnesses orally and in open court.[39] However, with the leave of the court such evidence may be given on affidavit but if the other party contests the evidence then the witness will be required to attend for cross-examination.[40] In the case of a bed-ridden witness such evidence may have to be taken by deposition[41] or the court may have to adjourn to the place where the witness resides.[42]

Construction of boundary features

In addition to the presumptions and considerations of the boundary features mentioned above, the mode of construction of features may also be relevant. For example, it is customary to build brick walls and close-boarded fences so that the piers, or the posts and arris rails, are on the land of the owner of the feature so as not to cause a trespass. Whilst this state of affairs may be prima facie evidence of ownership, it does not derive, in itself, from any principle of law. The possibility of prescriptive rights should, however, be borne in mind. In the absence of any direct evidence as to ownership, it is fairly safe to presume (especially in London) that the feature is a party structure.[43]

---

[34] *Earl of Dunraven* v. *Llewellyn* (1850) 15 Q.B. 791.
[35] R.S.C. Ord. 38, rr. 20–29 etc.; C.C.R. Ord. 20, rr. 14–22 etc.
[36] See also *Ecroyd* v. *Coulthard* (1897) 2 Ch. 554.
[37] R.S.C. Ord. 38, rr. 35, 37–44; C.C.R. Ord. 20, rr. 27–28.
[38] Normally at least 28 days beforehand.
[39] R.S.C. Ord. 38, r. 1; C.C.R. Ord. 20, r. 4.
[40] R.S.C. Ord. 38, r. 2; C.C.R. Ord. 20, rr. 5 to 6. See also Chap. 6 below.
[41] R.S.C. Ord. 39, r. 1; C.C.R. Ord. 20, r. 13.
[42] *St. Edmundsbury and Ipswich Diocesan Board of Finance* v. *Clark* [1973] Ch. 323.
[43] See further pp. 76–77.

Acts of ownership

Such evidence is admissible but is not necessarily conclusive. For example, if such acts have been carried out without the knowledge of the neighbour (and, thereby, his acquiescence) they are not good evidence.[44]

Local custom

This evidence may help to establish the position of boundaries in the absence of any other primary evidence.[45] As already stated, by way of example, it is the local custom in North Norfolk for the hedge on the northern side of the land to be in the ownership of the adjoining owner.

In this context, evidence of the reputation of the witness giving such evidence is admissible[46] and may be relevant. However, it is only of particular use where the general or public interest is concerned (*e.g.* the bounds of a parish).[47]

Variation of boundaries

Agreement

A deed is necessary[48] to give effect to any agreement varying a boundary. However, if such agreement is as the result of a genuine attempt to settle a doubtful boundary, then no deed nor any memorandum in writing is required since no land has changed hands.[49] The settlement itself can be treated as sufficient consideration to make the agreement mutually enforceable.[50] In practice, it is always prudent to ensure that there is a properly drafted memorandum, together with a sufficiently detailed and accurate plan to avoid further uncertainty.

Adverse possession

Principles   Under the Limitation Act 1980,[51] time runs against the paper owner of the land from the moment that the claimant encroaches and takes possession of that land.[51a] Such possession must be continuous and exclusive,[51b] coupled with the necessary *animus*

---

[44] *Henniker* v. *Howard* (1904) 90 L.T. 157.

[45] *e.g. Collis* v. *Amphlett* [1918] 1 Ch. 232; [1920] A.C. 271.

[46] Civil Evidence Act 1968, s.9(4). It can also include documents.

[47] *Thomas* v. *Jenkins* (1837) 6 Ad. & El. 525.

[48] L.P.A. 1925, s.52.

[49] For the same reason, the agreement is not registrable as a Class IV estate contract under the L.C.A. 1972 unless the boundary line is varied (*Neilson* v. *Poole* (1969) 20 P. & C.R. 909). See p. 23 for position regarding registered land.

[50] *Penn* v. *Lord Baltimore* (1750) 1 Ves.Sen. 444.

[51] Sched. 1, paras. 1, 8.

[51a] Adverse possession can even take place of a subterranean building or the sub-soil despite the paper owner's continuing possession of the surface (*see Rains* v. *Buxton* (1880) 14 Ch.D 537: cellar)

[51b] See *e.g. Tecbild Ltd.* v. *Chamberlain* (1969) 20 P. & C.R. 633: periodic absences by the landowner not sufficient to amount to abandonment. The Court of Appeal stressed the need for strong evidence; probably still good law, even after *Treloar* v. *Nute* [1976] 1 W.L.R. 1295.

possidendi i.e. the intention to exclude the world at large, so far as reasonably practicable,[51c] *e.g.* by the erection of fencing.[52]

Although the erection of fencing may cause inconvenience to the paper owner unless he takes direct steps to remove the claimant from the land before the limitation period expires or can establish that he has some specific purpose for the land in the future, a court will tend to support the claimant's case.[53] Moreover, as a matter of law, a claimant is not now to be treated as being in possession by means of an implied licence or permission, merely by virtue of the fact that his occupation is not inconsistent with the paper owner's present or future use of the land, although such an interpretation of events may be imputed, if justified by the facts.[54]

Generally   Ordinarily a period of 12 years must be shown.[55] In the case of land owned by a spiritual or charitable corporation sole or by the Crown (other than the foreshore),[56] proceedings for recovery of possession must be brought within 30 years.[57]

Exceptions   **Trust land**   Where land is held on trust, adverse possession by the claimant will not bar the trustees' title until all the beneficiaries have been barred.[58] Accordingly, if the land is held on trust for X for life with remainder to Y, time will not start to run against Y's interest until X's death.

Disability   If on the date when the right of action accrues (*i.e.* when adverse possession was taken) the paper owner was under a disability,[59] then a further period of six years must be added, being the time allowed to the paper owner to recover possession after his disability has ceased or to his successor after he has died.[60] If there is a succession of disabilities, then time runs from the ceasing of the first disability. A maximum period is

---

[51c] *Buckinghamshire County Council* v. *Moran, The Times*, March 2, 1988 (what is necessary to show the required *animus possidendi* is not an intention to own or acquire ownership of the land but merely an intention to possess.

[52] But see *George Wimpey & Co. Ltd.* v. *Sohn* [1967] Ch. 487 where it was held that the mere fencing of land in itself did not amount to an act of exclusion because it might have been done only for the purpose of protecting a garden from the public rather than from the true owner.

[53] See *Treloar* v. *Nute* [1976] 1 W.L.R. 1295 (land fenced off and prepared for building) distinguishing *Wallis's Cayton Bay Holiday Camp* v. *Shell-Mex B.P. Ltd.* [1975] Q.B. 94 (in which a majority of the Court of Appeal held that the claimant's possession had not been adverse because the paper owners had an eventual use for the land as a site for a new filling station). See also *Redhouse Farms (Thorndon)* v. *Catchpole* (1976) 244 E.G. 295 (Area of land used solely by D for shooting. *Held* that D had acquired "squatter's title" after 12 years had elapsed. *Wallis's* case distinguished on basis that there the land was still awaiting development whereas here P had no use for the land); and *Williams* v. *Usherwood* (1983) 45 P. & C.R. 235 (land fenced, driveway paved and cars parked. *Held* sufficient acts).

[54] Limitation Act 1980, Sched. 1, para. 8(4); but see *Powell* v. *McFarlane* (1979) 38 P. & C.R. 452. (Implied licence granted to P. from age of 14, to graze cow plus other activities on land over period of 16 years not regarded as compelling evidence of *animus possidendi*).

[55] Limitation Act 1980, s.15.

[56] *Ibid.* By Sched. 1, para. 11 the period is extended to 60 years.

[57] *Ibid.* Sched. 1, para. 10.

[58] *Ibid.* s.18.

[59] *i.e.* a minor or a person of unsound mind (*ibid.* s.38).

[60] *Ibid.* s.28(1).

prescribed of 30 years from the date when the right of action first accrued, after which time the claimant's occupation is protected.[61]

Fraud, deliberate concealment or mistake   Evidence of such acts may postpone the running of time until the date upon which they were discovered or could, with reasonable diligence, have been discovered.[62] However, such a plea must form the primary basis of the action for benefit to be obtained from this exception. Indeed, it cannot be utilised in respect of an action following a subsequent purchase for value if the purchaser has no knowledge or reason to believe that such an act has occurred.[63]

Computation   Time runs in favour of the claimant from the moment that he takes physical possession of the land in question. The fact that he has not personally occupied it throughout the relevant period will not bar a claim being made by him so long as he can establish that his predecessor or predecessors in title and

Time   himself have, cumulatively, enjoyed possession and there has been no abandonment during any of the intervening periods.[64]

Since the foregoing periods limit the period within which the paper owner can recover possession, once the necessary time has

Effect of adverse possession claim   elapsed, the paper owner's claim to possession is simply extinguished.[65] In effect, his title to the land will also cease[66] so that the claimant will have a new freehold title which will prevail unless a better title can be shown.[67] A restrictive covenant will, however, still be binding on the claimant in equity.[68]

Estoppel

In the context of this section,[69] a variation may arise as a result of the evidential rule that one person may be estopped by the acts or conduct of himself (or those of his predecessor in title) from taking action in respect of an encroachment upon his boundaries by his neighbour if he has caused the neighbour to act to his detriment.[70] Such a right arises independently of adverse possession. Resort is likely to be made to it where the latter claim cannot be sustained.

---

[61] *Ibid.* s.28(4).
[62] *Ibid.* s.32.
[63] *Ibid.* s.32(3).
[64] See *Asher* v. *Whitlock* (1865) L.R. 1 Q.B. 1; *Trustees, Executors and Agency Co. Ltd.* v. *Short* (1888) 13 App.Cas. 793 and Sched. 1, para. 8(2) to the 1980 Act.
[65] 1980 Act, s.17. See also, *e.g.* facts of *Treloar* v. *Nute* [1976] 1 W.L.R. 1295.
[66] Where the title is registered, the paper owner will, however, remain the registered proprietor holding on trust for the claimant until the register is rectified; L.R.A. 1925, s.75.
[67] *e.g.* by a lessor where a lessee's title has been defeated.
[68] See *Re Nisbet and Potts' Contract* [1906] 1 Ch. 386; and also *Spectrum Investment Co.* v. *Holmes* [1981] 1 All E.R. 6.
[69] See pp. 29 and 33 (n. 41) below for position concerning proprietary estoppel leading to the grant of licences and equitable easements.
[70] *e.g. Hopgood* v. *Brown* [1955] 1 W.L.R. 213 where one owner was estopped from asserting that the boundary was anywhere other than as agreed where his predecessor has consented to the erection of a garage between two and three feet over the boundary line.

Registered land

Introduction

Registration of title was designed in 1925 as a wholly new system of conveyancing by which a single established title to land could be guaranteed by the State. However, unlike the Land Charges Register, the Land Register is not open to public inspection save in respect of an index map and a parcels index. These simply show whether a particular piece of land has been registered. Accordingly, unless the authority of the registered proprietor is obtained,[71] the details contained therein will remain confidential. Although over three-quarters of the population of England and Wales are in compulsory registration areas, and in excess of eight million titles are now on the register, this system should, but still does not, simplify disputes over the extent of ownership. However, if one neighbour is confident about his rights, invariably he will disclose a copy of his land certificate setting out the extent of his registered title. The advantages and limitations of this form of proof are set out below.

The register

Meaning   The term "register"[72] has four distinct meanings of which the first two below are the most common:

(1) It is the official typewritten record of one estate owner's title to a particular property which is described by reference to an official plan kept at the Land Registry. Each separate register has an individual title number. Each registered proprietor has a certificate of title ("the land certificate") and every mortgagee a certificate relating to his incumbrance ("the charge certificate").

Divisions   (2) It may also refer to an individual part of the three divisions of the foregoing record,[73] namely,
(a) The Property Register;
(b) The Proprietorship Register;
(c) The Charges Register.

(3) It can also refer to the complete record of ownership of all registered titles *viz.* "There shall continue to be kept at H.M. Land Registry a *register* of title to freehold and leasehold land."[74] This register is kept at the Land Registry in London and in 13 district registries, formerly on a card index but now, increasingly, on computer.

(4) It is sometimes used to refer not only to the written record of title but also to the filed plan, *e.g.* "the *register* may be rectified pursuant to an order of the court or by the registrar" (if and when an error or an omission occurs).[75] Here all that would be required would be an adjustment of

---

[71] L.R.A. 1925, s.112; L.R.R. 1925, rr. 12, 287, 288; and S.I. 1981 No. 1135.
[72] See generally, Ruoff & Roper, *The Law and Practice of Registered Conveyancing* (5th ed. 1986); see also *Strand Securities Ltd.* v. *Caswell* [1965] Ch. 958 at 977.
[73] L.R.A. 1925, s.2.
[74] *Ibid.* s.1.
[75] *Ibid.* s.82(1).

the boundaries shown on the plan to which the register refers.

The property register   This contains a description of the registered property. Invariably, it will also refer to an individual plan relating to the particular title ("the filed plan"). When a parcel of land is added, a note will be made on this register that "the land edged and lettered 'A' in red on the filed plan" was added to the title on a certain date. Equally, where land has been removed from the title, a similar note will be made in green. There may also be a general note added as to easements granted and reserved when land is taken out of title. If there have been a number of transactions, a new edition of the register and plan are often prepared.[76] In the case of registered leasehold land, the property register will also contain short particulars of the lease and any prohibition against alienation without licence.

In addition to the date of first registration, this register will also include details of any mines and minerals, conditions and covenants, appurtenant easements, profits and similar interests and benefits.

The proprietorship register   This will state the nature of title (*i.e.* absolute, good leasehold, qualified or possessory) and particulars of the present registered proprietor (*i.e.* his name, address, description and capacity if, *e.g.* he is a trustee).[77] It is in this register that cautions are registered, *e.g.* to protect a claim by adverse possession. The address of any person entered in this register will, unless he directs otherwise, be his address for service.[78]

The charges register   This contains particulars of all incumbrances which were in existence at the date of first registration and particulars of all subsequent charges and incumbrances (*e.g.* leases, restrictive covenants and agreements constituting the other classes of land charge). It will also contain any notes relating to covenants, conditions and other rights adversely affecting the land and all dealings which are capable of registration.

Maps and plans

Public index maps

Public index maps show the position and extent of every registered estate in England and Wales and are either the Ordnance Survey map (with or without a parcels index) or are based on such a map. Where no parcels index is shown, the title number will be shown under which each estate was first registered.

They may be inspected by any member of the public[79] who wishes to discover whether a title is registered or the extent of such registration. This is shown by means of a pink tint enclosed by a red edging with the title number in red ink. A leasehold title

---

[76] L.R.R. 1925, r. 4.
[77] *Ibid.* r. 6.
[78] L.R.A. 1925, s.79(1).
[79] *Ibid.* s.12.

is indicated by the additional suffix "L"; by "M" where there is only title to mines and minerals; and by "R" if there is a rentcharge.

General map   The term "general map" covers the series of maps held by the Land Registry indicating the extent and details of registered land in particular areas. This map is based, once again, on the appropriate Ordnance Survey extract.

A parcels index is kept containing the numbers and titles of each parcel of registered land. In the case of an old title, the plan will be bound up with the land, or charge, certificate. Where an office copy or extract from the general map is annexed to any land certificate, it is deemed to be contained in the certificate itself for the purposes of admissibility.[80] General maps may also be inspected by the general public.

Filed plans   Filed plans are the title plans for individual properties, the only function of which is to identify the land in question. Where practicable, the Chief Land Registrar may have used the plan attached to the conveyance or transfer as an adjunct to or in substitution for the filed plan.[81] Such a practice tends to be adopted where restrictive covenants and easements are described by reference to colours or hatching on the deed plan.

Practice   By convention, the Registry has used certain colours for particular situations:

Red edging   Shows the extent of the registered plan.

Green edging   Indicates land removed from a title.

Green tinting   Shows excluded "islands" of land not registered with the surrounding.

Brown tinting   Indicates the benefit of a right of way over the registered land.

Blue tinting   Indicates that part of the registered land which is subject to a right of way.

Broken lines   Are often used to indicate where no physical feature yet exists, *e.g.* where a fence has still to be erected.

"T" marks   These are shown on post-1962 filed plans in the following circumstances:

(1) Where such marks are referred to in positive or restrictive covenants;
(2) Where such marks appeared on a plan to which reference has been made in a pre-registration deed but without any explanation in the deed of their significance, and where the applicant for first registration has specifically asked for their inclusion. The fact that no reference has been made to such marks will be recorded on the register.

Limitations   Since the function of both the general map and the filed plan is to identify the registered land, the boundaries

[80] L.R.R. 1925, r. 275.
[81] Registered Land Practice Notes 1982/3, p. 24, F3.

General boundaries marked indicate only general boundaries.[82] Therefore they will not indicate who owns the feature or where exactly the boundary line runs. As already stated, since such maps and plans normally either comprise or are based upon Ordnance Survey extracts, boundary lines will usually be drawn in accordance with Ordnance Survey practice, namely, down the middle of physical features. However, where practicable, not only the boundaries themselves but also any requisite details (*e.g.* ownership of fences) will have been entered on the register or filed plan or general map[83] if they are clear cut. Field numbers and areas, though, will not be shown.

Classification of interests

Registered interests   These comprise either a legal fee simple absolute in possession or a legal term of years absolute, subject to the following qualifications:

(1) That registration is prohibited even in a compulsory area, if the lease was granted for a term of 21 years or less,[84] or if it contains an absolute prohibition against assignment, or if it is a mortgage term subject still to a right of redemption[85];

Registered interests

(2) That registration is compulsory if it is in a designated area and the transaction consists either of the grant of a lease for 21 years or more or is the assignment or sale of a lease with a term of 21 years or more unexpired,[86] or if the transaction consists of the grant of a lease for more than 21 years if the title out of which the lease has been granted is registered.[87]

Overriding interests   Such rights which bind a purchaser whether or not they are expressly disclosed on the register.[88] These include the following:

(1) Rights of common, drainage rights, customary rights (until extinguished), public rights, *profits à prendre*, rights of sheepwalk, rights of way, watercourses, rights of water, and other easements, not being equitable easements required to be protected by notice on the register (*viz.* appurtenances and quasi-easements)[89] and arguably equitable easements[90] but *not* restrictive covenants[91];

---

[82] L.R.R. 1925, r. 278.
[83] L.R.A. 1925, s.76 and Registered Land Practice 1982/3 p. 17 or 7, C4.
[84] *Ibid.* s.19(2).
[85] *Ibid.* s.8(1), (2).
[86] *Ibid.* s.123(1) (as amended by L.R.A. 1986, s.2(1) with effect from January 1, 1987).
[87] L.R.A. 1925, s.19(2).
[88] *Ibid.* s.70(1).
[89] *Ibid.* s.258.
[90] See *Celsteel Ltd.* v. *Alton House Holdings* [1986] 1 W.L.R. 512 where Scott J. decided that an equitable easement (a right of way to a garage) did constitute an overriding interest by virtue of s.258.
[91] See *Hodges* v. *Jones* [1935] Ch. 657 at 671.

(2) Liability to repair highways, channels, embankments and sea and river walls and tenurial liabilities;

(3) Rights acquired or being acquired under the Limitation Act 1980 (*i.e.* by adverse possession) and by prescription;

Overriding interests

(4) "The rights of every person in actual occupation of the land or in receipt of the rents and profits thereof, save where enquiry is made of such person and the rights are not disclosed," proprietary rights such as estate contracts, equitable interests and mere equities[92] as well as leases not under (7) below[93];

(5) Local land charges;

(6) Fishing, sporting, seignorial and manorial rights and franchises;

(7) Leases granted for a term not exceeding 21 years[94] including an agreement for a lease which creates a tenancy.[95]

Minor interests   These are rights which need to be protected by an entry on the register. The principal examples are restrictive covenants, legal rent charges, estate contracts[96] and charging orders. Protection will be given by one of the following means:

(1) A notice   This is entered on the charges register and ensures that any subsequent dealing with the land will take effect subject to the notice. A copy of the land certificate will be required by the applicant which will preclude most neighbours. The Chief Land Registrar can vary the notice on such terms and evidence as he deems appropriate.[97] Upon the production of satisfactory evidence he may also cancel the notice if he is satisfied that the notice has determined, ceased, been discharged, or for any other reason no longer affects the registered land.[98]

(2) A caution   This is a short-term measure which entitles the cautioner to notice of an intended transaction or "dealing."[99] It is usually the only means of protection available to a person who cannot obtain a copy of the land certificate. The benefit, and disadvantage of a caution is that it cannot be transferred to another person. The registered proprietor is not obliged to wait until he is about to deal with the land before he may "warn off" the cautioner by giving notice to such effect.[1] The caution will

---

[92] *Hodgson v. Marks* [1971] Ch. 892; *Blacklocks v. J.B. Developments (Godalming) Ltd.* [1982] Ch. 183.

[93] *e.g. Mornington Permanent B.S.* v. *Kenway* [1953] Ch. 382.

[94] As amended by L.R.A. 1986, s.4.

[95] See also *City Permanent B.S.* v. *Miller* [1952] Ch. 840.

[96] *i.e.* all land charges under the L.C.A. 1972.

[97] L.R.R. 1925, r. 204.

[98] L.R.A. 1925, s.59(4); L.R.R. 1925, r. 16.

[99] "Dealing" is not defined by the L.R.A. 1925 but will include any power of disposition, *e.g.* transfer of land, creation of rentcharges and easements, charges and mortgages. A caution may also be used as an alternative to a pending action charge (see p. 26) if the circumstances permit (see, *e.g. Regan & Blackburn Ltd.* v. *Rogers* [1985] 1 W.L.R. 870).

[1] L.R.A. 1925, s.55; L.R.R. 1925, r. 218.

Minor interests

then cease to have effect if the cautioner is unable to defend the interest protected within the time prescribed.[2]

(3) An inhibition   This is either an order of the court or the Chief Land Registrar which forbids any dealings in the land until a certain time or event or absolutely. Terms and conditions may be imposed and a discharge or cancellation may be ordered.[3] The most common examples are where a receiving order in bankruptcy is registered as a land charge, where the land certificate has been stolen or there is a suspicion of fraud.[4]

(4) A restriction   This also prevents any dealing with the land until some condition has been complied with. It is usually made by the registered proprietor (*e.g.* where he is the tenant for life) or by the Chief Land Registrar (*e.g.* where there is a transfer of registered land to trustees for sale). It may also be appropriate to protect the beneficiary under a bare trust or to prevent an unauthorised lease by a mortgagor.

Title

There are four types of title which guarantee the degree of effectiveness of the registration:

(1) Absolute   This is a complete guarantee of ownership subject only to those third party rights which are protected as overriding interests on the register.[5]

(2) Possessory   This has the same force as an absolute title except that it is subject to any estate, right or interest adverse to or in derogation of the title of the first proprietor and subsisting or capable of arising at the time of registration of that proprietor.[6] It will normally arise when a proprietor cannot prove his ownership on an application for first registration when, for example, the title

Types of title

deeds have been lost. Accordingly, the title cannot be guaranteed at this stage.

(3) Qualified   This is where there is some particular defect which is noted on the register *e.g.* where the Chief Land Registrar is not satisfied with the title before a certain date. As with possessory title, if no adverse interest appears, it can in due course be converted into absolute title.[7]

(4) Good leasehold   This guarantees the title to the leasehold, subject to interests noted on the register and to overriding

---

[2] Within 14 days of the service of the notice the cautioner must lodge his objections in the form of a written statement signed by himself or his solicitor setting out his grounds for maintaining the caution. The Chief Land Registrar ("C.L.R.") may extend or reduce the prescribed period, so long as it is no less than seven days (r. 218(2)) or written representations can then be made to the C.L.R. showing cause why the caution should be continued (r. 220(1)). The C.L.R. has power to order security (L.R.A. 1925, s.55(2)).
[3] L.R.A. 1925, ss.57(1), (2).
[4] For discharge by C.L.R. see r. 231. See also L.R.A. 1986, s.5 for abolition of Minor Interests Index.
[5] L.R.A. 1925, s.5.
[6] *Ibid.* s.6.
[7] *Ibid.* s.17.

interests, but does not guarantee the title to the freehold reversion,[8] unlike an absolute title in the case of a leasehold.

Fixed boundaries

Indemnity claim

Fixed boundaries are not often found due to the initial expense of making the application and the lack of practical advantages to the applicant and his successor in title. Where they occur, a note will have been made on the property register and on the filed plan or general map that the boundaries have been fixed.[9] Such a state of affairs guarantees the boundary line. Accordingly, even the slightest adjustment by rectification can lead to an indemnity claim under section 83 of the Land Registration Act 1925, for the consequences of an application to fix are that a comprehensive and accurate survey will have been undertaken in conjunction with the owners of adjoining lands.

Variations

The boundaries of registered land can only be varied if the alteration is shown on the register following an application to the Chief Land Registrar. In the absence of a normal transfer this can only be done under his powers of rectification[10] to give effect to orders of the court, to alter entries obtained by fraud, to give effect to an agreement of all interested parties and to correct any error or omission.[11] Such powers are exercised, *e.g.* where there has been a misinterpretation of deeds where the title was investigated at the time of first registration. There is also power[12] to give effect to an acquisition by adverse possession.

Land charges

Introduction

Separate registers

Where the title to the land is still unregistered reference may need to be made to the Land Charges Register.[13] This is divided into five separate registers:

(1) a register of land charges;
(2) a register of pending actions;
(3) a register of writs and orders affecting land;
(4) a register of deeds of arrangement affecting land;
(5) a register of annuities.

In the context of this work, specific reference is made to the first three registers. It should also be borne in mind that a land charge must be registered in the name of the owner of the legal estate[14]

---

[8] *Ibid.* s.8(1), 10.
[9] L.R.R. 1925, r. 277.
[10] L.R.A. 1925, s.82.
[11] See pp. 14–16.
[12] L.R.A. 1925, s.75.
[13] L.C.A. 1972, s.1(1).
[14] *Ibid.* s.3(1), *viz.* "the estate owner" is defined by s.17(1) by reference to L.P.A. 1925, ss.1(1) and 205(1)(v). For the purposes of registration any legal estate will suffice (see *Barrett* v. *Hilton Developments* [1975] Ch. 237).

of the affected land, although a version of the proper name will not render the registration a nullity.[15]

The main advantage of the land charges system over land registration remains the fact that any member of the public may search any register himself or have an official search carried out under section 10 of the Land Charges Act 1972. Accordingly, in the context of litigation much useful "spadework" can be achieved before positions are taken in subsequent inter-solicitor correspondence.

Land charges register

Land charges are classified as follows:

Class A   This charge is either,

(1) *a rent or annuity or principal money* payable by instalments or otherwise, with or without interest, which is not a charge created by deed but is a charge upon land (other than a rate) created pursuant to the application of some person under the provisions of any Act of Parliament[16] for securing to any person either the money spent by him or the costs, charges and expenses incurred by him under such Act, or the money advanced by him for repaying the money spent or the costs, charges and expenses incurred by another person under the authority of an Act of Parliament; or

(2) *a rent or annuity or principal money* payable as mentioned above which is not a charge created by deed but is a charge upon land rather than a rate) created pursuant to some person under the enactments set out under Schedule 2 to the Land Charges Act 1972, *e.g.* the Landlord and Tenant Act 1927, Schedule 1, para. 7 (charge in respect of improvements to business premises); the Civil Defence Act 1939, sections 18(4) and 19(1) (charge in respect of civil defence works); the Corn Rents Act 1963, section 1(5) (charge under a scheme for the apportionment of redemption of corn rents or other payments in lieu of tithes).[17]

Classification of charges

Class B   This is a charge on land (not being a local land charge within the meaning of the Local Land Charges Act 1975[18]) of any of the kinds described in respect of Class A (1) above, created otherwise than pursuant to the application of any person, which has been acquired under a conveyance made on or after January 1, 1926.[19]

Class C   These charges are any of the following[20]:

---

[15] See *Oak Co-Operative Society* v. *Blackburn* [1968] Ch. 730.
[16] Now regulated by the Improvement of Land Act 1864.
[17] See also the Agricultural Holdings Act 1986, s.85(2), (3). (Compensation to tenant; payment of rent to landlord as trustee).
[18] *i.e.* any charge acquired by the local authority under, *e.g.* Public Health Act 1936, Highways Act 1980 or Building Act 1984 (s.1(1) of 1975 Act).
[19] s.2(8).
[20] s.2(4) of the Land Charges Act 1972 provides a statutory definition of each type of charge in the terms set out below.

(1) A puisne mortgage   This is a legal mortgage which is not protected by a deposit of documents relating to the legal charge affected.

(2) A limited owner's charge   This is an equitable charge acquired by a tenant for life or statutory owner under the Inheritance Tax Act 1984[21] or any other statute by reason of the discharge by him of any death duties or other liabilities and to which special priority is given by the statute.

(3) A general equitable charge   This is any equitable charge which, (a) is not secured by a deposit of documents relating to the legal estate affected; (b) does not arise or affect an interest arising under a trust for sale or a settlement; (c) is not a charge given by way of indemnity against rents equitably apportioned or charged exclusively on land in exoneration of other land and against the breach or non-observance of covenants or conditions; and (d) is not included in any other class of land charge.[22]

(4) An estate contract   This is a contract by an estate owner[23] or by a person entitled at the date of the contract to have a legal estate conveyed to him to convey or create a legal estate, including a contract conferring either expressly or by statutory implication a valid option to purchase a right of pre-emption or any other like right.[24]

Class D   This charge is any of the following, namely:

(1) An Inland Revenue charge   This relates to a charge on land being a charge acquired in respect of capital transfer tax for "death duties liable or payable on any death occurring on or after January 1, 1926.[25]

(2) A restrictive covenant   This is defined as a covenant or agreement (other than a covenant or agreement between a lessor and a lessee) restrictive of the user of land and entered into on or after January 1, 1926.[26]

---

[21] See s.212(2) of the 1984 Act under which a person, having a limited interest in any property who pays the tax attributable to the value of that property, is entitled to a charge as if the tax so attributable had been raised by means of a mortgage to him. By s.100(1) of the Finance Act 1986 the tax charged under the Capital Transfer Tax 1984 is now known as "inheritance tax". The title of the 1984 Act is also re-named.

[22] See *Georgiordes* v. *Edward Wolfe & Co. Ltd.* [1965] Ch. 487 (estate agents' commission not registrable as Class C (iii) charge).

[23] For definition see above n.14.

[24] See *Pritchard* v. *Briggs* [1980] Ch. 338 (right of pre-emption, unlike an option, does not create an interest in land so therefore requires registration for purposes of protection. See also *Gardner* v. *Coutts & Co.* [1968] 1 W.L.R. 173 (no avoidance by means of a gift to another).

[25] L.C.A. 1972, s.2(5)(i) as amended by the Capital Transfer Tax Act 1984, Sched. 8; para. 3(1).

[26] L.C.A. 1972, s.2(5)(ii). Covenants between lessor and lessee are, therefore, not registrable (see *Newman* v. *Real Estate Debenture Corpn.* [1940] 1 All E.R. 131) even though the covenant relates to land not within the demise (see *Dartstone Ltd.* v. *Cleveland Petroleum Co. Ltd.* [1969] 1 W.L.R. 1807—covenant restricting development of adjoining plot as petrol filling station).

(3) An equitable easement This is defined as an easement, right or privilege over or affecting land created or arising on or after January 1, 1926, and being merely an equitable interest.[27]

Class E This charge will protect an annuity created before January 1, 1926 and not registered in the register of annuities.

Class F This charge protects the rights of a spouse under the Matrimonial Homes Act 1983.

Register of pending actions

A "pending land action" is defined[28] as "any action or proceeding pending in court relating to land or any interest in or charge on land." A petition in bankruptcy filed on or after January 1, 1926 may also be registered here.

Benefits In neighbours' disputes considerable tactical benefit can be gained from the registration of this type of charge since it will "warn off" any prospective purchaser of the adjoining land and, indeed, may restrict the ability of the adjoining owner to raise money on the property. However, the use of this weapon to bring the other side to the negotiating table has come under considerable judicial scrutiny in recent years by Megarry V.-C. in the context of what constitutes an interest or charge sufficient to come within the statutory definition given above.[29]

Power to vacate The court also has power under section 5(10) of the 1972 Act either upon the determination or during the pendency of the proceedings, to make an order vacating a registration and to direct that the party concerned should pay all costs if it is satisfied that the proceedings are not being presented in good faith.[30] The court also had an inherent jurisdiction to order such a charge to be vacated.[31]

Duration The registration of such a charge will cease to have effect at the end of the period of five years from the date on which it was made. However, it may be renewed from time to time and, if so renewed, will take effect for a further five years from the date of renewal.[32]

---

[27] L.C.A. 1972, s.2(5)(iii) and p. 33 below.

[28] L.C.A. 1972, ss.5(1) and 17(1). It is also known as "lis pendens."

[29] See *Calgary and Edmonton Land Co. Ltd.* v. *Dobinson* [1974] Ch. 102 (the action or proceeding must claim some proprietary right in the land and not merely involve a claim that the owner should be retrained from exercising his powers of disposition); see also *Greenhi Builders Ltd.* v. *Allen* [1979] 1 W.L.R. 156 (claim in respect of easement of support held a pending land action); *Selim Ltd.* v. *Bickenhall Engineering Ltd.* [1981] 3 All E.R. 210 (forfeiture proceedings for tenant's breach of repairing obligations) but not in *Haslemere Estates Ltd.* v. *Baker* [1982] 3 All E.R. 525 (claim for pre-contract expenditure based on proprietary estoppel held not to be a pending land action).

[30] See R.S.C. Practice Note 93/10/3 for procedure; see also *Calgary and Edmonton Land Co. Ltd.* v. *Discount Bank (Overseas) Ltd.* [1971] 1 All E.R. 551 (action seeking direction that certain mortgages of land and an injunction to restrain mortgagee from exercising its power of sale *held* not to have been presented in good faith).

[31] See *Heywood* v. *B.D.C. Properties Ltd.* [1963] 1 W.L.R. 975 (in which Harman L.J. stated that the application should have been made by motion invoking the general jurisdiction of the court rather than by summons—action by P for declaration that no contract existed between parties).

[32] L.C.A. 1972, s.8. It is doubtful whether the registration of a bankruptcy petition may be renewed (see *Re Receiving Order (in Bankruptcy)* [1947] Ch. 498.

Register of writs and orders

The following writs and orders[33] may be registered:

(1) any writ or order affecting land issued or made by any court for the purpose of enforcing a judgment or recognisance;

(2) any order appointing a receiver or sequestrator of land;

(3) any receiving order in bankruptcy made on or after January 1, 1926 whether or not it is known to affect land.

Benefits This register deals with the enforcement of judgments and orders of the court. Accordingly, in the context of this work, it may be of benefit in ensuring that the recalcitrant neighbour is kept to his duties and obligations as finally declared by the court. Once again the charge may serve as a useful tactical weapon since it is effective for five years from the date of registration and may be renewed for a further period of five years.[34]

Cancellation

An application to cancel the entry of the charge must be made by way of a *pro forma*[35] supported by sufficient documentary evidence of the applicant's title to apply for such cancellation, if the registration was not made for the applicant's own benefit, and/or an office copy of the order of the court or the Lands Tribunal justifying the cancellation. This procedure may be relaxed if the Registrar is satisfied that the applicant would suffer "exceptional hardship or expense" by complying with the foregoing requirements.[36]

[33] L.C.A. 1972, s.6(1).
[34] *Ibid.* s.8.
[35] L.R.R. 1925, Form K11 and Land Charges Rules 1974, r. 10.
[36] *Ibid.* Form K12 and proviso to r. 10.

2 RIGHTS AND RESTRICTIONS

Legal principles

Licences

Bare licence   A bare licence is a permission, without valuable consideration, which allows a landowner to do an act on his neighbour's land which would otherwise amount to a trespass, *e.g.* to enter and retrieve a ball. Accordingly, even if the licence is granted by deed, it may be revoked on the giving of reasonable notice at any time.[1] However, the revocation will not affect the legality of acts already done whilst the licence was in operation.[2] Such licence cannot, of course, bind third parties.

Licence coupled with an interest   A licence coupled with a right to hunt or fish permits the licensee both to enter at will or on reasonable notice and to remove the subject matter of the right, *e.g.* the ubiquitous deer[3] or tree.[4] In law, such a licence amounts to the grant of an incorporeal hereditament.[5] It is often **Incorporeal** linked to a *profit à prendre*.[6] As a form of proprietary interest, **hereditament** reasonable notice must be given[7] to revoke such a licence and cannot be given where it is limited to the *profit à prendre*. Both forms of licence can be protected by an injunction[8] against the licensor (landowner) and third parties.

Contractual licence   The purpose of a contractual licence is to create a finite permission which is sufficiently binding upon the licensee to prevent him revoking it at will or without reasonable notice during the currency of the contract period,[9] *e.g.* whilst a building contractor is on site.[10]

Such a right may be protected by ordinary contractual remedies including specific performance[11] and an injunction.

---

[1] *Wood* v. *Leadbitter* (1845) 13 M. & W. 838 at 845.

[2] *e.g. Armstrong* v. *Sheppard & Short Ltd.* [1959] 2 Q.B. 384 (oral assent to the construction of a manhole and sewer held to be sufficient to defeat plaintiff's claim in trespass although plaintiff was unaware of his legal title to the land at the material time).

[3] *Thomas* v. *Sorrell* (1673) Vaugh. 330 at 351.

[4] *e.g.* but no proprietary interest in the timber is created until the tree is felled (*Kursell* v. *Timber Operators and Contractors Ltd.* [1927] 1 K.B. 298).

[5] *i.e.* a right in land which does not give the owner physical possession.

[6] See p 41 below. Sporting and fishing rights can only be let by deed (*Swayne* v. *Howells* [1927] 1 K.B. 385).

[7] *e.g.* one month's notice at the end of the shooting season (*Lowe* v. *Adams* [1901] 2 Ch. 598).

[8] *Frogley* v. *Earl of Lovelace* (1859) John 333; *McManus* v. *Cooke* (1887) 35 Ch.D. 681.

[9] *Winter Garden Theatre (London) Ltd.* v. *Millenium Productions* [1948] A.C. 173 .

[10] *London Borough of Hounslow* v. *Twickenham Garden Developments Ltd.* [1971] Ch. 233.

[11] *Verrall* v. *Great Yarmouth B.C.* [1981] Q.B. 202 (repudiation of licence letting hall to National Front).

Exclusive occupation   Where the licensee has exclusive occupation of the land, then the circumstances may well lead to the inference that a tenancy has been created. Since the decision of the House of Lords in *Street* v. *Mountford*,[12] the stated intention of the parties, as manifested in the agreement, is no longer the deciding factor but whether, on the true construction of the agreement, the occupier has been granted exclusive possession of the property in question for a fixed or a periodic term. Accordingly, unless special circumstances exist (*e.g.* where from the outset there was no intention to create legal relations or where possession is granted pursuant to a contract of employment) it will be presumed that a tenancy will have been created.[13] Therefore, the deciding factor is likely to be the quality of the occupation. Certainly, cases like *Clore* v. *Theatrical Properties Ltd.*,[14] dealing with "front of house" rights, will continue to be decided in favour of the licensor where the circumstances of the letting negative the presumption of a tenancy. Where a doubt is likely to exist, the most expedient course will be to apply to the local county court under section 38(4) of the Landlord and Tenant Act 1954 for an order contracting out of the business tenancy code. In an agricultural context the previous practice of creating "grass keep" licences or "grazing agreements"[15] for a specified period of 364 days a year, or with longer break periods, should continue to be adopted, particularly in view of the more relaxed provisions for the conversion of a succession of licences into a tenancy under section 2(2)(*b*) of the Agricultural Holdings Act 1986.[16]

Quality of occupation

Estoppel licences   An irrevocable licence may also be acquired under the principles of estoppel, namely, where the landowner encourages or knowingly permits his neighbour to act in the belief that he is acquiring an irrevocable licence to occupy or use the land, *e.g.* by the expenditure of money.[17] Arguably, such a licence is only effective against the other party; but the Court of Appeal, in recent years, has assumed that an estoppel licence is capable of binding third parties to the extent of being a proprietary interest even though the original agreement may not have been supported by consideration nor evidenced in working.[18]

---

[12] [1985] A.C. 809.

[13] See recent application in *Crancour* v. *Da Silvaesa* (1986) 278 E.G. 618 (sham lettings) and *Bretherton* v. *Paton* (1986) 278 E.G. 615 (prospective purchaser in occupation).

[14] [1936] 3 All E.R. 483.

[15] *e.g. Reid* v. *Dawson* [1955] 1 Q.B. 214 and *Luton* v. *Tinsey* (1978) 249 E.G. 239 under the statutory exception created by s.2(1) at the A.H.A. 1948; s.2(3)(*a*) of the A.H.A. 1986 now uses the expression "grazing and mowing." See *Lory* v. *Brent L.B.C.* [1971] 1 W.L.R. 823 where ploughing and producing crops created a tenancy.

[16] *e.g. Lampard* v. *Barker* (1984) 272 E.G. 783 (tenancy created where no indication in agreement that grazing rights were to be for less than a year). See also *Bahamas International Trust Co. Ltd.* v. *Threadgold* [1974] 1 W.L.R. 1514.

[17] See *Hopgood* v. *Brown* [1955] 1 All E.R. 550 and see p. 16 above.

[18] *Crabb* v. *Arun D.C.* [1976] Ch. 179 (equitable easement) and p. 33 (n. 41) below; but see *Western Fish Products* v. *Penwith D.C.* [1981] 2 All E.R. 204 where the Court of Appeal held that the equitable principle of "proprietary estoppel" was confined, with certain exceptions, to rights and interests created in and over the land of another and was inapplicable to a landowner spending money to take advantage of existing or supposedly existing rights over his own land (*viz.* planning rights).

Rentcharges

Definition Section 1 of the Rentcharges Act 1977 defines a rentcharge as "any annual or other periodic sum charged on or issuing out of land except:

    (1) rent reserved by a lease or tenancy, or
    (2) any sum payable by way of interest."

It arises where land is charged with a rent under a deed or will but the owner of the rent has no reversion on the land. It is enforceable by a power of distress for the payment of it.[19] In the context of rentcharges, reference is sometimes made to "rent-seck." This form of payment is now obsolete.[19a] It differed from a rentcharge to the extent that it reserved a rent without any express power of distress, for which reason it has been colloquially known in the past as "barren rent."[20] A rent-seck cannot issue out of a term of years.[21]

Creation In addition to a deed or a will, a legal rentcharge may be created by statute or under the powers conferred thereby.[22] An equitable rentcharge may be created by a document in writing.[23]

However, under section 2(4) of the 1977 Act, no new rentcharge may be created whether at law or in equity after August 22, 1977, except for a rentcharge:

    (1) which has the effect of making the land on which the rent is charged settled land by virtue of section 1(1)(v) of the Settled Land Act 1925:
    (2) which would have that effect but for the fact that the land on which the rent is charged is already settled land or is held on trust for sale;
    (3) which is an estate rentcharge[24];

Limitations imposed by the 1977 Act
    (4) under any Act of Parliament providing for the creation of rentcharges in connection with the execution of works on land (whether by way of improvements, repairs or otherwise) or the commutation of any obligation to do any such work; or
    (5) by, or in accordance with the requirements of, any order of a court.

---

[19] Pursuant to L.P.A. 1925, s.121.
[19a] By reason of s.2(4) of 1977 Act.
[20] However, under Landlord & Tenant Act 1730, s.5 provision was made for an express right to distrain.
[21] See *Langford* v. *Selmes* (1857) 3 K. & J. 220 at 229.
[22] *e.g.* Improvement of Land Act 1864.
[23] L.P.A. 1925, s.53.
[24] s.2(4) defines "estate rentcharge" as a rentcharge created for the purpose (a) of making covenants to be performed by the owner of the land affected by the rentcharge enforceable by the rent owner against the owner for the time being of the land; or (b) of meeting, or contributing towards, the cost of the performance by the rent owner of covenants for the provision of services, the carrying out of maintenance or repairs, the effecting of insurance or the making of any payment by him for the benefit of the land affected by the rentcharge or for the benefit of that and other land, and that the amount payable, if more than a nominal amount, is reasonable in relation to that covenant. See further p. 64 for use to enforce positive covenants where a "flying freehold" exists.

Enforcement   The owner of the rentcharge may enforce it in a number of ways:

Action for money   This may be pursued against the current freehold owner[25] in possession of the land or any part of it upon which the rentcharge is payable, even though it may exceed the value of that land.[25a]

Distress   If no express power of distress is given in the instrument creating the rentcharge, then, subject to any contrary intention, the owner of the rentcharge can distrain as soon as the rent or any part of it is more than 21 days in arrear.[26]

Enforcing a rentcharge

Re-entry   If the rent or any part of it is more than 40 days in arrear, the owner of the rentcharge may enter the land and take possession of it without causing damage and receive the income until he has paid himself all rent due, with costs.[26a]

Demise to a trustee   In like circumstances, after 40 days, the owner of the rentcharge may let the land to a trustee for a term of years, on trust to raise the money due, with all costs and expenses, by creating a mortgage, receiving the income or any other reasonable means.[27] Moreover, where the rentcharge has been created after July 15, 1964 the rule against perpetuities will not apply to this remedy.[27a]

Rentcharge charged on another rentcharge   In such circumstances, if the rent is more than 21 days in arrears, the owner of the primary rentcharge may appoint a receiver.[28]

Lapse of time

Extinguishment   Under section 3 of the 1977 Act, every rentcharge will be extinguished at the expiration of 60 years from August 22, 1977 or the date when the rentcharge first became payable, except where the rentchargeable is payable in relation to land wholly or partly in lieu of tithes or is one of the statutory exceptions set out under section 2(3). In addition, under the Limitation Act 1980[28a] the right of recovery will be extinguished if the rentcharge is not paid for 12 years and no sufficient acknowledgment of the owner's title has been made.

Release   The owner of a rentcharge may release the land, wholly or in part, from all the rent or part of it.[29] If the release is not effected by deed, it may still be valid in equity.

Redemption   Under sections 8 to 10 of the 1977 Act, the landowner can redeem certain rentcharges[30] by paying a sum

[25] Known as the "terre tenant." A lessee for a term of years is not liable (*Re Herbage Rents* [1896] 2 Ch. 811).
[25a] *Pertwee* v. *Townsend* [1896] 2 Q.B. 129.
[26] L.P.A. 1925, s.121(2). For rentcharges created before 1882 an immediate right to distrain exists under the Landlord and Tenant Act 1730, S.5.
[26a] L.P.A. 1925, s.121(3) for rentcharges created after 1881.
[27] L.P.A. 1925, s.121(4).
[27a] Perpetuities and Accumulations Act 1964, s.11 amending L.P.A. 1925, s.121(6). The other powers are also expressly excepted.
[28] L.P.A. 1925, s.122. The receiver has the same powers as a receiver appointed under a mortgage.
[28a] ss.15, 38.
[29] L.P.A. 1925, s.70.
[30] *i.e.* those which are not exempt from the 60-year rule under s.3(3).

equal to the capital value according to the formula set out under
section 10(1). Following payment, a redemption certificate will
be issued by the Secretary of State. This will discharge the land
from the rentcharge but without prejudice to the recovery of any
outstanding arrears.

Easements

General principles   An easement is an interest in land which
entitles a landowner to use, or restrict the use of, his neighbour's
Definition   land in a particular way without giving him possession of it. Most
easements are positive in character in that they entitle the
dominant owner to do something on the servient owner's land
(*e.g.* to enter on to the servient land to repair a wall). Save for an
easement requiring a neighbour to maintain a fence,[31] a positive
easement will not require the servient owner to do something. An
easement may be negative in that it may require the servient
owner to refrain from doing something, *e.g.* an easement of light
or of support.[32]

Requirements   A right can only exist as an easement if all the
following requirements are satisfied:

(1) It must belong to the list of recognised easements. A
landowner can only create property interests that are
recognised in law and, as a general rule, the courts will not
create new property interests for him.[33] Accordingly, at
various times, certain rights have **not** been recognised as
easements. These have included the right to a view[34] and
the right to have a building protected from the weather by
another building.[35]

(2) There must be a dominant and a servient property.[36]

(3) The dominant and servient properties must be separately
owned.

(4) The right must benefit the dominant property and not be
for the personal benefit of the dominant owner. The two
factors which will be relevant in this regard are (a) the
proximity of the two properties and (b) the use to which
the dominant property is put.[37]

Types of easement   Legal easements can only be created if the
Legal easements   right is:

(1) for an interest equivalent to a fee simple absolute in
possession or a term of years absolute.[38] and

---

[31] *Ward* v. *Kirkland* [1967] Ch. 194.
[32] See further pp. 43–47.
[33] See *Hill* v. *Tupper* (1863) 2 H. & C. 121 at 127; *Phipps* v. *Pears* [1965] 1 Q.B.
76 at 83.
[34] *Browne* v. *Flower* [1911] 1 Ch. 219 at 225.
[35] *Phipps* v. *Pears* [1965] 1 Q.B. 76.
[36] See *e.g. Re Ellenborough Park* [1956] Ch. 131: pleasure garden in a building
estate held to be servient property.
[37] *e.g. Chapman* v. *Edwards* [1938] 2 All E.R. 507, where the provision in a lease
giving the right to use the flank walls of the adjoining premises for advertising
purposes did not create an easement since the user was not limited to the
requirements of the dominant property.
[38] L.P.A. 1925, s.1(2)(*a*).

(2) created by deed, assent,[39] prescription or statute.

A legal easement passes by conveyance of the land to which it is annexed without necessarily having to be mentioned expressly.[40] Since it cannot be over-reached, having all the incidents of a legal estate, it is not necessary to register it as a land charge.

Equitable easements

Any easement which fails to satisfy the foregoing requirements can only be an equitable easement. By section 2(3)(*iii*) of the Law of Property Act 1925 it has been defined as meaning:

> "any easement, liberty or privilege over or affecting land created or arising after the commencement of this Act and being merely an equitable interest."

Such rights must be registered to be fully enforceable.[41] A quasi-easement is a right (equivalent to an easement in type) which exists for the benefit of certain land over other land in the same ownership.[42]

Creation   An easement may be created by one of the following three methods:

(1) Express grant or reservation   This must take place by deed, the contents of which should:

(1) identify the dominant property and show an intention to annexe the benefit of the easement to it; and
(2) identify and show an intention to burden the servient property.

Express

In practice, most express easements arise where a person sells part of his land and either grants easements over the retained land or reserves them over the sold land.[43] Whether the deed creates an easement or some lesser right (*e.g.* a licence) will depend upon the particular form of words that has been used. Extrinsic evidence is allowed to identify the property intended to receive the benefit[44] but only if the words in the deed are not clear.[45] In the absence of identification of the land there is a rebuttable presumption that the dominant tenement is the land conveyed by the deed granting the easement.[46]

(2) Implied grant or reservation

Easements of necessity   These will be implied where a property cannot be used at all without the easement (*e.g.* a right of way[47] or of lateral support[48]). They do not extend to rights which are

---

[39] L.P.A. 1925, s.52(1); *i.e.* an instrument under seal.
[40] This is irrespective of L.P.A. 1925, s.62.
[41] See L.P.A. 1925, s.199(*d*)(*i*). For creation by proprietary estoppel see *Crabb* v. *Arun D.C.* [1976] Ch. 179; *E. R. Ives Investment Ltd* v. *High* [1967] 2 Q.B. 379; *Ward* v. *Kirkland* [1967] Ch. 194 and p. 29 (n. 18) above.
[42] See *Bolton* v. *Bolton* (1879) 11 Ch.D. 968 at 970.
[43] See pp. 3–4 for definition of "reservation."
[44] See, *e.g. Johnstone* v. *Holdway* [1963] 1 Q.B. 601.
[45] *(The) Shannon Ltd.* v. *Venner Ltd.* [1965] Ch. 682.
[46] *Ibid.*
[47] *e.g. Cory* v. *Davies* [1923] 2 Ch. 95.
[48] *e.g. Rigby* v. *Bennett* (1882) 21 Ch.D. 559 where a man built two houses adjoining one another and retained one.

necessary for the reasonable enjoyment of that property (*e.g.* a right to light[49]). This principle does not, however, rest in itself on a basis of public policy but on the foregoing implication. This may be excluded by express agreement.[50] Usually, an easement of necessity will arise where a vendor sells part of his land and retains a portion. However, if some of the surrounding land belongs to third parties, a way of necessity can still be implied[51] so long as the necessity exists at the outset and does not subsequently.[52] In such circumstances, the extent of the right of way will be limited to the needs of the land at this time and will not cover all purposes.[53] It is doubtful whether such a right is lost, however, if the necessity subsequently ceases.[54]

Implied

Ancillary easements   These are incidental easements necessary to the reasonable enjoyment of an express easement, *e.g.* the right to water sheep in addition to common grazing rights[55] or a right of way to a spring in addition to a right to draw from it.[56]

Intended easements   These are implied where it is necessary to grant additional rights to give effect to the common intention of the parties.[57]

Rule in Wheeldon v. Burrows[58]   Where a landowner has any quasi-easements over adjoining land, these will ripen into proper easements upon the sale of that land if it can be established that the right is:

(1) "continuous" (*i.e.* constant) and "apparent" (*i.e.* readily discoverable);
(2) reasonably necessary for the enjoyment of the land sold;
(3) in use at the time of the sale.

Examples of rights upheld have included a right to light,[59] the right to use a drain[60] and a watercourse through visible pipes,[61] but not to take water from a neighbour's pump from time to time.[62]

Rights of way do not automatically come within the *Rule* but will be upheld if clear evidence of way can be shown *e.g.* by means of a visible and made road[63] or a worn track.[64]

---

[49] *Ray* v. *Hazeldine* [1904] 2 Ch. 17; see also *Hansford* v. *Jago* [1921] 1 Ch. 322.
[50] See *Nickerson* v. *Barraclough* [1981] 2 W.L.R. 773.
[51] *Barry* v. *Hasseldine* [1952] Ch. 835.
[52] *Midland Rly.* v. *Miles* (1886) 33 Ch.D. 632.
[53] *Maguire* v. *Browne* (1921) 1 Ir.R. 148; *Corporation of London* v. *Riggs* (1880) 13 Ch.D. 38; *Carr-Saunders* v. *McNeil (Dick) Associates* [1986] 1 W.L.R. 922.
[54] *Proctor* v. *Hodgson* (1855) 10 Ex. 824 at 828 casting doubt on *Holmes* v. *Goring* (1824) 2 Bing. 76 at 83.
[55] *White* v. *Taylor (No. 4)* [1968] 2 W.L.R. 1402.
[56] *Pwllbach Colliery Co. Ltd.* v. *Woodman* [1915] A.C. 634 at 646.
[57] *e.g.* an easement to have a duct fitted to the outside of premises let as a restaurant (*Wong* v. *Beaumont Property Trust Ltd.* [1965] 1 Q.B. 173).
[58] (1879) 12 Ch.D. 31.
[59] *e.g. Birmingham, Dudley and District Banking Co.* v. *Ross* (1888) 38 Ch.D. 295; *Godwin* v. *Schweppes Ltd.* [1902] 1 Ch. 926.
[60] *Pyer* v. *Carter* (1857) 1 H. & N. 916.
[61] *Watts* v. *Kelson* (1870) 6 Ch.App. 166.
[62] *Polden* v. *Bastard* (1865) L.R. 1 Q.B. 156.
[63] *Hansford* v. *Jago* [1921] 1 Ch. 322.
[64] *Borman* v. *Griffith* [1930] 1 Ch. 493 at 498.

Law of Property Act 1925, section 62 The material parts of the section read as follows:

"(1) A conveyance of land shall be deemed to include and shall by virtue of this Act operate to convey, with the land, all buildings, erections, fixtures, commons, hedges, ditches, fences, ways, waters, watercourses, liberties, privileges, easements, rights, and advantages whatsoever, appertaining or reputed to appertain to the land or any part thereof, or, at the time of conveyance, demised, occupied, or enjoyed with, or reputed or known as part or parcel of or appurtenant to the land or any part thereof,

(2) A conveyance of land, having houses or other buildings thereon, shall be deemed to include and shall by virtue of this Act operate to convey, with the land, houses, or other buildings all outhouses, erections, fixtures, cellars, areas, courts, courtyards, cisterns, sewers, gutters, drains, ways, passages, lights, watercourses, liberties, privileges, easements, rights, and advantages whatsoever, appertaining or reputed to appertain to the land, houses, or other buildings conveyed, or any of them, or any part thereof, or, at the time of conveyance, demised, occupied, or enjoyed with, or reputed or known as part or parcel of or appurtenant to, the land, houses, or other buildings conveyed, or any of them, or any part thereof."

The object of the "general words" implied by section 62 was to shorten deeds. Accordingly, it only applies to a conveyance[65] whereas the rule in *Wheeldon* v. *Burrows* applies to the contract as well as to the conveyance. However, the operation of section 62 is much wider since the only requirement is that the right must have been enjoyed at the time of the conveyance[66] but only "if and so far as a contrary intention is not expressed in the conveyance and has effect subject to the terms of the conveyance."[67]

Such rights will include a *profit à prendre*[68] but not matters of general enjoyment of the property which amount to matters of personal contract, *e.g.* the right to park a car near to a house[69] or to use a back entrance effectively on convenient occasions only[70] or to the supply of hot water and central heating.[71] On the other hand, it has been held that a right to have a neighbour "keep up the fences and walls" is a right capable of being passed under section 62.[72]

[65] By L.P.A. 1925, s.205(1)(ii) a "conveyance" includes a "mortgage, charge, lease, assent, vesting declaration, vesting instrument, disclaimer, release, and every other assurance of property, or of an interest there, by any instrument except a will."
[66] This can sometimes lead to the ripening of a quasi-easement into a full easement where the land is divided into separate ownership (see *Ward* v. *Kirkland* [1967] Ch. 194) or to the enlarging of an existing easement (see *Graham* v. *Philcox* [1984] Q.B. 747—right of way extended to whole building of which purchaser formerly tenant of part).
[67] L.P.A. 1925, s.62(4).
[68] *White* v. *Williams* [1922] 1 K.B. 727 and see pp. 41–42.
[69] *Le Strange* v. *Pettefar* (1939) 161 L.T. 300.
[70] *Green* v. *Ashco Horticulturist* [1966] 1 W.L.R. 889.
[71] *Regis Property Co.* v. *Redman* [1959] A.C. 370.
[72] *Crow* v. *Wood* [1971] Q.B. 77.

Non-derogation from grant   Allied to the foregoing types of implied easements is the general principle that a grantor must not derogate from his grant.[73] This may result in the imposition of an obligation which runs with the land as a proprietary interest, although an easement cannot be granted, *e.g.* where the servient tenement is in the possession of a tenant at the time of the grant.[74]

(3) Presumed grant or prescription

Principles   Since in law there is a presumption that a right of enjoyment of property derives from a lawful origin, the courts will uphold such enjoyment, provided the following conditions can be fulfilled:

(1) The essential requirements of a valid easement are fulfilled.[75]

(2) The use has been:

(a) As of right (*nec vi, nec clam, nec precario*). *Nec vi* (without force)—The claimant must not commit acts of violence (*e.g.* breaking down gates and fences) nor continue the use if continuous and unmistakeable protests come from the servient owner.[76] *Nec clam* (without secrecy)—This requirement relates not only to the nature of the use (*e.g.* by stealth or at night) but also to the nature of the easement itself (*e.g.* secret excavations leading to a claim of an extraordinary degree of support[77]). *Nec precario* (without permission)—The claimant must establish that his enjoyment does not arise under a licence or permission from the servient tenant or that such permission has expired or been revoked expressly or by implication.[78] In addition to the foregoing it must also be established that the use has not arisen under a mistaken view of the other party's rights.[79]

(b) Continuous—Depending upon the nature of the easement claimed, this condition is fulfilled if regular use can be shown.[80] Breaks in such use are permitted[81] whenever circumstances so require but such intervals in time must not be excessive.[82] The parties may vary the line of a right of way by agreement without breaking the continuity of use.[83]

---

[73] See *Browne* v. *Flower* [1911] 1 Ch. 219 at 224.

[74] See *Cable* v. *Bryant* [1908] 1 Ch. 259.

[75] See p. 32.

[76] *Dalton* v. *Angus* (1881) 6 App.Cas. 786.

[77] *Partridge* v. *Scott* (1838) 3 M. & W. 229 and *Dalton* v. *Angus* at first instance (1878) 4 Q.B.D. 162.

[78] See *Healey* v. *Hawkins* [1968] 1 W.L.R. 1967.

[79] See *Earl de la Warr* v. *Miles* (1881) 17 Ch.D 535 and *Thomas W. Ward Ltd.* v. *Alexander Bruce (Grays) Ltd.* [1959] 2 Lloyd's Rep. 472; but see also *Bridle* v. *Ruby, The Times*, January 13, 1988 (n. 94 below) for success under the doctrine of lost modern grant.

[80] *Dare* v. *Heathcote* (1856) 25 L.J. Ex.245.

[81] For a claim under Prescription Act 1832, s.2, such enjoyment must be without a break (see *Hollins* v. *Verney* (1884) 13 Q.B.D. 304).

[82] See *Hollins* v. *Verney* (1884) 13 Q.B.D. 304 at 307, 308. See also *e.g. Goldsmith* v. *Burrow Construction Co. Ltd.*, *The Times*, July 31, 1987 where the locking of gate and path for substantial periods defeated claim.

[83] *Davis* v. *Whitby* [1974] Ch. 186.

Prescription

(c) In Fee Simple—This means that the user must be by or on behalf of the owner in fee simple of the dominant property[84] against his counterpart of the servient property,[85] except in respect of profits acquired by prescription at common law[86] or under the doctrine of lost modern grant and easements of light under the Prescription Act 1832.[87]

(3) Enjoyed for a sufficient length of time. This aspect is of particular importance in connection with the three methods of prescription:

(a) *At Common Law*—The claimant must show that enjoyment has continued by himself and his predecessors for so long a period as man can remember. The relevant date has been fixed at A.D. 1189.[88] In practice, if he can establish enjoyment for a period in excess of 20 years and that the easement could have or has existed[89] since 1189, then he will succeed. It follows that if evidence can be given of unity of ownership during this period or that the building in question had not been constructed,[90] then the claim will fail.

(b) *Lost Modern Grant*—This doctrine presumes that the grant was made just before the relevant period of enjoyment began but that it has been lost. Since the presumption is based on a fiction, the claimant is not obliged to give particulars of the alleged grant but he must plead whether it was made before or after a particular date.[91] Whilst such a claim cannot be defeated by evidence that no grant was actually made,[92] a defendant will succeed if he can prove that there was nobody who could lawfully have made the grant during the entire period when it could have been made,[93] *e.g.* where the land has been held under a strict settlement. Generally, 20 years' enjoyment will be sufficient to prove the presumption.[94]

(c) *Prescription Act 1832*—The relevant sections can be summarised as follows:

(i) Section 1 (*profits à prendre*)—At least 30 years uninterrupted enjoyment as of right must be shown.

---

[84] In this respect a tenant can claim on behalf of his landlord (*Gateward's Case* (1607) 6 Co. Rep. 59b; *Dawney* v. *Cashford* (1697) Carth. 432).

[85] Thus no prescriptive easement will arise if the land is occupied by a tenant for years (*Daniel* v. *North* (1809) 11 East. 372) or a tenant for life (*Robert* v. *James* (1903) 89 L.T. 282).

[86] *Johnson* v. *Barnes* (1873) L.R. 8 C.P. 527 but not under the Prescription Act 1832.

[87] Including one tenant against another tenant of the same landlord (*Morgan* v. *Fear* [1907] A.C. 425).

[88] By the *Statute of Westminster 1275* and the first of the reign of Richard I.

[89] *Hulbert* v. *Dale* [1909] 2 Ch. 570 at 577.

[90] *e.g.* in a claim of a right to light (*Duke of Norfolk* v. *Arbuthnot* (1880) 5 C.P.D. 390).

[91] *Tremayne* v. *English Clays Lovering Pochin & Co. Ltd.* [1972] 1 W.L.R. 657.

[92] *Tehidy Minerals Ltd.* v. *Norman* [1971] 2 Q.B. 528.

[93] *Neaverson* v. *Peterborough R.D.C.* [1902] 1 Ch. 557.

[94] *Roberts* v. *James* (1903) 89 L.T. 282. Indeed, in the recent case of *Bridle* v. *Ruby, The Times*, January 13, 1988, the Court of Appeal *held* that a right of way could be acquired under the doctrine of lost modern grant even when the 20 years' uninterrupted grant was based on the parties' mistaken view as to existing rights.

If such enjoyment can be established over a period of 60 years, then the right is deemed to be absolute unless it has arisen as a result of a written consent or agreement. The Crown is bound by this provision.

(ii) Section 2 (easements other than of light)—This lays down periods of 20 years and 40 years on a comparable basis. Any consent which is given intermittently during the relevant period will defeat a claim. However, whereas a written consent given at the beginning of the period will defeat all claims, an oral consent given at the beginning will only defeat a claim based on the shorter period of 20 years.[95]

(iii) Section 3 (right of light)—If it can be established that access and use of light to and for any dwelling, house, workshop or other building[96] has been enjoyed without interruption and without written consent or agreement for 20 years, then an absolute right is created. It is not necessary to show user by or on behalf of one freeholder against the other. Accordingly, the fact that the servient tenement has been held under a lease for the whole of the period in question does not prevent the easement being effective against the landlord and against the subsequent owners of the land.[97]

Prescription Act 1832

Unlike sections 1 and 2, the Crown is neither named nor bound by this provision.

The right cannot become absolute and indefensible until it is called into question in legal proceedings.[98] It is sufficient, however, if evidence of "actual enjoyment"[99] in the character of an easement is established[1] but the quantum of light that can be claimed is not diminished if the full extent of such light has not been admitted continuously[2] or the user of the room requires less than the normal amount of light.[3] However, whilst fluctuating or temporary obstructions on the servient land may not necessarily amount to an interruption,[4] the erection of a screen

[95] See *Healey* v. *Hawkins* [1968] 1 W.L.R. 1967.
[96] "Other building" has been held to include a church (*Ecclesiastical Commissioners* v. *Kind* (1880) 14 Ch.D. 213), a greenhouse (*Clifford* v. *Holt* [1899] 1 Ch. 698) and an open-side garage (*Smith & Co.* v. *Morris* (1962) 112 L.J. 702) but not a structure for storing timber (*Harris* v. *De Pinna* (1886) 33 Ch.D. 238) nor, seemingly, to a trade fixture removable by the tenant at the end of the tenancy (*Maberley* v. *Dowson* (1827) 5 L.J. (o.s.) K.B. 261). It should also be borne in mind that under s.3 of the Act the dominant owner's right is an easement for access to light to a building and not to a particular room within it (see *Carr-Saunders* v. *McNeil (Dick) Associates* [1986] 1 W.L.R. 922).
[97] *Morgan* v. *Fear* [1907] A.C. 425.
[98] See s.4 and *Colls* v. *Home & Colonial Stores* [1904] A.C. 179 at 189; *Hyman* v. *Van den Bergh* [1908] 1 Ch. 167 at 172.
[99] *Smith* v. *Baxter* [1900] 2 Ch. 138.
[1] *i.e.* separate dominant and servient tenements; but it does not matter if the dominant tenement has been unoccupied continuously (*Courtauld* v. *Legh* (1869) L.R. 4 Exch. 126).
[2] *Cooper* v. *Straker* (1888) 40 Ch.D. 21; *Smith* v. *Baxter* [1900] 2 Ch. 138; *e.g.* a scullery.
[3] *Price* v. *Hilditch* [1930] 1 Ch. 500; see *Harbidge* v. *Warwick* (1849) 3 Exch. 552.
[4] *e.g.* stacking of empty packing cases *Presland* v. *Bingham* (1889) 41 Ch.D. 268.

or hoarding can defeat a claim.[5] As a result of the Rights of Light Act 1959, a servient owner may now provide a notional obstruction by registering a notice in the register of local land charges identifying the dominant and servient tenements and specifying the size and position of the notional obstruction.[6] The notice then takes effect as an acquiesced obstruction for a period of a year,[7] during which time the dominant owner can sue for cancellation or variation of the registration.[8] However, as an initial step, a certificate must be obtained from the Lands Tribunal that adequate notice has been given to all persons likely to be affected or that the case is of exceptional urgency.[9]

(iv) Section 4 (periods of enjoyment)—These are calculated backwards from the date of the proceedings in which the prescriptive claim is brought into question. Therefore, the vital period is that (*e.g.* of 20 years) "next before some action." It should also be borne in mind that the prescriptive right always remains inchoate until this event occurs. If any interruption[10] takes place, then the act will not be treated as such (and thereby defeat the prescriptive claim) so long as the claimant has not submitted to, or acquiesced, in the obstruction for one year after he learns both of the obstruction and of the person responsible for it.[11]

(v) Section 5 (pleadings)—This provides that the claimant need only plead that his enjoyment has been "as of right" during the relevant period. If the other party intends to rely upon any proviso, exception, incapacity, disability, contract agreement or other fact or matter upon which reliance will be placed to defeat the claim, then these must be specifically pleaded.[12]

(vi) Section 6 (no presumptions)—This provides that enjoyment for less than the statutory periods shall not give rise to any claim under the Act and that no presumption shall be allowed or made to enable reliance to be placed upon a lesser period.

(vii) Section 7 (disabilities)—This provides that a deduction must be made from the statutory periods in respect of the time when the person capable of resisting the claim is a minor or mentally incapacitated or a tenant for life. The period during

---

[5] *e.g. Bonner* v. *G.W.R.* (1883) 24 Ch.D. 1.
[6] s.2 of the 1959 Act and Local Land Charges Rules 1966 (S.I. 1966 No. 579), r. 16.
[7] s.3.
[8] For this purpose, he may treat his enjoyment as having begun a year earlier.
[9] s.2 and Land Tribunal Rules 1975 (S.I. 1975 No. 299), Part VI.
[10] In this context, the term means some "hostile obstruction" and not mere non-user (see *Smith* v. *Baxter* [1900] 2 Ch. 138 at 143) nor commencement of proceedings by the servient owner (*Reilly* v. *Orange* [1955] 2 Q.B. 112).
[11] *Seddon* v. *Bank of Bolton* (1882) 19 Ch.D. 462; and see *e.g. Goldsmith* v. *Burrow Construction Co. Ltd., The Times*, July 31, 1987 (and n. 81 above).
[12] See *Colls* v. *Home & Colonial Stores* [1904] A.C. 179 at 205.

which the action is pending and actively prosecuted must also be deducted. The section applies to prescriptive claims in respect of profits and easements other than of light.

(viii) Section 8 (further deductions)—This applies only to the period of 40 years[13] and therefore does not concern profits or rights to light. It provides that if the servient tenement has been held under a "term of life," or any term of years exceeding three years from the date of grant, then that term shall be excluded in computing the period of 40 years (where the claim concerns a right of way over land or water, a watercourse or the use of water) provided the reversioner resists the claim within three years of the determination of the term.

Commons   Under the Commons Registration Act 1965[14] an additional right of deduction is available in respect of both the shorter and the longer periods where, during the period in question, the right to graze animals cannot be exercised due to animal health or because the common has been requisitioned by a Government department. Non-user for such reasons does not rank, though, as an interruption.

Extinguishment   There are three circumstances in which an easement may be extinguished.

Express release   In order to be effective, this must be by deed.[15]

Implied release   This arises where the actions of the owner of the dominant tenement shows an intention to abandon the easement in the following circumstances:

(1) By licence—*e.g.* if the dominant owner, whether orally or in writing, authorises an obstruction of a permanent nature on the servient land, then an abandonment will be presumed.[16]

(2) By cessation or alteration of user—An intention to abandon must be shown, *e.g.* by alterations to the dominant land which make the enjoyment of the easement impossible or unnecessary.[17] Mere non-user will not imply a release in itself although non-user for a long period may raise a presumption of abandonment, certainly if it is as long as 20 years.[18] In the case of rights of way, occasional substitution of another track may be considered as substantially the exercise of the existing right.[19] Mere

Release

---

[13] See *Park* v. *Skinner* (1852) 18 Q.B. 568.
[14] s.16.
[15] Co. Ltt. 264b; see also *Poulton* v. *Moore* [1915] 1 K.B. 400.
[16] *Treweeke* v. *36 Wolseley Road Property Ltd.* (1973) 128 C.L.R. 274. See also *Armstrong* v. *Sheppard & Short Ltd.* [1959] 2 Q.B. 384 at 399–401.
[17] *e.g. Ecclesiastical Commissioners for England* v. *Kind* (1880) 14 Ch.D. 213 and *Scott* v. *Pape* (1886) 31 Ch.D. 554—as to rights of light; see also *Tehidy Minerals Ltd.* v. *Norman* [1971] 2 Q.B. 528.
[18] *Moore* v. *Rawson* (1824) 3 B. & C. 332 at 339.
[19] *Payne* v. *Shedden* (1834) 1 Mood. & R. 382.

non-user, where no occasion for user arises, will also not constitute abandonment in itself.[20]

(3) By unity of ownership and possession—Both these elements must be established. The absence of one merely leads to the right being suspended.[21]

Release by statute   This may be express, *e.g.* by section 295(1) of the Housing Act 1985 which provides, *inter alia*, that all private rights of way over land acquired by a local authority under a clearance order shall be extinguished or under section 118(1) of the Town & Country Planning Act 1971 in respect of land compulsorily acquired. Alternatively, it may be implied, *e.g.* by failure to register under the Commons Registration Act 1965[22] or where it was shown that the construction of a pier authorised by statute would be physically inconsistent with the existence of a public right of way.[23]

Profits á prendre

Definition   A *profit à prendre* or *profit* (for short) is a right to remove something capable of ownership from the servient land, whereas an easement relates only to user of that land. Examples include the right to graze sheep[24] or to exercise sporting rights.

Where the profit is enjoyed to the exclusion of all other persons, it is known as a "sole" or "several" *profit(s)*. Where such enjoyment takes place with others, including the owner of the servient land, then it is termed a *profit* "in common" or a right of common.

As with an easement, a *profit* may be appurtenant to the dominant tenement and thereby run with the land for the benefit of subsequent owners. However, it must be limited by reference to a definite limit or to the needs of the dominant tenement.[25]

Profits in gross are unconnected with the ownership of the dominant land and are, therefore, not limited to the needs of it, *e.g.* the right to take fish from a canal without stint.[26] They are an interest in land and, therefore, can be devolved in any of the usual ways.

Profits can now only be created by statute, express grant or by prescription. Whilst the same rules relating to easements in general apply, a *profit* in gross cannot be obtained under the Prescription Act 1832 nor will it be implied under the rule in *Wheeldon* v. *Burrows*. Profits in common are subject to

---

[20] *James* v. *Stevenson* [1893] A.C. 162. (Dominant owner not using some of the roads over which way existed coupled with servient owner's use of those parts for farm purposes held not to constitute abandonment). See also *Ward* v. *Ward* (1852) 7 Exch. 838 (non-user for period in excess of 20 years held not to be abandonment although dominant owner had a more convenient access through his own land).

[21] *e.g. Richardson* v. *Graham* [1908] 1 K.B. 39.

[22] New rights may be created and registered. However, in respect of land over which no rights have previously been registered (see S.I. 1969 No. 1843).

[23] *Yarmouth Corporation* v. *Simmons* (1878) 10 Ch.D. 518.

[24] *White* v. *Taylor (No. 4)* [1968] 2 W.L.R. 1402.

[25] See *Lord Chesterfield* v. *Harris* [1908] 2 Ch. 397.

[26] *Staffordshire & Worcestershire Canal Navigation* v. *Bradley* [1912] 1 Ch. 91.

registration under the Commons Registration Act 1965[27] and only for a definite number of animals.

(1) Profit of estovers   This is the right to take wood from the servient land for the specific purposes of repairing fences ("lay-bote"), making or repairing agricultural implements ("plough-bote") or repairing a house or for domestic heating ("house-bote").

(2) Profit of pasture   This can take the following forms:

(*a*) *Appendant*   This is limited to the number of horses, oxen, cows and sheep which are "levant and couchant" on the land, *i.e.* the number which the dominant land is capable of maintaining during the winter.[28]

(*b*) *Appurtenant*   This depends on the terms of the grant or the type of animals habitually turned out to pasture. The number must be fixed either by agreement or by levancy and couchancy.

Types of Profit

(*c*) *Pur cause de vicinage*   This relates to commons and limits the commons to the number of cattle which the land can maintain.

(*d*) *In gross*   This can exist for a fixed number of cattle or "without stint," though the latter right is limited to the number of cattle that the servient tenement can maintain in addition to any existing burdens.

(3) Profit of piscary   This is the right to catch and take away fish. It can exist in gross or as an appurtenant right.[29]

(4) Other sporting rights   They may also exist as profits. Of consideration is that the right to hunt, shoot or fowl is not infringed if the servient owner drives away game as a result of cutting timber "in the ordinary way"[30] but infringement will occur if fundamental changes are made to the land.[31]

(5) Profit of turbary   This is the right to dig and remove peat or turf for use as fuel in a house on the dominant tenement.

Specific considerations

Rights to air

Whilst a general right to the access to air passing over servient land cannot be acquired by prescription,[32] if a definite aperture or channel can be shown, then such a right will be upheld, *e.g.*

[27] See pp. 8 and 40.
[28] *Robertson* v. *Hartopp* (1889) 43 Ch.D. 484 at 516.
[29] See *Lord Chesterfield* v. *Harris* [1908] 2 Ch. 397.
[30] *Gearns* v. *Baker* (1875) 10 Ch.App. 355.
[31] *Peech* v. *Best* [1931] 1 K.B. 1.
[32] *e.g. Bryant* v. *Lefever* (1879) 4 C.P.D. 172. No right of free access to air to chimneys.

where a skylight placed over a yard materially impedes the passage of air to the plaintiff's kitchen window.[33] Moreover, following the principle that a grantor may not derogate from his grant if land is specifically let or sold for the plaintiff's particular business, then an interruption of the air supply will be actionable on the basis of derogation from grant.[34] Likewise, a grantee may have an implied easement of necessity to enter upon the grantor's land to erect an airduct so that he may carry on his business legally.[35] However, the right to prevent the access of impure air is a right of property in itself and does not require an easement to uphold the injured party's rights.[36]

Rights to light

Acquisition   A landowner does not have a natural right to light. Accordingly, for the purposes of enforcement, it must be established that the right has been obtained by grant, agreement or prescription. In this last respect, the right to light can be claimed not only under the Prescription Act 1832[37] but also at common law or by lost modern grant. However, it must be established (i) that the actual enjoyment is of right and (ii) that there is a presumption of a grant if these latter two methods are to be relied upon.[38] For this reason reliance is rarely placed upon these two methods of acquisition.

Vacant land   No right can be acquired in respect of vacant land. Accordingly, an adjoining owner can, prima facie, build to the extremity of his land and thereby obstruct the free passage of light and air.[39] Therefore, no action can be maintained at common law for disturbing a neighbour's privacy by opening windows which overlook the adjoining property.[40] However, the adjoining owner is equally at liberty to obstruct such windows at **User**   any time during the next 20 years,[41] subject to the question of planning permission, and thus prevent the acquisition of an easement of light.[42] The provisions of the Rights to Light Act 1959 can equally be utilised both to prevent and promote development of the adjoining land.[43] In this context it must always be borne in mind that the necessity of planning permission,[44] bye-law approval or consent under the Building Acts[45] will mean that the line of such building will be made the

[33] *Gale* v. *Abbott* (1862) 8 Jur. (N.S.) 987; see also *Dent* v. *Auction Mart Co.* (1866) L.R. 2 Eq. 238.

[34] *Aldin* v. *Latimer Clerk, Murhead & Co.* [1894] 2 Ch. 437—timber drying sheds.

[35] *Wong* v. *Beaumont Property Trust Ltd.* [1965] 1 Q.B. 173.

[36] See *Curriers' Co.* v. *Corbett* (1865) 4 De G.J. & S.M. 764.

[37] See pp. 38–40.

[38] See *Colls* v. *Home & Colonial Stores* [1904] A.C. 179 at 205–206.

[39] See, *e.g. Potts* v. *Smith* (1868) L.R. 6 Eq. 311 at 318; *Harris* v. *De Pinna* (1886) 33 Ch.D. 238.

[40] See *Chandler* v. *Thompson* (1811) 3 Camp. 86; *Tapling* v. *Jones* (1865) 11 H.L.C. 290 at 305; *Dalton* v. *Angus* (1881) 6 App.Cas. 740 at 764; *Browne* v. *Flower* [1911] 1 Ch. 219 at 225.

[41] *e.g.* from the date of construction.

[42] See *Tapling* v. *Jones* (1865) 11 H.L.Cas. 290.

[43] See pp. 66–70 for position with restrictive covenants.

[44] See pp. 121–136.

[45] See pp. 114–116.

subject of consultation and review before actual construction can take place.

Built land   Under the Prescription Act 1832,[46] the enjoyment must relate to a "building"[47] in which there must be an "aperture."[48] It is the aperture which defines the area which is to be kept free on the servient land.[49] Indeed, as a general rule it can be said that an easement of light can only exist in such circumstances, whatever the method of acquisition. However, it is only under the 1832 Act that no actual enjoyment (in the sense of user and occupation) need be established. It is sufficient, therefore, to show that the aperture existed and that the light will have been used during the relevant period.[50]

Alterations   Where an alteration takes place to the dominant tenement, the preservation of the right to light will depend upon the identity of the light and not on the identity of the aperture.[51] Accordingly, if there is an alteration in the size or position of the aperture, the burden of the servient owner will not be increased, even if most of the light to the altered aperture is obstructed.[52] However, where an obstruction by the servient owner not only infringes an easement of light to one set of windows but also obstructs another set for which no easement exists, the dominant owner can recover damages in respect of both sets on the basis that the obstruction of both is a direct and foreseeable consequence.[53]

"Ordinary user" test   An owner, generally speaking, is entitled to "sufficient light according to the ordinary notions of mankind for the comfortable use and enjoyment of his house as a dwellinghouse if it is a dwellinghouse, or for the beneficial use and occupation of the house if it is a warehouse, shop or other

Extent   place of business."[54]

It follows that the standard of light will vary, to some extent, depending upon the particular neighbourhood.[55] Regard also has to be paid to other sources of light but only to the extent that such light is already enjoyed by reason of a grant or by prescription.[56]

---

[46] See pp. 37–40.

[47] See p. 67 for definition.

[48] *e.g.* a skylight (*Easton* v. *Isted* [1903] 1 Ch. 405; *Smith* v. *Evangelization Society (Incorporated) Trust* [1933] Ch. 515); the glass roof and sides of a greenhouse (*Clifford* v. *Holt* [1899] 1 Ch. 698; *Born* v. *Turner* [1902] 2 Ch. 211) but not an ordinary doorway (*Levet* v. *Gas Light & Coke Co.* [1919] 1 Ch. 24).

[49] *Scott* v. *Pape* (1886) 31 Ch.D. 554 at 575.

[50] *e.g.* window with iron shutters only opened occasionally (*Cooper* v. *Straker* (1888) 40 Ch.D. 21); windows obscured by shelves (*Smith* v. *Baxter* [1900] 2 Ch. 138); see also pp. 38–39 above.

[51] *Andrews* v. *Waite* [1907] 2 Ch. 500.

[52] *Ankerson* v. *Connelly* [1907] 1 Ch. 678.

[53] *Re London, Tilbury & Southend Railway and Gower's Walk School Trustees* (1889) 24 Q.B.D. 326.

[54] *Colls* v. *Home & Colonial Stores* [1904] A.C. 179 at 204; see also *Allen* v. *Greenwood* [1980] Ch. 119.

[55] *Fishenden* v. *Higgs & Hill Ltd.* (1935) 153 L.T. 128; see also p. 88.

[56] *Jolly* v. *Kine* [1907] A.C. 1.

Quantum   Where an obstruction occurs the question of infringement should be viewed in terms of the extent of the light that remains rather than what has been removed. In this context, regard will have to be paid to all sources (*e.g.* a skylight)[57] before sufficient obstruction can be established to found a claim in nuisance. Use of a room for a purpose requiring a reduced amount of light will not, though, normally diminish the extent of such entitlement. On the other hand, a right to an extraordinary amount of light may be acquired by prescription if the use in question has taken place with the knowledge of the servient owner for the full period of 20 years. Where the dominant premises have been let for a particular purpose (*e.g.* an artist's studio) requiring an additional amount of light, such entitlement may also be upheld against the lessor on the basis that he cannot derogate from his grant.

Measurement   As a matter of factual evidence, there is no hard and fast rule as to how loss of light is to be assessed other than by the "ordinary user" test.[58] Before *Colls*,[59] some judges had attempted to establish a specific test that if a person retained 45 degrees of unobstructed light through a particular window, he could not maintain an action for nuisance. This is no longer to be treated as a rule of law.[60] Similarly, the "Waldram" test (*viz.* that so long as half the room was adequately lit, there was no infringement) was not treated as decisive; rather whether it was established that the diminution of light to the room in question was such as to make it uncomfortable for ordinary use[61] having regard to the locality and to the higher standard of lighting at the present day.[62] Other attempts have included the "grumble line" (*viz.* where a line is drawn across the room to establish what part of it is receiving less than 0·4 of the sill light which would thereby cause "ordinary common sense people to grumble"[63]) and the 50–50 test (*viz.* how much of the room remains adequately lit.[64]) This latter test, whilst by no means a hard and fast rule, has come to be regarded in some cases as a minimum.[65]

---

[57] *Smith* v. *Evangelisation Society (Incorporated) Trust* [1933] Ch. 515.
[58] For further assistance see, *e.g.* Simplified Daylight Tables published by Building Research Tables; see also *Lyme Valley Squash Club Ltd.* v. *Newcastle under Lyme B.C.* [1985] 2 All E.R. 405.
[59] [1904] A.C. 179 at 210.
[60] See also *Sheffield Masonic Hall Co.* v. *Sheffield Corporation* [1932] 2 Ch. 17 where Maugham J. doubted another test in which an estimate was made of the amount of direct sky which could reach a hypothetical table two feet nine inches in height.
[61] *Ough* v. *King* [1967] 1 W.L.R. 1547.
[62] It was also suggested by Lord Denning M.R. in *Ough* v. *King* that it would be helpful for the judge to have a view of the premises.
[63] See *Charles Semon & Co. Ltd.* v. *Bradford Corporation* [1922] 2 Ch. 737 (action dismissed where even the worst-hit parts of the dominant building were receiving double the amount of light which would cause grumbles).
[64] See "Light Matters" by H. W. Wilkinson (1985) 135 New L.J. 1005 and "Light for Inadequate Windows" by A. Hudson (1984) Conv. 408.
[65] See *Lyme Valley Squash Club Ltd.* v. *Newcastle under Lyme B.C.* [1985] 2 All E.R. 405 at 413, *per* Blackett-Ord V.-C.

Rights to support

Natural right   The prima facie rule is that the owner of land has a common law right of support, wholly independent of any grant, where the land exists in its natural state.[66] This natural right, however, does not extend to the support of any building on the land[67] unless it can be established that the withdrawal of support not only affects the land in its natural state but also the buildings upon it, in which event recovery may be made for the damage to the building on the basis of consequential injury.[68]

Extent   This natural right of support does not extend to any subterranean water. Accordingly, if as a consequence of an adjoining owner draining his land, subsidence is caused, no right of action will lie.[69] However, there may be right of support from sand, silt,[70] liquid pitch[71] or brine.[72] Equally, in the absence of express or implied authority, inevitable subsidence resulting from the abstraction of minerals will also give rise to cause of action.[73]

Form   The nature of the right is, therefore, a negative one, namely, that the servient owner shall refrain from any act that will diminish support. Accordingly, the servient owner is not obliged to take any active steps to maintain the means of support.[74] Indeed, if he prevents subsidence by the use of an artificial means of support, no cause of action will arise unless, in accordance with the general rule, actual injury is caused to the dominant land.[75]

Buildings   As has already been stated above, there is no natural right to the support of a building for which purpose an easement must be acquired either by express grant or by implication.[76]

Repairs   Irrespective of whether such right is acquired expressly or by implication, neither owner is under any obligation to carry out any necessary repairs to ensure the continuation of such support.[77] However, the dominant owner is entitled to enter the

---

[66] *Dalton* v. *Angus* (1881) 6 App.Cas. 740; *Butterknowle Colliery Co.* v. *Bishop Auckland Industrial Cooperation Co.* [1906] A.C. 305; *Warwickshire Coal Co.* v. *Corporation of Coventry* [1934] Ch. 488.

[67] *Dalton* v. *Angus* (1881) 6 App.Cas. 740.

[68] *e.g. Hamer* v. *Knowles* (1861) 6 H. & N. 454; *Att.-Gen.* v. *Conduit Colliery Co.* [1895] 1 Q.B. 301 at 312.

[69] *Popplewell* v. *Hodkinson* (1869) L.R. & Ex. 248; but see *Brace* v. *South East Regional Housing Association Ltd.* (1984) 270 E.G. 1286 (n. 79 below).

[70] *Jordeson* v. *Sutton, Southcoates & Drypool Gas Co.* [1899] 2 Ch. 217.

[71] *Trinidad Asphalt Co.* v. *Ambard* [1899] A.C. 594.

[72] *Lotus Ltd.* v. *British Soda Co. Ltd.* [1972] Ch. 123 (and generally on this aspect).

[73] See *Warwickshire Coal Co. Ltd.* v. *Corporation of Coventry* [1934] Ch. 488 and see pp. 107–108 for current statutory position.

[74] *Sack* v. *Jones* [1925] Ch. 235; *Bond* v. *Nottingham Corporation* [1940] Ch. 429 at 438; *Macpherson* v. *London Passenger Transport Board* (1946) 175 L.T. 279.

[75] See *Backhouse* v. *Bonomi* (1861) 9 H.L.Cas. 503.

[76] See, *e.g. Ray* v. *Fairway Motors (Barnstaple) Ltd.* (1968) 20 P. & C.R. 261 (collapse of wall without interference to natural right of support. Court of Appeal held there would be no duty of care in absence of easement of support); and at pp. 38–40 for position under s.2 of the Prescription Act 1832.

[77] *Southwark & Vauxhall Water Co.* v. *Wandsworth Board of Works* [1898] 2 Ch. 603 at 612.

servient land and to take such steps as are necessary to ensure that such support continues.[78] It follows, therefore, that he cannot sit back and watch a gradual deterioration.

Duties   Where a building is demolished, sufficient support must be provided to maintain the adjoining building.[79] However, so long as such an obligation is observed, there is no subsequent duty to protect that building from the weather or from consequent damp penetration.[80] A cause of action will not arise though, until actual injury is caused to the dominant land.[81] If a series of subsidences occur, then each will create a separate cause of action in nuisance. Awareness of such a hazard, whether **Duty of care**   natural or artificial, may also place a duty of care to take reasonable steps to prevent or minimise the risk,[82] thereby giving rise to an action in nuisance.

Private rights of way

Express grant or reservation   Where there is an express grant, the rule of construction is that the grant should be construed against the person making it. However, where there is a **Rules of**   reservation, it will be construed in favour of the grantor. **construction**   In each instance, the wording of the grant and the surrounding circumstances must be considered together.[83] Accordingly, the nature and use of the dominant tenement and the type and condition of the way will be of particular significance.

Dwellinghouses   The grant of a right of way to a dwellinghouse, **General**   prima facie, gives the grantee the right to use the way for all **presumptions**   reasonable purposes connected with the use and enjoyment of the dwellinghouse[84] (*e.g.* the right to have a van draw up at the door).[85]

Commercial premises   The grant of a right of way to commercial premises, prima facie, gives the grantee a right to use the way for such purposes and times[86] as are reasonable in relation to the business in question[87] (*e.g.* loading and unloading vehicles in a yard).

---

[78] *Bond* v. *Nottingham Corporation* [1940] Ch. 429 at 438–439.
[79] *Bond* v. *Nottingham Corporation* [1940] Ch. 429; see also *Brace* v. *South East Regional Housing Association Ltd.* (1984) 270 E.G. 1286 (demolition of adjoining property affecting easement of support for plaintiff's building as a result of shrinkage of clay) due to lack of moisture).
[80] *Phipps* v. *Pears* [1965] 1 Q.B. 76; *Marchant* v. *Capital & Counties Property Co. Ltd.* (1982) 263 E.G. 661.
[81] *Backhouse* v. *Bonomi* (1861) 9 H.L. Cas. 503.
[82] See *Leakey* v. *National Trust* [1980] Q.B. 485.
[83] See *St. Edmundsbury and Ipswich Diocesan Board of Finance* v. *Clark (No. 2)* [1975] 1 W.L.R. 468.
[84] *Cannon* v. *Villars* (1878) 8 Ch.D. 415 at 421; *Keefe* v. *Amor* [1965] 1 Q.B. 334 .
[85] *McIlraith* v. *Grady* [1968] 1 Q.B. 468.
[86] See *Cannon* v. *Villars* (n. 84 above) and *McIlraith* v. *Grady* above.
[87] *Bulstrode* v. *Lambert* [1953] 1 W.L.R. 1064.

Roads Where the road is metalled with a pavement on each side, it can be presumed that the use covers pedestrians, motor vehicles and other vehicular traffic.[88]

Phrases The following more commonly used phrases have been judicially considered as follows:

(1) "As at present enjoyed"—These words have been held to restrict the quality of the user (*viz.* on foot or with vehicles) to that existing at the time of the grant but do not limit the quantity of such user.[89]

(2) "For horses and carriages"—This expression was held to give a right of way for motor cars[90] and motor vehicles.[91]

(3) "With or without horses, carts and agricultural machines and implements"—It was held that such terms permitted the use of the way by lorries removing large quantities of sand from the dominant tenement.[92]

Purpose

Unless there is any restriction arising from the wording of the grant or the surrounding circumstances, the right of way may be used by the grantee (dominant owner) for such purposes as are authorised by the terms of the grant and not by the purpose for which the dominant tenement was used at the date of the grant.[93]

Physical extent

Terms of the grant These will, prima facie, give a right to use every part of the way but there must be evidence of substantial interference before an action can lie.[94] If the right is not physically apparent, the onus is upon the servient owner to indicate the limits of the way. It follows that, once such express delineation has taken place (or by usage), it cannot be altered except by agreement.[95] Likewise, the right of way will be restricted to the dominant land and cannot otherwise be extended to provide a means of access to adjacent land.[96]

Deviation A right to deviate can only be exercised if an obstruction[96a] is placed across the way by the owner or occupier of the servient land[97] which cannot be easily removed.[98] It follows, therefore, that if the way becomes impassable, by reason of other causes (including want of repair) then no right will

---

[88] *Watts* v. *Kelson* (1870) 6 Ch.App. 166 at 170n; *Robinson* v. *Bailey* [1948] 2 All E.R. 791.

[89] *Hurt* v. *Bowmer* [1937] 1 All E.R. 797.

[90] *White* v. *Grand Hotel, Eastbourne* [1913] 1 Ch. 113.

[91] *Lock* v. *Abercester Ltd.* [1939] Ch. 861.

[92] *Kain* v. *Norfolk* [1949] Ch. 163.

[93] See *White* v. *Grand Hotel, Eastbourne, Ltd.* [1913] 1 Ch. 113.

[94] *Pettey* v. *Parsons* [1914] 2 Ch. 653 (dominant owner held entitled to place an unlocked gate at one end and to fence in small portion at wider end of way).

[95] *Deacon* v. *South Eastern Railway* (1889) 61 L.T. 377.

[96] *Harris* v. *Flower* (1905) 74 L.J. Ch. 127; *Bracewell* v. *Appleby* [1975] Ch. 408; *Nickerson* v. *Barraclough* [1981] 2 W.L.R. 773.

[96a] "Obstruction", in this context, means some physical barrier but not an owner's failure to clear frozen rutted ice and snow from the road (see *Cluttenham* v. *Anglian Water Authority, The Times*, August 14, 1986; [1986] C.L.Y. 1115.

[97] And, arguably where the obstruction is placed by any third party (see *Stacey* v. *Sherrin* (1913) 29 T.L.R. 555).

[98] *Selby* v. *Nettleford* (1873) 9 Ch.App. 111 (tenant for life); See also *Mann* v. *R. C. Eayrs Ltd.* (1973) 231 E.G. 843 (servient land requisitioned for 20 years—use of alternate way—original right held to persist).

Trespass arise.[99] Such deviation can only be across the servient owner's land. Otherwise it would amount to a trespass. It is a question of fact whether the exercise of such a right is reasonable or not.[1] The route taken over the servient land must be similarly judged.[2] Normally, the erection of a gate across the way will not be an obstruction unless the restriction that it places on free passage is substantial.[3] The right to deviate can continue only for so long as the obstruction is in existence and/or for the duration of the tenure of the obstructing party.[4] Accordingly, long acquiescence may make it harder for the dominant owner to have the obstruction removed, although he is not obliged himself to go to law to have it removed.[5]

Quality of user Apart from any qualifying words in the grant, the method or quality of the dominant owner's use will only be limited by the physical capacity of the way itself.[6] However, if the use is excessive, then the dominant owner can be liable in trespass.[7] If such excessive user cannot be abated and the proper use restored, then the servient owner may stop all use by the dominant owner.[8]

Persons using the way As a general principle, a right of way may be used by anyone (with the authority of the dominant owner) whose user is not inconsistent with the quality or purpose of the user envisaged by the grant.[9] Accordingly, the right of way to a dwelling-house will extend to the dominant owner, members of his family, visitors, guests, employees and tradespeople, even though no express reference is made to them in the grant.[10] Equally, the identity of the person using a right of way to business premises is immaterial.[11] This prevents any limitation being placed on the type of customers in the absence of any restriction in the grant itself.

Repairs Subject to any provision in the grant,[12] the dominant owner is not required to keep the way in repair.[13] However, he

---

[99] *Taylor* v. *Whitehead* (1781) 2 Doug. K.B. 745; *Bullard* v. *Harrison* (1815) 4 M. & S. and see *Repairs*, below.

[1] *Hawkins* v. *Carbines* (1857) 27 L.J. Ex. 44.

[2] *Hawkins* v. *Carbines*, above; *Selby* v. *Nettleford*, above.

[3] *Pettey* v. *Parsons* [1914] 2 Ch. 653.

[4] *Selby* v. *Nettleford* (1873) 9 Ch.App. 111.

[5] *Selby* v. *Nettleford*, above.

[6] *Cannon* v. *Villars* (1878) 8 Ch.D. 415 at 420, 421; *Robinson* v. *Bailey* [1948] 2 All E.R. 791 at 793; *Bulstrode* v. *Lambert* [1953] 1 W.L.R. 1064.

[7] *Milner's Safe Co. Ltd.* v. *Great Northern & City Railway Co.* [1907] 1 Ch. 208 at 229; and liable to an injunction to prevent such excessive use (see, *e.g. Rosling* v. *Pinnegar* (1987) 54 P. & C.R. 124). Alternatively, the court can make a declaration coupled with liberty to apply for an injunction (see *Jelbert* v. *Davis* [1968] 1 All E.R. 1182).

[8] *Bernard and Bernard* v. *Jennings and Hillaire* (1968) 13 W.I.R. 501, Trinidad and Tobago C.A.

[9] See *White* v. *Grand Hotel (Eastbourne) Ltd.* [1913] 1 Ch. 113.

[10] *Baxendale* v. *North Lambeth Liberal and Radical Club Ltd.* [1902] 2 Ch. 427 at 429.

[11] *Woodhouse & Co. Ltd.* v. *Kirkland (Derby) Ltd.* [1970] 1 W.L.R. 1185.

[12] *Newcomen* v. *Coulsen* (1877) 5 Ch.D.133 (construction of roadway); *Jones* v. *Pritchard* [1908] 1 Ch. 630 at 638.

[13] *Duncan* v. *Louch* (1845) 6 Q.B. 904 at 909, 910. See also *Weston* v. *Weaver* [1961] 1 Q.B. 402.

may be obliged to do so in practice,[14] for which purpose he has a
right of entry onto the servient land.[15] The right to repair is not,
however, limited to making good defects in the original surface
but enables the dominant owner to make the way reasonably fit
for the purpose for which it was granted.[16] Arguably, therefore, a
right of way "at all times and all purposes" entitles the dominant
owner to construct a hard-wearing surface by means of concrete
or asphalt. If the dominant owner is under a duty to contribute to
the upkeep of the way, then it is arguable that he could be
restrained from using the way until his stipulated obligation had
been performed.[17] As a covenant it could also be enforceable
against the original grantee.[18]

Unless it is by reason of local custom or an express provision
in the grant, the servient owner is under no obligation to
construct or to effect repairs himself.[19] Apart from the dominant
owner's right to go onto the servient land to effect the repairs
himself, the servient owner is not obliged to permit the dominant
owner to use another part of his land so as to reduce the cost of
such repairs or whilst they are being carried out.[20]

Implied grant or reservation   The following points should be
borne in mind:

(1) That the implied grant will only be made where there is no
other means of reaching the land[21];

(2) That the necessity must exist at the outset and not arise
subsequently[22];

(3) That the extent, nature and use of the right of way will be
limited to the needs of the dominant land at the time when
the necessity arose[23];

Creation

(4) That the dominant owner will be limited to one right of
way[24];

(5) That the servient owner is entitled to select the route to be
taken by the way, but such route should be reasonably
convenient to the needs of the dominant owner[24];

(6) That it is doubtful whether the right is subsequently lost if
the necessity ceases as a result of the dominant owner
acquiring another source of access other than over the
servient land.[25]

---

[14] *Duncan* v. *Louch* (1845) 6 Q.B. 904; *Miller* v. *Hancock* [1893] 2 Q.B. 177 at 181
(approved in part in *Liverpool City Council* v. *Irwin* [1976] 2 W.L.R. 562);
Ingram v. *Morecraft* (1863) 33 Beav. 49.

[15] *Newcomen* v. *Coulsen* (1877) 5 Ch.D. 133 at 143; *Goodhart* v. *Hyett* (1883) 25
Ch.D. 182.

[16] *Newcomen* v. *Coulsen* (1877) 5 Ch.D. 137.

[17] *Duncan* v. *Louch* (1845) 6 Q.B. 904.

[18] *Brookes* v. *Drysdale* (1877) 3 C.P.D. 52; see also, *passim*, *Smith and Snipes Hall
Farm Ltd.* v. *Robert Douglas Catchment Board* [1949] 2 K.B. 500.

[19] *Newcomen* v. *Coulsen* and *Duncan* v. *Louch*, above; *Stokes* v. *Mixconcrete
(Holdings) Ltd.* (1978) 38 P. & C.R. 488.

[20] *Birkenhead Corporation* v. *LNWR Co.* (1885) 15 Q.B.D. 572.

[21] *Proctor* v. *Hodgson* (1855) 10 Exch. 824; *Union Lighterage Co.* v. *London
Gravity Dock Co.* [1902] 2 Ch. 557.

[22] *Midland Railway* v. *Miles* (1886) 33 Ch.D. 632.

[23] *Corporation of London* v. *Riggs* (1880) 13 Ch.D. 798.

[24] *Bolton* v. *Bolton* (1879) 11 Ch.D. 968.

[25] *Proctor* v. *Hodgson* (1855) 10 Ex. 824 at 828 casting doubt on *Holmes* v. *Goring*
(1824) 2 Bing. 76 at 83; and see *Deacon* v. *South Eastern Railway Co.* (1889) 61
L.T. 337 at 379.

Deviation As with an express grant (see p. 48) the same considerations are likely to apply in deviation.

Repairs As a matter of practice, the dominant owner will be obliged to maintain the way if he is to justify his use of it.[26] Arguably, he will also have to construct it for the purposes of making the implied grant effective.[26a]

Creation

Prescription The extent and purpose of the way will be dictated by the nature of the use and the character of the dominant tenement during the relevant period.[27] If the way is used for several purposes, then a right of way for all purposes may be inferred. Otherwise, the right will be restricted to the particular purpose or purposes for which the way has been used but not the frequency of such use, unless there is a significant change in the nature of the dominant tenement itself.[28]

Deviation A positive act of obstruction is likely to break the running of time. However, if the deviation continues for a sufficient length of time, then the revised route will, of course, be upheld.

Repairs Maintenance of the way by the prospective dominant owner will, of course, be useful evidence in support of his claim.

Public rights of way

Generally Apart from by express grant, it should be borne in mind that where a way has been actually enjoyed by the public as of right and without interruption for a full period of 20 years, then the way will be deemed to have been dedicated as a highway, unless there is sufficient evidence that there was no intention during the period to dedicate it.[29] Moreover, once the way is delineated on official maps, then such evidence will be conclusive of the rights shown.[30] In this regard, local authorities are required to maintain definitive maps and statements of all public footpaths and bridleways in their areas, subject to the hearing and determination of objections.[31]

Conclusive evidence of creation

Extinguishment Other than by natural destruction, neither an obstruction of the way nor a failure by the public to use it will extinguish a public right of way.[32] This can only take place if it is

[26] See generally *Newcomen v. Coulsen* (1877) 5 Ch.D. 133 at 143.
[26a] *Duncan v. Louch*; *Newcomen v. Coulsen*, above.
[27] See *Wimbledon and Putney Commons Conservations v. Dixon* (1875) 1 Ch.D. 362 (right of way used for agricultural purposes held not to extend to cover cartage of building materials); *British Railways Board v. Glass* [1965] Ch. 538.
[28] *British Railways Board v. Glass* (n. 27 above); *Woodhouse & Co. Ltd. v. Kirkland (Derby) Ltd.* [1970] 1 W.L.R. 1185.
[29] s.31(1) of the Highways Act 1980; see also National Parks and Access to the Countryside Act 1949. For a detailed study of this area of law see J.F. Garner, *Rights of Way and Access to the Countryside*.
[30] ss.55 and 56 of the Wildlife and Countryside Act 1981. Although the map may only show a footpath this will not exclude evidence that the public may have wider rights (s.56(1)(*a*)); see further *Halsbury's Laws of England*, Vol. 21.
[31] See Pt. III of the 1981 Act.
[32] *R. v. Bamber* (1843) 5 Q.B. 279; *Dawes v. Hawkins* (1860) 8 C.B.(N.S.) 848 at 858.

closed or diverted under certain statutory powers (*e.g.* Town and Country Planning Act 1971, s.209 or Highways Act 1980, s.116).

Repairs and maintenance   The liability of adjoining owners or occupiers may arise by reason of a special enactment or because of the nature of the tenure, enclosure or by prescription.[33] Whilst at common law trees and herbage growing along the side of the way belong to the owner of the soil,[34] it follows that he must keep them properly trimmed to comply with his repairing obligations.

Public rights

Extent of private use   The owner of premises abutting on a public highway is entitled to make a reasonable use of the highway for the purpose of obtaining access to his own premises and of loading and unloading goods at his premises, but such private rights must yield to the public rights if serious obstruction is caused, since the right of the public is higher than that of the occupier.[35] Nevertheless, the adjoining owner retains a private right of access to which the public are subject,[36] thereby entitling the owner to maintain an action in nuisance.[37]

Rights over water

Introduction   A landowner[38] does not actually own the water which either percolates through his land[39] or flows through a defined channel,[40] but rather is entitled only to the use of it as it passes along for the enjoyment of his property.[41]

Extent of proprietary interest

This body of proprietary rights is not an easement capable of being granted or reserved but is part of the fee simple.[42] However, if it is desired to alter or modify these rights then this state of affairs can only be achieved by the grant or reservation of an easement.

Abstraction   The right of abstraction,[43] which is both natural and proprietary in nature, is limited to drawing such water as is necessary for all "ordinary purposes" connected with the land (*e.g.* domestic use and for watering cattle[44]) and may be extended to include "extraordinary purposes" (*e.g.* certain manufacturing purposes[45]) and for irrigation but not spray irrigation[46]), so long as such use is reasonable, connected with the "riparian

Common law

---

[33] See s.50(1) of the Highways Act 1980 for continuing obligations.
[34] *Turner* v. *Ringwood Highway Board* (1870) L.R. 9 Eq. 418; *Nicol* v. *Beaumont* (1883) 53 L.J.Ch. 853; see also pp. 8–9.
[35] See *Vanderpant* v. *Mayfair Hotel Co.* [1930] 1 Ch. 138 at 152.
[36] See *Marshall* v. *Blackpool Corporation* [1935] A.C. 16 at 22.
[37] See, *e.g. Rowley* v. *Tottenham U.D.C.* [1914] A.C. 95.
[38] In the context of this section includes the owner of land abutting on water (*viz.* "the riparian owner").
[39] *Ballard* v. *Tomlinson* (1885) 29 Ch.D. 115 at 121.
[40] *Mason* v. *Hill* (1833) 5 B. & Ad. 1 at 24.
[41] *Wood* v. *Waud* (1849) 3 Exch. 748 at 776.
[42] See *Portsmouth Borough Waterworks Co.* v. *London, Brighton and South Coast Rly.* (1909) 26 T.L.R. 173.
[43] See *Bradford Corporation* v. *Ferrand* [1902] 2 Ch. 655.
[44] *Miner* v. *Gilmour* (1858) 12 Moo. P.C. 131 at 156 and cases under "Flow" pp. 53–54.
[45] See, *e.g. Swindon Waterworks Co.* v. *Wilts and Berks Canal Navigation Co.* (1875) L.R. 7 H.L. 697 at 704.
[46] *Rugby Joint Water Board* v. *Walters* [1967] Ch. 397.

tenement" and so long as the water is returned substantially undiminished in quantity and unaltered in character.[47]

Under section 23(1) of the Water Resources Act 1963[48] "no person shall abstract water in a river authority area, or cause or permit any other person so to abstract any water, except in pursuance of a licence under this Act granted by the river authority and in accordance with the provisions of that licence."

Statute "Abstract" is defined by the Act[49] as meaning to remove water from a source of supply whereby it either ceases (either permanently or temporarily) to be comprised in the water resources of the area or is transferred to another source of supply in the area.

"Source of supply" means any inland water[50] or underground strata[51] situated in a river authority area.

Under section 24, the principal exceptions are as follows:

Exceptions
(1) any abstraction of a quantity of water not exceeding 1,000 gallons if it does not form part of a continuous operation, or a series of operations, whereby in the aggregate more than 1,000 gallons of water are abstracted[52];
(2) domestic purposes of the occupier's household[53];
(3) agricultural purposes[54] (other than spray irrigation[55])

The grant of a licence provides a statutory defence to the holder of the licence[56] and to any person whom he causes or permits to abstract water in pursuance of the licence[57] so long as all the terms are complied with. Accordingly, common law rights are still of considerable importance.

Flow The landowner is entitled to such flow of water in volume or quantity as results from the ordinary and reasonable use of such water by the upper riparian owners.[58] At common law, the **Extent** expression "ordinary and reasonable use" has included the watering of cattle,[59] drinking and culinary purposes,[60] and, subject to the qualifications expressed above, "extraordinary purposes" such as irrigation and manufacturing processes.[61]

---

[47] *Attwood* v. *Llay Main Collieries Ltd.* [1926] Ch. 444 at 458.

[48] As amended by the Water Act 1973, s.9 (creating new Water Authorities).

[49] s.135(1).

[50] "Inland water" means *inter alia* any river, stream or other watercourse, whether natural or artificial and whether tidal or not, any lake or pond whether natural or artificial (s.135(1)) but "source of supply" does not include a lake or pond which does not discharge into any other inland water or one of a group or lakes or ponds where none discharge outside that group (s.2(3)).

[51] Strata subjacent to the surface of any land (s.135(1)).

[52] s.24(1).

[53] Including abstraction from underground strata (s.24(3)).

[54] s.24(2).

[55] *i.e.* watering land by jets or sprays from hoses and the like (s.135(1)).

[56] s.31(1) of the 1963 Act.

[57] *Ibid.* s.23(1).

[58] See *John Young & Co.* v. *The Bankier Distillery Co.* [1893] A.C. 698. See also *e.g. Home Brewery Co.* v. *Davis (William) & Co. (Loughborough)*, *The Times*, August 13, 1986; [1986] C.L.Y. 2822 (filling in of lower land causing flooding to upper land held to be reasonable use of land on basis that upper owner has no right to discharge water over lower land).

[59] *McCartney* v. *Londonderry and Lough Swilly Rly* [1904] A.C. 301 at 306.

[60] *Kensit* v. *Great Eastern Rly* (1883) 23 Ch.D. 556 at 574.

[61] See *Swindon Waterworks Co.* v. *Wilts and Berks Canal Navigation Co.* (1875) L.R. 7 H.L. 697.

If the taking of water for these purposes lowers the level and exhausts the water altogether, the lower riparian owners may not ordinarily complain[62] unless damage or nuisance can be established.[63] In this context, upper riparian owners must not send water down in an irregular manner but if water is collected for the ordinary use of the land (*e.g.* draining and improving it) then lower riparian owners are bound to receive it. Conversely, lower riparian owners must not interfere with and stop the natural flow of water to their land.[64]

Types of watercourse　The rights of the landowner will vary according to whether the watercourse is:

Natural channels

(1) Defined　The right to the flow of water only applies where it flows in some "known and defined channel."[65] This applies whether the water in question runs on the surface or is underground[66] (where the course is known and defined or can be presumed to be known).[67]

(2) Undefined　If the water rises at source on the land from, for example, a spring, pond or swamp and does not flow in a regular or definite channel, he can use it, draw it or direct it as he pleases.[68] In the case of subterranean water and percolating water below, the same considerations equally apply.[69] In such circumstances, a neighbour cannot complain that the water does not come onto his land.[70]

Artificial watercourses

(3) Artificial　The relevance of artificial watercourses is of particular importance in relation to the acquisition of prescriptive rights. Usually, the extent of flow will have been regulated by some express grant of arrangement.[71] However, if the origin of the channel is unknown, then the same considerations in connection with a defined natural channel will apply.[72] Where artificial watercourses exist in temporary circumstances, no right to an uninterrupted flow can be acquired by prescription.[73]

---

[62] See *McCartney* v. *Londonderry and Lough Swilly Rly* [1904] A.C. 301.

[63] See *Orr-Ewing* v. *Colquhoun* (1877) 2 App.Cas. 839; *Robinson* v. *Lord Byron* (1785) 1 Bro.C.C. 588; *Gibbons* v. *Lnnfwey* (1915) 84 L.J.P.C. 158; *Tate & Lyle Industries Ltd.* v. *Greater London Council* [1983] 2 A.C. 509.

[64] See *John Young & Co.* v. *The Bankier Distillery Co.* [1843] A.C. 698.

[65] "Known" means by reasonable inference from existing and observable facts in the natural or pre-existing condition of the surface of the ground; "defined channel" means a constructed or bounded channel (*Chasemore* v. *Richards* (1859) 7 H.L.Cas. 349; *Bradford Corporation* v. *Ferrand* [1902] 2 Ch. 655 at 660)—the onus of proof is on the person claiming riparian rights without opening up the ground or having recourse to obstruct speculations (*Black* v. *Ballymena Township Commrs.* (1886) 17 L.R. Ir 459 at 474, 475).

[66] *Dickinson* v. *Grand Junction Canal Co.* (1852) 7 Exch. 282 at 301; *Bleachers' Association Ltd.* v. *Chapel-en-le-Frith R.D.C.* [1933] Ch. 356.

[67] See *Bradford Corporation* v. *Ferrand* [1902] 2 Ch. 655.

[68] *Broadbent* v. *Ramsbotham* (1856) 11 Exch. 602.

[69] *Chasemore* v. *Richards* (1859) 7 H.L.Cas. 376; *Ballard* v. *Tomlinson* (1885) 29 Ch.D. 115 at 123.

[70] *e.g. R.* v. *Metropolitan Board of Works* (1863) 3 B. & S. 710.

[71] *Rameshur* v. *Koonj* (1878) 4 App.Cas. 121 at 126.

[72] *e.g. Whitmores (Edenbridge) Ltd.* v. *Stanford* [1909] 1 Ch. 427.

[73] *Burrows* v. *Lang* [1901] 2 Ch. 502.

Diversion

Restrictions   Unless authorised by express grant or by statute (*e.g.* for drainage works),[74] any diversion of water from a known and defined channel will be actionable without proof of special damage.

Culverting   It should also be borne in mind that the covering or culverting of any stream or watercourse requires the express written permission of the relevant local authority in accordance with approved plans and sections.[75] The owner or occupier of the land is also liable to repair, maintain and cleanse such culverts, in default of which the local authority may, by notice, require him to execute such works of repair, maintenance or cleansing as may be necessary.[76]

Obstruction   In addition to the rights and duties in respect of the flow of water, a landowner is also under an obligation to preserve the bed of the stream from all obstructions which could reasonably interfere with the rights of other riparian owners[77] or with rights of navigation[78] except where the obstruction is a natural one or where it has been formed by natural accumulation, and such removal would cause injury to a lower riparian owner.[79]

Purity   Since every land owner is entitled to a flow of water without significant adulteration in its character or quality,[80] it follows that he is entitled to insist that it is not polluted[81] nor raised in temperature[82] or altered in type (*e.g.* from very soft water to very hard water).[83] This natural right to purity extends

Common law

to underground water.[84] As a right of property, an action to restrain pollution can be maintained without the need to prove actual damage,[85] and the fact that the water has already been polluted by one person is not a defence to an action to restrain pollution by another.[86] Equally, if the combined acts of several persons caused pollution when individually they would not, each may still be restrained.[87]

Statutory control of pollution must be regarded, in this context, as lying in the public domain. In addition to the Control of Pollution Act 1974, other legislation contains numerous specific prohibitions. The most relevant to this work are listed below:

[74] *e.g.* by the relevant authority under the Land Drainage Act 1976 or the Highways Act 1980.

[75] Public Health Act 1936, s.263(1); Local Government Act 1972, s.180(2), Sched. 14, para. 4.

[76] Public Health Act 1936, s.264. For powers in relation to a land drainage authority s.266(1)(i).

[77] *Palmer* v. *Persse* (1877) 1 R.11 Eq. 616 and *Hanley* v. *Edinburgh Corporation* [1913] A.C. 488.

[78] *Orr-Ewing* v. *Colquhoun* (1877) 2 App.Cas. 839.

[79] *Withers* v. *Purchase* (1859) 60 L.T. 819; *Fear* v. *Vickers (No. 1)* (1911) 27 T.L.R. 558.

[80] *John Young & Co.* v. *The Bankier Distillery Co.* [1893] A.C. 698.

[81] *e.g. Crossley & Sons* v. *Lightowler* (1867) 2 Ch.App. 478.

[82] *e.g. Pride of Derby and Derbyshire Angling Association* v. *British Celanese Ltd.* [1953] Ch. 149.

[83] *John Young & Co.* v. *The Bankier Distillery Co.* [1893] A.C. 698.

[84] *Hodgkinson* v. *Ennor* (1863) 4 B. & S. 229.

[85] *Jones* v. *Llanrwst U.D.C.* [1911] 1 Ch. 393.

[86] *Crossley & Sons* v. *Lightowler* (1867) 2 Ch.App. 478.

[87] *Pride of Derby* (see n. 82 above).

Statute

(1) animal carcasses[88];
(2) cemeteries[89];
(3) escapes from pipe-lines[90];
(4) sewage[91];
(5) throwing of rubbish into the existing watercourses.[92]

Local by-laws should also be borne in mind.

Rights of access and passage   A riparian owner is entitled, as
Generally   of right, to access and free passage over the boundary of his land
abutting onto water, whether it is a tidal[93] or non-tidal river[94] or
lake[95] or the sea,[96] so long as that boundary is in daily contact[97]
with that water.[98] In the case of tidal rivers and the sea, it is
sufficient if this touching occurs at high tide, following the
presumption that the boundary extends to the highwater mark.[99]
Such a right does not depend upon ownership of the bed of the
water.[1] However, in exercising such rights of passage, he must
not interfere with any public rights of navigation, though such
rights are limited to passage and do not include a right to fish.[2]

In principle, the same considerations apply with mooring
Boats   and beaching boats. Any mooring must not interfere with a right
of access by another riparian owner or with a public right of
navigation.[3] There is also a general right to moor or beach a boat
for the purposes of loading and unloading it but, seemingly, for
any other purpose.[4] However, the landowner is not entitled to
have a particular depth of water maintained.[5]

Fishing rights   A landowner has the exclusive right to fish all
Generally   the area of water within his ownership[6] unless it constitutes tidal
waters.[7] Unlike the right of way, the general public cannot
acquire a right to fish by effluxion of time, however long this
period may have been.[8]

So far as tidal waters are concerned, the public have the
general right to fish but only as far as the mean high water mark

---

[88] Animal Health Act 1981, s.35(4)(*a*).
[89] Cemeteries Clauses Act 1847, ss.20–22.
[90] Pipe-Lines Act 1962, s.27.
[91] Public Health Act 1936, ss.30, 31.
[92] Control of Pollution Act 1974, s.31(1); see also Salmon and Freshwater
    Fisheries Act 1975, s.4 (causing waters to be injurious or poisonous to fish as a
    result of effluents and the like).
[93] *Lyon* v. *Fishmongers' Co.* (1876) 1 App.Cas. 662.
[94] *Hindson* v. *Ashby* [1896] 2 Ch. 1.
[95] *Marshall* v. *Ullswater Steam Navigation Co.* (1871) L.R. 7 Q.B. 166.
[96] *Att.-Gen. of Straits Settlement* v. *Wemyss* (1888) 13 App.Cas. 192.
[97] Either laterally or vertically.
[98] *North Shore Rly Co.* v. *Pion* (1889) 14 App.Cas. 612.
[99] See pp. 7, 8 and 10.
[1] *e.g. Hindson* v. *Ashby* [1896] 2 Ch. 1.
[2] *Pearce* v. *Scotcher* (1882) 9 Q.B.D. 162.
[3] *Macey* v. *Metropolitan Board of Works* (1864) 3 New Rep. 669.
[4] *e.g. ibid.*
[5] *Tate & Lyle Industries Ltd.* v. *Greater London Council* [1983] 2 A.C. 509.
[6] *Ecroyd* v. *Coulthard* [1898] 2 Ch. 358 at 366; *Stephens* v. *Snell* [1939] 3 All E.R.
    622.
[7] *Malcolmson* v. *O'Dea* (1863) 19 H.L.Cas. 593; *Att.-Gen.* v. *Emerson* [1891]
    A.C. 649.
[8] *Pearce* v. *Scotcher* (1882) 9 Q.B.D. 162.

Tidal waters

of ordinary tides.[9] Accordingly, the landowner retains his exclusive right to fish in tidal waters where such waters overtop that mark.[9] The public has no general right of access to go on land above the mean high-water mark in the exercise of their right to fish nor to beach or leave boats or nets except by special custom[10] or by Acts of Parliament.[11] However, the public has the right to cross the foreshore to and from the sea for the purpose of fishing but only from such places as usage or necessity have appropriated to that purpose.[12]

Licences

Finally, it should be borne in mind that a fishing licence is required from the regional Water Authority to fish any water for salmon and trout and for other fish in fresh water.[13]

Bathing rights   The same considerations apply. More particularly, there is no common law right for the public to use even the foreshore for such purpose though, once again, it may be gained by custom or prescription.[14]

Acquisition of rights   The use of the following terminology should be borne in mind:

"Watercourse"   This can mean:

(1) the right to running water, or
(2) the drain[15] which contained the water, or
(3) the land over which the water flows.[16]

Express grant

However, in the absence of words to the contrary, a grant of a watercourse will be held to mean the grant of the right to the running water.[16] The reservation of a right to make a watercourse includes the right to divert water and to use such water.[17]

"Spring of water"   This means a natural source of water of a definite and well-marked extent.[18]

"Stream"   This covers water which runs in a defined course so as to be capable of diversion[18] but does not include either the spring or water soaking through marshy ground.[19]

---

[9] *Thames Conservators* v. *Smeed, Dean & Co.* [1897] 2 Q.B. 334; see also *Hanbury* v. *Jenkins* [1901] 2 Ch. 401.

[10] *e.g.* in Kent; see also *e.g. Mercer* v. *Denne* [1904] 3 Ch. 534.

[11] Herring fishers in all parts of Great Britain can use land within 100 yards of the highest high water mark for landing fish and drying nets (White Herring Fisheries Act 1771, s.11) and special rights have been granted to certain fishermen in Somerset, Devon and Cornwall for fishing herring, pilchard and other fish caught with seine nets (1 Jac. 1 c.23 (1603–1604)).

[12] See *Brinckman* v. *Matley* [1904] 2 Ch. 313.

[13] See Salmon & Freshwater Fisheries Act 1975, s.25.

[14] See *Brinckman* v. *Matley* [1904] 2 Ch. 313.

[15] *i.e.* the channel, whether natural or artificial, through which the water flows—*Remfry* v. *Natal (Surveyor-General)* [1896] A.C. 558 at 560. A "drain" is an underground pipe or open channel for the carrying of water, sewage, etc. into a cesspool or sewer within the same curtilage as the building or premises so served. A "sewer" is any trench, channel or pipe through which water or sewage flow (see Jowitt, *Dictionary of English Law* (2nd ed., 1977)).

[16] *Taylor* v. *St. Helens Corporation* (1877) 6 Ch.D. 264 at 271.

[17] See *Remfry* v. *Natal* (at n. 15 above).

[18] See *Taylor* (at n. 16 above).

[19] *McNab* v. *Robertson* [1897] A.C. 129.

A grant of all streams that might be found on land includes the underground water in the land.[20] On the other hand, a grant of an artificial watercourse (on a plan) with the stream and springs flowing into or feeding the same did not justify the grantees enlarging the channel so as to carry off more water.[21]

Prescription   In the context of prescriptive rights a riparian owner may by user acquire a right to use the water passing through his land in a manner different from that under his natural rights. However, this right does not affect the natural rights of an upper or lower riparian owner *unless* the presumption of a grant can be raised so that such adjoining land can be regarded as the servient tenement.[22]

Flow   The position differs regarding:

(1) Defined channels   Both at common law[23] and under the Prescription Act 1832[24] at least 20 years' undisturbed possession of the water is required, *e.g.* by diversion[25] or the raising of it in height (*e.g.* by a weir)[26] or to bank up the stream on the land of an upper riparian owner[27]; and

(2) Undefined channels   No right to an uninterrupted flow can be acquired since no grant can be presumed.[28]

Abstraction   Both riparian and non-riparian owners may acquire the right to go onto other land to draw water from a spring[29] or a pump[30] or to turn water from a natural stream into an artificial channel.[31]

Discharge and eavesdrop   In the case of eaves, whilst a landowner should not construct a building in such a manner as to overhang neighbouring land or to cause water to discharge onto it, such a right may be acquired by user.[32] This right of "eavesdrop" will not be lost by raising the height of the house.[33]

In other circumstances, the mere discharge of water onto adjoining land is likely to establish such a right but not necessarily to have the same flow continued.[34] No prescriptive right is acquired, however, in respect of water which escapes through lack of repair.[35]

---

[20] *Whitehead* v. *Parks* (1858) 2 H. & N. 870.
[21] *Taylor* v. *St. Helens Corporation* (1877) 6 Ch.D. 264.
[22] *Sampson* v. *Hoddinott* (1857) 1 C.B.(N.S.) 590.
[23] *Prescott* v. *Phillips* (1798) 6 East 213; 102 E.R. 1268; *Mason* v. *Hill* (1833) 5 J.B. & Ad. 23.
[24] s.2.
[25] *Holker* v. *Porritt* (1875) L.R. 10 Exch. 59 but not in a navigable river (*Vooght* v. *Winch* (1819) 2 B. & Ald. 662).
[26] Likewise fishing rights at a weir in a non-navigable river, see, *e.g. Leconfield* v. *Lonsdale* (1870) L.R. 5 C.P. 657.
[27] *Roberts* v. *Fellowes* (1906) 94 L.T. 279.
[28] *Chasemore* v. *Richards* (1859) 7 H.L.Cas. 349.
[29] *Race* v. *Ward* (1855) 4 E.&B. 702.
[30] *Polden* v. *Bastard* (1865) L.R. 1 Q.B. 156.
[31] *Beeston* v. *Weate* (1856) 5 E. & B. 986.
[32] *Thomas* v. *Thomas* (1835) 2 C.M. & R. 34; *Pyer* v. *Carter* (1857) 1 H. & N. 916.
[33] *Harvey* v. *Walters* (1872–73) L.R. 8 C.P. 162.
[34] *Chamber Colliery Co.* v. *Hopwood* (1886) 32 Ch.D. 549 at 558.
[35] *Brymbo Water Co.* v. *Lesters Line Co.* (1894) 8 L.R. 329.

Pollution As with user and flow, a right may be acquired by prescription to pollute but only if it can be established by the continuance of perceptible injury for 20 years.[36]

Custom Water rights may also be acquired by custom.[37]

---

[36] *Goldsmid* v. *Tunbridge Wells Improvement Commrs.* (1866) 1 Ch.App. 349; *Liverpool Corporation* v. *Coghill* [1918] 1 Ch. 307.
[37] *e.g. Carlyon* v. *Lovering* (1857) 1 H. & N. 784 (customary right to pollute); *Harrop* v. *Hirst* (1868) L.R. 4 Exch. 43 (customary right to use water).

3 COVENANTS

Legal principles

Classification A covenant is simply an agreement under seal relating to a particular obligation. A restrictive covenant is both a covenant and an interest in property, the purpose of which is to prevent the covenantor from doing something on or concerning his land for the benefit of the covenantee's land.[1] A positive covenant stands somewhere between a mere contractual right and a proprietary interest in that the benefit can be made to run with both freehold and leasehold land but the burden, with certain exceptions, can only run with a leasehold property.[2] The pre-requisite of a positive covenant is that it involves the carrying out of a function of an active character or the expenditure of money. Where the nature of the function is restrictive, then the covenant or the terms of the covenant are in part restrictive, and the covenant will be construed on such a basis.[3]

Creation Formal words are not required to make a covenant[4] so long as the language shows a sufficient intention between the parties to carry out a particular obligation or to refrain from doing a particular act.[5]

Construction If the language of the covenant is ambiguous, then it may be implied from the recital.[6] However, when provision is made for an express covenant, no other covenants can be implied relating to the same subject matter.[7] A restrictive covenant will not be implied unless the court is satisfied that the restriction was fairly within the contemplation of the parties to the contract.[8]

The Law of Property Act 1925 Regard must also be paid to the following word-saving provisions:

Section 78. Benefit of covenants relating to land Section 78 provides that:

(1) A covenant relating to any land of the covenantee[9] shall be deemed to be made with the covenantee and his successors in title and the persons deriving title under him or them,

---

[1] *Formby* v. *Barker* [1903] 2 Ch. 539; see *Tulk* v. *Moxhay* (1848) 2 Ph. 774.

[2] Lack of space and the subject matter of this book mean that no detailed critique can be given on this aspect.

[3] *Clegg* v. *Hands* (1890) 44 Ch.D. 503.

[4] *Mackenzie* v. *Childers* (1889) 43 Ch.D. 265; and *Westacott* v. *Hahn* [1918] 1 K.B. 495 at 504.

[5] *Re Cadogan and Hans Place Estate Ltd., ex p. Willis* (1895) 73 L.T. 387.

[6] *Re Coghlan* [1894] 3 Ch. 76; *Re Weston* [1900] 2 Ch. 164. As to the wording of the covenant making it void for uncertainty see *National Trust* v. *Midlands Electricity Board* [1952] Ch. 380.

[7] *Stephens* v. *Junior Army & Navy Stores Ltd.* [1914] 2 Ch. 516 (covenant to repair did not imply covenant to build).

[8] *e.g. Holford* v. *Acton U.D.C.* [1898] 2 Ch. 940 (covenant to erect shops and dwelling houses not limited only to this type of building).

[9] See *Federated Homes Ltd.* v. *Mill Lodge Properties Ltd.* [1980] 1 W.L.R. 594 (automatic statutory annexation to the land without the need for express words. There a break had occurred in the chain of assignments of a restrictive covenant affecting part of the covenantee's land). See also *Roake* v. *Chadha* [1984] 1 W.L.R. 40 (and below p. 65).

and shall have effect as if such successors and other persons were expressed.

For the purposes of this subsection in connection with covenants restrictive of the user of land "successors in title" shall be deemed to include the owners and occupiers for the time being of the land of the covenantee intended to be benefited.

(2) This section applies to covenants made after the commencement of this Act, but the repeal of section 58 of the Conveyancing Act 1881 does not affect the operation of covenants to which that section applied.

Section 79. Burden of covenants relating to land   Section 79 provides that:

(1) A covenant relating to any land of a covenantor or capable of being bound by him, shall, unless a contrary intention[10] is expressed, be deemed to be made by the covenantor on behalf of himself his successors in title and the persons deriving title under him or them, and, subject as aforesaid, shall have effect as if such successors and other persons were expressed.

L.P.A. 1925   This subsection extends to a covenant to do some act relating to the land, notwithstanding that the subject-matter may not be in existence when the covenant is made.

(2) For the purposes of this section in connection with covenants restrictive of the user of land "successors in title" shall be deemed to include the owners and occupiers for the time being of such land.

(3) This section applies only to covenants made after the commencement of this Act.

Section 80. Covenants binding land   Section 80 provides that:

(1) A covenant and a bond and an obligation or contract under seal made after December 31, 1881, binds the real estate as well as the personal estate of the person making the same if and so far as a contrary intention is not expressed in the covenant, bond, obligation, or contract.

This subsection extends to a covenant implied by virtue of this Act.

(2) Every covenant running with the land, whether entered into before or after the commencement of this Act, shall take effect in accordance with any statutory enactment affecting the devolution of the land, and accordingly the benefit or burden of every such covenant shall vest in or bind the persons who by virtue of any such enactment or otherwise succeed to the title of the covenantee or the covenantor, as the case may be.

(3) The benefit of a covenant relating to land entered into after the commencement of the Act may be made to run with the land without the use of any technical expression if the covenant is of such a nature that the benefit could

[10] *i.e.* not a personal covenant (see *Re Fawcett & Holmes' Contract* (1889) 42 Ch.D. 150; *Powell* v. *Hemsley* [1909] 2 Ch. 252).

have been made to run with the land before the
commencement of this Act.

(4) For the purposes of this section, a covenant runs with the
land when the benefit or burden of it, whether at law or in
equity, passes to the successors in title of the covenantee
or the covenantor, as the case may be.

Section 81. Effect of covenant with two or more jointly   Section 81
provides that:

(1) A covenant, and a contract under seal, and a bond or
obligation under seal, made with two or more jointly, to
pay money or to make a conveyance, or to do any other
act, to them or for their benefit, shall be deemed to
include, and shall, by virtue of this Act, imply, an
obligation to do the act to, or for the benefit of, any other
person to whom the right to sue on the covenant, contract,
bond, or obligation devolves, and where made after the
commencement of this Act shall be construed as being
also made with each of them.

(2) This section extends to a covenant implied by virtue of
this Act.

(3) This section applies only if and so far as a contrary
intention is not expressed in the covenant, contract, bond,
or obligation, and has effect subject to the covenant,
contract, bond, or obligation, and to the provisions
therein contained.

(4) Except as otherwise expressly provided, this section
applies to a covenant, contract, bond, or obligation made
or implied after December 31, 1881.

Enforceability   The enforceability of the covenant will depend upon at least
one of the following criteria being satisfied:

(a) Privity of contract   If this exists, then positive and restrictive
covenants will be enforceable by the covenantee against the
original covenantor[11] personally and, after his death, against his
estate,[12] unless an express reservation is made.[13]

(b) Privity of estate   In such circumstances, only covenants which
touch and concern[14] the land will be enforceable by the
covenantee.

*(c) Exceptions when neither privity of contract nor of estate
exists*   Here the benefit of the covenant will only pass if either the
benefit is capable of being assigned (*e.g.* a covenant as to title[15])
or the covenant is a restrictive covenant taking effect in equity.[16]

---

[11] *e.g. Smith & Snipes Hall Farm* v. *River Douglas Catchment Board* [1949] 2 K.B.
500.
[12] *S.E. Railway Co.* v. *Associated Portland Cement Manufacturers (1900) Ltd.*
[1910] 1 Ch. 12.
[13] *Sefton* v. *Tophams Ltd. (No. 2)* [1967] 1 A.C. 50.
[14] See below and n. 18.
[15] See below and nn. 24, 28.
[16] See below and n. 33.

Positive freehold covenants

Contractual enforcement   As has already been seen, a covenant creating a contractual relationship will bind the parties in accordance with the ordinary rules of the law of contract. In this regard, the benefit of the covenant can be assigned to a third party as a chose in action.[17]

The following conditions must be fulfilled if the benefit of the covenant is to pass with the land without the need for an express assignment:

(1) The covenant must "touch and concern" the land of the covenantee. This has been held to mean that "the covenant must either affect the land as regards mode of occupation or it must be such as *per se*, and not merely from collateral circumstances, affects the value of the land. . . . "[18] Examples include the supply of pure water by a mill owner for the benefit of the covenantee's cattle[19] and a covenant to construct and maintain new banks to a stream to prevent flooding.[20]

Benefit running with land

(2) The land must be ascertainable with reasonable accuracy.[21]

(3) The wording of the covenant must also indicate that it is intended to run with the land, *i.e.* that it is not a personal right. This will normally be presumed in the absence of express provision to the contrary.[22]

(4) The benefit must be enforceable by a subsequent owner who has the same legal estate, as the original covenantee. By sections 56(1)[23] and 78(1) of the Law of Property Act 1925, the successors in title of the original covenantee can enforce so long as they are identifiable at the time when the covenant is made, *e.g.* prospective assignees but not subsequent lessees.[24]

The burden of a positive freehold covenant cannot generally be assigned and be made to run with the burdened land save in the following circumstances:

(1) Where the benefit is made conditional on the performance of positive obligations, *e.g.* to contribute to the cost of maintaining roads and sewers on a housing estate.[25]

---

[17] *Griffith* v. *Pelton* [1958] Ch. 205 where the court held that a transfer of a lease implied an assignment of an option to purchase the freehold reversion contained in the lease.

[18] *Rogers* v. *Hosegood* [1900] 2 Ch. 388 at 395, *per* Farwell J.

[19] *Sharp* v. *Waterhouse* (1857) 7 E. & B. 816.

[20] See *Smith & Snipes Hall Farm* v. *River Douglas Catchment Board* [1949] 2 K.B. 500.

[21] See again *Smith & Snipes Hall Farm* v. *River Douglas Catchment Board* above.

[22] See, *e.g. Shayler* v. *Woolf* [1946] Ch. 320 (covenant to supply water and maintain pump).

[23] *viz.* "a person may take an immediate or other interest in land or other property, or the benefit of any condition, right of entry, covenant or agreement over or respecting land or other property, although he may not be named as a party to the conveyance or other instrument."

[24] See *Westhoughton U.D.C.* v. *Wigan Coal and Iron Co. Ltd.* [1919] 1 Ch. 159; *Re Ecclesiastical Commissioners for England's Conveyance* [1936] Ch. 430.

[25] *Halsall* v. *Brizell* [1957] Ch. 169.

Running of the burden

(2) Where the property is made subject to a rentcharge and a covenant by way of a right of entry is reserved. A right of entry is itself a legal interest in land and is exempt from the rule against perpetuities.[26] Accordingly, it can be utilised to enforce the performance of a positive covenant (*e.g.* to build or repair) rather than the payment of money, reserving the right of re-entry to enter and make good in default.[27]

(3) Where there is a chain of personal covenants of indemnity. This arises where the covenantor (and, thereafter, his successors in title) secures an undertaking from the incoming purchaser to indemnify him against any future breach of the covenant in question, *e.g.* to build or maintain a wall.[28]

Flying freeholds

The problems associated with making positive covenants run with the land most frequently occur with the sale of freehold flats and maisonettes where arrangements have to be made for the repair of the block in which they are situated, the maintenance of the common parts, the provision of common parts, the provision of common services and the general management of the block.

Although, as has been seen above, a chain of positive covenants may be made to run with the land, by means of a deed of covenant entered into by all purchasers and renewed on each change of ownership, the scheme tends to break down in due course.

Management company

A means of overcoming this difficulty is by creating a management company in which the flat-owners are shareholders and officers. The common parts can then be vested in the company and the titles of the flat-owners can be registered accordingly. Arrangements can then be made for a restriction to be entered against each title ensuring no transfer without the consent of the management company. The use of an estate rentcharge may equally assist in ensuring that a sanction is available to secure performance of the covenants in question.[28a]

Restrictive covenants

Requirements

A valid restrictive covenant will be created if the following requirements are satisfied:

(1) The covenant is restrictive or negative in form;

(2) There is a dominant and a servient property which must

---

[26] L.P.A. 1925, s.4(3); Perpetuities and Accumulations Act 1964, s.11.

[27] Rentcharges Act 1977, s.2(3)(*c*) and (4) permit the continued use of an estate rentcharge for the purpose of making covenants enforceable against successive owners. See also *Shiloh Spinners* v. *Harding* [1973] A.C. 691.

[28] See *Radford* v. *De Froberville (Lange third party)* [1977] 1 W.L.R. 1262 for measure of damages for failure to build a brick wall.

[28a] See further above p. 30.

be sufficiently ascertainable[29] and within sufficient proximity of one another[30];

Principles

(3) The covenant "touches and concerns" the dominant land[31];

(4) The covenantee has some interest[32] in the dominant land;

(5) The covenantor identifies and indicates an intention to annex (a) the burden to the servient land and (b) the benefit to the dominant land; or

(6) There is a scheme of development which includes both the dominant and servient land.

Contractual enforcement   As with a positive covenant, the original covenantor will remain liable even though he may have assigned his interest in the servient land.

Running of the burden

Provided that the burdened land is identified as the one to which the restrictive covenant relates, the words implied by section 79 of the Law of Property Act 1925 will be sufficient to make the burden of the covenant run with the land. The effect in law will be that the covenant will run in equity, *i.e.* it will be enforceable by an injunction or specific performance as well as damages and it must be registered to bind a bona fide purchase of the servient land[33] but not a subsequent occupier such as a squatter who does not acquire the land by purchase.[34]

Running of the benefit

Following the decision of the Court of Appeal in *Federated Homes Ltd.* v. *Mill Lodge Properties Ltd.*[35] it will be presumed, unless the contrary appears, that the annexation of the benefit will be to each and every part of the dominant land, subject only to the qualification that the area must be of a size sufficient to benefit from the covenant.[36] This will not only turn on the wording of the covenant but on the particular circumstances of the area.[37] The covenantee must also be in a position to show either that he has had the benefit of the covenant assigned to him expressly at the time of the conveyance of the dominant land[38] or

---

[29] *L.C.C.* v. *Allen* [1914] 3 K.B. 642; *Miles* v. *Easter* [1933] Ch. 611.

[30] *viz.* a covenant binding land in Hampshire will be too remove to benefit land in Clapham (*Kelly* v. *Barrett* [1924] 2 Ch. 379 at 404); see also *Re Tiltwood, Sussex* [1978] Ch. 269 (covenant extinguished where lands owned and occupied by same person).

[31] See n. 18 above. Covenants preventing competition come within this phrase (see *Newton Abbot Cooperative Society* v. *Williamson & Threadgold Ltd.* [1952] Ch. 286).

[32] This will be sufficiently established if the covenantee can establish either (a) that the covenant was made for the whole or part of the dominant land (*Drake* v. *Gray* [1936] Ch. 451; *Russell* v. *Archdale* [1964] Ch. 38) or (b) if the benefit of the covenant has been expressly assigned to him (*Stilwell* v. *Blackman* [1968] Ch. 508).

[33] See *Wilkes* v. *Spooner* [1911] 2 K.B. 473 and L.P.A. 1925, s.2(5).

[34] See *Fairweather* v. *St. Marylebone Property Co.* [1963] A.C. 510 and *Marten* v. *Flight Refuelling Ltd.* [1962] Ch. 115. For registration see L.C.A. 1972, s.2(5) (Class D(II)) and as a Minor Interest under L.R.A. 1925, s.101.

[35] [1980] 1 All E.R. 371. (Therefore evidence of claim of assignments no longer necessary).

[36] See *Zetland, Marquess of* v. *Driver* [1939] Ch. 1 distinguishing *Re Ballard's Conveyance* [1937] Ch. 473 (covenant only running with whole of estate).

[37] *Formby* v. *Barker* [1903] 2 Ch. 539; *Marten* v. *Flight Refuelling Ltd.*

[38] *Chambers* v. *Randall* [1923] 1 Ch. 149.

part of it.[39] It will be a question of construction of the covenant whether such annexation was permitted[40] and therefore has taken effect. If the benefit of the covenant has been annexed to the dominant land, then the covenant will pass, even though the purchaser may have been unaware of the existence of the covenant at the time of purchase.[41]

Implied annexation under development schemes

Where there is a scheme of development or building scheme, the annexation of the benefit will be implied in relation to each property within the scheme whose purchaser, in turn, can enforce against neighbouring properties.

For such a scheme to exist, the following conditions[42] will have to be met:

Conditions

(1) The original owner (or owners) of the land must have created a scheme by:
  (a) selling off a defined area[43] of land in individual plots and
  (b) imposing a common set of restrictions at the time of the sale of each plot for the benefit of every other plot.[44]
(2) The purchaser of each plot (and his successors in title) must have each:
  (a) bought from the original owner[45]; and
  (b) agreed to be bound by the common set of restrictions and have been aware of the purpose of such restrictions (*viz.* for the benefit of the other plots in the scheme).

If a plot is divided into sub-plots, then the scheme can still be enforced by and between the respective purchasers.[46] Equally, if a fully-built estate is sold on a plot by plot basis, with each sale being subject to the same conditions, then the covenants will be equally enforceable as under a building scheme.[47]

Scope of covenants

Generally

Construction   As a general rule of construction, the whole of the instrument should be considered and, in particular, the form of words used. Where, however, the "contract" as expressed in writing would be futile and would not carry out the intention of the parties, the law will imply any term obviously intended by the

---

[39] *Re Union of London and Smith's Bank Ltd.'s Conveyance* [1933] Ch. 611 at 632; *Russell* v. *Archdale* [1964] Ch. 38.
[40] *Stilwell* v. *Blackman* [1968] Ch. 508.
[41] See *Re Selwyn's Conveyance* [1967] Ch. 674.
[42] See *Elliston* v. *Reacher* [1908] 2 Ch. 374; *Baxter* v. *Four Oaks Properties Ltd.* [1965] Ch. 816 and *Brunner* v. *Greenslade* [1971] Ch. 993.
[43] *Reid* v. *Bickerstaff* [1909] 2 Ch. 305.
[44] *Tucker* v. *Vowles* [1893] 1 Ch. 195.
[45] *Re Dolphin's Conveyance* [1970] 1 Ch. 654.
[46] *Brunner* v. *Greenslade* [1971] Ch. 993. See also *Texaco Antilles Ltd.* v. *Kernochan* [1973] A.C. 609 (covenants in a scheme only suspended where ownership of dominant and servient land united).
[47] *Torbay Hotel Ltd.* v. *Jenkins* [1927] 2 Ch. 255 at 241; see also *Hudson* v. *Cripps* [1896] 1 Ch. 265 for similar application to a block of flats for residential purposes only.

parties which is necessary to make the contract effectual.[48]
Whilst a particular (or further) restriction may be implied, the
court will be required to be very careful before imposing such an
interpretation unless it is satisfied that it was fairly within the
contemplation of the parties.[49]

Examples The following examples are given to illustrate the
construction of different types of covenant:

Building works *"To submit plans"* This means that no work can commence until
the plans of the proposed building have been submitted to, and
approved by, the covenantee[50] but subject to the implied term
that consent will not be unreasonably withheld.[51]

"Against alterations" A covenant against alterations will be
broken if a permanent alteration to the fabric of the building
takes place, *e.g.* forming a window opening,[52] a doorway in a
party wall[53] or the conversion of a dwelling-house into flats with
new partition walls and doorways.[54]

"Building" This will turn upon the particular context of the
covenant.[55] It has been held that extensions and alterations to a
house, *e.g.* a bay window,[56] an advertisement hoarding,[57] a
barbecue 10 feet high[58] amount to the erection of a "building"
but a wooden, garden type shed[59] or a wall do not.[60]

"Erection" or "structure" This has been held to include a petrol
pump,[61] a scaffolding[62] and poles carrying overhead electric
cables.[63]

Residential covenants *"House"* Means a building intended for "some purpose of
habitation."[64]

"Bungalow" Means a building of which the walls are no higher
than the ground floor and the roof starts at a point no higher than
the top of such walls.[65]

---

[48] *Oriental Steam Ship Co. v. Tylor* [1893] 2 Q.B. 518.
[49] *Holford v. Acton U.D.C.* [1898] 2 Ch. 240 at 247.
[50] *Powell v. Hemsley* [1909] 2 Ch. 252. Nominal damages are only likely to be awarded in default; but if buildings are erected then an injunction will issue.
[51] *Wrotham Park Estate Co. v. Parkside Homes Ltd.* [1974] 1 W.L.R. 798. See also *e.g. Bower & Bower v. Goodyear* [1986] C.L.Y. 2827.
[52] *Sharp v. Harrison* [1922] 1 Ch. 502.
[53] *British Empire Mutual Life Assurance Co. v. Cooper* (1888) 4 T.L.R. 362.
[54] *Day v. Waldron* (1919) 88 L.J.K.B. 937.
[55] See *Paddington Corpn. v. Att.-Gen.* [1906] A.C. 1 at 3.
[56] *Manner v. Johnson* (1875) 1 Ch.D. 673.
[57] *Nussey v. Provincial Billposting Co.* [1909] 1 Ch. 734 but not in *Foster v. Fraser* [1893] 3 Ch. 158.
[58] *Windsor Hotel (Newquay) Ltd. v. Allen* (1981) J.P.L. 274.
[59] *Gardiner v. Walsh* [1936] 3 All E.R. 870.
[60] *Urban Housing Co. Ltd. v. Oxford Corpn.* [1940] Ch. 70.
[61] *Mackenzie v. Abbott* (1926) 24 L.G.R. 444.
[62] *R. v. Whittingham* (1840) 9 C. & P. 234.
[63] *National Trust v. Midlands Electricity Board* [1952] Ch. 380 (in the context of not being a "building").
[64] *Reckitt v. Cody* [1920] 2 Ch. 452 (iron corrugated shed used as a temporary classroom held to be a house).
[65] *Ward v. Paterson* [1929] 2 Ch. 396.

"Private dwelling-house"   This qualification is broken when another type of building is put up (*e.g.* commercial premises)[66] but not by the usual appurtenances of a residence (*e.g.* a stable[67] or a swimming pool[68]) or if the use is altered (*e.g.* to a guest-house[69]).

"Multiple occupation"   Contemplates in excess of a single residence, *e.g.* where rooms or flats in a house are let.[70]

"Limited to (two) houses"   A restriction on the number and size of housing units that can be erected will normally be strictly enforced.[71] Flexibility appears to be introduced only by the manner of internal communication and entrances as to whether the property as a whole is to be treated as a single house.[72]

"Minimum cost"   Where the figure is fixed, this will continue to bind the developer even though this may produce a property different from that contemplated.[73]

"Minimum area"   As a more flexible restraint this will usually preserve the type of house originally contemplated.[74]

Commercial covenants   *"Any trade or business"*   This phrase usually is taken as one. The word "trade" connotes a business activity usually involving buying and selling.[75] The word "business" includes almost all "serious occupations"[76] including the taking in of lodgers on a regular basis[77] but not a single paying guest.[78] Neither actual business activity[79] nor the intention of making a profit[80] are pre-requisites for the purposes of enforcement.

"Offensive trade or business"   This term, together with similar epithets such as "noxious" "dangerous" or "noisome" should be viewed in the light of the character of the neighbourhood along the same lines as any intended action in nuisance.[81]

"Nuisance," "annoyance" and the like   The same considerations apply to these expressions. Where a number of such words occur together, effect must be given to all of them.[82] A covenant in

---

[66] *Reid* v. *Bickerstaff* [1909] 2 Ch. 305.
[67] *Russell* v. *Baber* (1870) 18 W.R. 1021 (and by analogy a garage).
[68] *Harlow* v. *Hartog* (1977) 245 E.G. 140.
[69] *Chatsworth Estates Co.* v. *Fewell* [1931] 1 Ch. 224.
[70] *e.g. Barton* v. *Keeble* [1928] Ch. 517; *Westminster (Duke of)* v. *Swinton* [1948] 1 K.B. 524.
[71] *Re Enderick's Conveyance* [1973] 1 All E.R. 843.
[72] *Ilford Park Estates Ltd.* v. *Jacobs* [1903] 2 Ch. 522.
[73] *Grant* v. *Derwent* [1929] 1 Ch. 390.
[74] *Drake* v. *Gray* [1936] Ch. 451.
[75] *Doe d. Wetherell* v. *Bird* (1834) 2 Ald. & E. 161.
[76] *Rolls* v. *Miller* (1884) 27 Ch.D. 71 at 88. See also *Cheryl Investments* v. *Saldanha; Royal Life Saving Society* v. *Page* [1979] 1 All E.R. 5 for a recent definition of "business" under Part II of the Landlord and Tenant Act 1954.
[77] *Thorn* v. *Madden* [1925] Ch. 847.
[78] *Segal Securities Ltd.* v. *Thoseby* [1963] 1 Q.B. 887.
[79] *Tubbs* v. *Esser* (1909) 26 T.L.R. 145 (letting gable-ends for advertisements a business).
[80] *Rolls* v. *Miller* (1884) 27 Ch.D. 71.
[81] *e.g. Adams* v. *Ursell* [1913] 1 Ch. 269 (fish-frying "offensive").
[82] *Re Davis and Carey's Contract* (1888) 40 Ch.D. 601 at 606; see also *Tod-Heatly* v. *Benham* (1888) 40 Ch.D. 80.

such terms may be qualified by words relating to the judgment and opinion of the covenantee or some other designated person.[83] The effect of this provision is to substitute their opinion for that of a court. Accordingly, no action will lie until the required opinion has been formed.[84] However, the designated person forming that opinion is not required to act judicially and so is not obliged to consider anything but his own convenience. He must nonetheless, act in good faith and not form his opinion capriciously.[85]

"Permit" or "suffer"   Normally, there is no difference between these two verbs and they will be treated as synonymous. The word "permit" has been held to mean one of two things, "either to give leave for an act which without that leave, could not be legally done," or, "to abstain from taking reasonable steps to prevent the act, where it is within a man's power to prevent it."[86] Where the two words appear together, "suffer" will, however, be treated as the wider term.[87]

"Only to use as"   This will regulate the extent of the trading activities within the particular class of user, *e.g.* where a covenant restricted the use of a supermarket to the sale of groceries, provisions, garden produce, fresh meat, confectionery, domestic and hardware and toilet requisites and also as an ancillary thereto the sale of such other articles or things as are usually sold in supermarkets, it was held that the sale of freezer cabinets was permitted.[88] Although self-service was the prime feature of a supermarket, this did not connote that no item should be too bulky to carry away, provided that substantially the greater part of the articles on display could be carried away from the checkout.

"Not to compete" and "not to carry on"   There must be a substantial degree of identity between the ranges of goods sold by each shop for the covenant to be enforceable.[89] A degree of overlap will be permitted.[90] The effect of the covenant must also not amount to an unreasonable restraint of trade.[91]

Enforcement

Injunction   The normal remedy for breach of a restrictive covenant is by way of an injunction. Proof of pecuniary damage is not necessary.[92] However, the defendant's lack of knowledge of the covenant may be material, *e.g.* when excluding certain

---

[83] *e.g. Zetland* v. *Driver* [1939] Ch. 1 ("the opinion of the vendor" . . . and his successors in title).
[84] *Barton* v. *Reed* [1932] 1 Ch. 362.
[85] *Zetland* v. *Driver* [1939] Ch. 1.
[86] *Barton* v. *Alliance Economic Investment Co.* [1922] 1 K.B. 742 at 759, *per* Atkin L.J. followed in *Sefton* v. *Tophams Ltd. (No. 2)* [1967] 1 A.C. 50.
[87] See *Barton* v. *Keeble* [1928] Ch. 517; *Barton* v. *Reed* [1932] 1 Ch. 362.
[88] *Calabar (Woolwich) Ltd.* v. *Tesco Stores* (1970) 245 E.G. 479.
[89] See *Labone* v. *Litherland U.D.C.* [1956] 1 W.L.R. 522; *Rother* v. *Colchester Corpn.* [1969] 2 All E.R. 600.
[90] See *Lewis and Co. (Westminster) Ltd.* v. *Bell Property Trust Ltd.* [1940] Ch. 345.
[91] See *Esso Petroleum Co.* v. *Harper's Garage (Stourport) Ltd.* [1968] A.C. 269.
[92] *Elliston* v. *Reacher* [1908] 2 Ch. 374 at 395.

activity from the scope of the injunction[93] or, more usually, when suspending its operation for a sufficient period to enable the defendant to make alternative arrangements. Since the decision of the House of Lords in *American Cyanamid Co.* v. *Ethicon Ltd.*,[94] the court will be concerned about the balance of convenience to the parties. Accordingly, in cases where buildings are to be erected, it will often be that an interlocutory injunction is more likely to be issued once their construction has commenced, since the only effective course by the date of trial would be a mandatory injunction to remove the building.[95] Each case will, of course, turn on its own facts. Likewise, where there is breach of a user covenant, the balance of convenience test will usually not favour an injunction. An injunction to prevent further breaches will, however, still lie.

Interlocutory injunction

Damages The remedy of damages will arise both as compensation in respect of past and continuing breaches as well as an alternative remedy to an interlocutory injunction. The measure of loss is a contractual one, namely, to place the plaintiff in the position in which he would have been had the covenant not been broken. One basis will be the diminution in value of the dominant land which might result in only a nominal award in the event. On the other hand, where appropriate, the sum of money that might reasonably have been expected for relaxing the covenant may be adopted as the appropriate yardstick.[96]

Measure of loss

Defences The following points may be relevant to the issue of enforceability:

(1) Change of character of neighbourhood Strict evidence of a complete change is required before a court will be prepared to hold that the plaintiff's covenant is valueless.[97] Normally, this consideration will affect the method of enforcement that will be adopted and the quantum of damages. Sometimes the court will grant a stay of proceedings on terms[98] pending an application to the Lands Tribunal under section 84(2) of the Law of Property Act for modification or discharge of the covenant in question.[99]

(2) Delay or acquiescence This will not deprive the plaintiff of his right of enforcement unless the acquiescence is of such a nature and in such circumstances that it would be dishonest or unconscionable for the plaintiff to seek to enforce it. However, such conduct will invariably preclude the grant of an injunction and may reduce the level of damages awarded.

---

[93] See, *e.g. Marten* v. *Flight Refuelling Ltd.* [1962] Ch. 115.
[94] [1975] A.C. 396.
[95] But see *Wakeham* v. *Wood* (1981) 43 P. & C.R. 40 (mandatory injunction normal remedy for infringement of covenant to preserve a view).
[96] *e.g.* in *Wrotham Park Estate Co.* v. *Parkside Homes Ltd.* [1974] 2 All E.R. 321 where Brightman J. assessed the sum as 5 per cent. of the developer's profit.
[97] *Sobey* v. *Sainsbury* [1913] 2 Ch. 513; *Chatsworth Estates Co.* v. *Fewell* [1931] 1 Ch. 224; *Westripp* v. *Baldock* [1939] 1 All E.R. 279.
[98] *Shaw* v. *Applegate* [1977] 1 W.L.R. 970.
[99] See *Richardson* v. *Jackson* [1954] 1 W.L.R. 447 and *Hanning* v. *Gable-Jeffreys Properties* [1965] 1 W.L.R. 1390.

(3) Merger This will occur when the identity of the two properties ceases.[1]

Declaration Provision is made under section 84(2) of the Law of Property Act 1925 for an application to the court[2] for a declaration to ascertain whether the land in question is still affected by any restriction[3] and, if so, the nature, extent and enforceability of the covenant.[4] A high likelihood of success is required because the court's role is limited since no power exists to modify.

Discharge or modification If an adjoining owner wishes to have the terms of a restrictive covenant varied or discharged then he must make an application to the Lands Tribunal under section 84(1) of the 1925 Act.[5] Such an applicant is required to bring his case under one of the following heads (grounds):

Restriction deemed obsolete *(1) That by reason of changes in the character of the property or the neighbourhood[6] and other circumstances which the Lands Tribunal may deem material, the restriction ought to be deemed obsolete (section 84(1)(a))* The burden of proof here is upon the applicant to show that the covenant is no longer of value because the original purpose of it is not being served[7] by reason of the foregoing factors. The ground is, however, a difficult one to establish for which reason section 84(1)(*aa*) and (*c*) tend to be more favoured by applicants.[8]

(2) That its continued existence would impede some reasonable user of the land for public or private purposes or would unless modified so impede such user[9] (section 84(1)(aa)) Under subsections 84(1A) and (1B), the Lands Tribunal is directed to have regard to the following matters:

    (a) that the restriction does not secure any practical benefits of substantial value or advantage to the person entitled to the benefit of it;

---

[1] See, *e.g. Golden Lion Hotel (Hunstanton) Ltd.* v. *Carter* [1965] 1 W.L.R. 1189 (where lessee purchased freehold reversion).

[2] This will be the county court if the land is unrated or its net annual value is less than £1,000.

[3] Under ss.84(1) and 84(2) freehold land; and by s.84(12) leasehold land for a term of 40 years where at least 25 years have expired, but not mining leases (see *Ridley* v. *Taylor* [1965] 2 All E.R. 51).

[4] *Preston and Newsom on Restriction Covenants* (7th ed.) pp. 193–198 recommends that a circular letter and a form of consent are sent to all houses in the immediate area that might be affected before such an application is made. The extent of the response can then be transcribed onto a large scale to measure the level of consent to the applicant's proposal (see *Re Freeman-Thomas Indenture* [1957] 1 W.L.R. 560 for practical example).

[5] As amended by s.28(11) of the L.P.A. 1969. The power of the Lands Tribunal is discretionary (*Driscoll* v. *Church Commissioners for England* [1957] 1 Q.B. 330).

[6] Neighbourhood need not be large (see, *e.g. Re Ling's Application* (1956) 7 P. & C.R. 233 (particular area within four roads held to be sufficient)).

[7] *Re Truman, Hanbury, Buxton & Co. Ltd.'s Application* [1956] 1 Q.B. 261.

[8] *e.g. Re Forestmere Properties Ltd.'s Application* (1980) 41 P. & C.R. 390 (building restricted to use as a cinema or residential estate was obsolete but not control—new restrictions limiting it to residential use imposed).

[9] See *Re Bass Limited's Application* (1973) 26 P. & C.R. 156.

Lands Tribunal considerations

(b) that it is contrary to the public interest;
(c) that money will be an adequate compensation for the loss or discharge (if any) which any such person will suffer from the discharge or modification;
(d) to the development plan and any declared or ascertainable pattern for the grant or refusal of planning permissions in the relevant areas;
(e) the period at which, and context in which, the restriction was created or imposed and any other material circumstances.

Under subsection 84(1C) the Lands Tribunal is also given the power to add further provisions restricting the user of or the building on the land affected as appear reasonable in view of the relaxation of existing provisions, subject to the applicant's consent. Section 84(1)(*aa*) is the ground most frequently pursued by applicants to the Lands Tribunal and reported decisions have frequently involved a wish to increase the density of housing[10] on the subject land or the development of flats.[11]

(3) That the persons of full age and capacity for the time being or from time to time entitled to the benefit of the restriction have agreed either expressly or by implication, by their acts or omissions to the same being discharged or modified (section 84(1)(b)) This ground is normally pursued where the applicant believes that the majority of the neighbouring owners will be in favour of a modification. It also

Binding order enables the Lands Tribunal to make an order binding on those owners who have either failed to lodge notices of objection or who have withdrawn their notices in respect of other grounds under section 84(1).[12]

(4) That the proposed discharge or modification will not injure the persons entitled to the benefit of the restriction (section 84(1)(c)) The purpose of this ground is to provide a "long stop"[13] against frivolous objections where the terms of a covenant, whilst still technically valid, need to be modified or discharged on certain terms, *e.g.* the provision of alcohol at a Chinese restaurant.[14] The successful applicant benefits since he is not obliged to pay any compensation to obtain the necessary relief.

Compensation The concluding words of section 84(1) deal with the question of compensation as follows:

"and an order discharging or modifying a restriction under this subsection may direct the applicant to pay to any person entitled to the benefit of the restriction such a sum by way of consideration as the Tribunal may think it just to award under one, but not both, of the following headings, that is to say, either
(1) A sum to make up for any loss or disadvantage suffered by that person in consequence of the discharge or modification, or

[10] *e.g. Re Brierfield's Application* (1976) 35 P. & C.R. 124.
[11] *e.g. Re Osborn & Easton's Application* (1978) 38 P. & C.R. 251.
[12] *Re Purkiss' Application* [1962] 1 W.L.R 902.
[13] *Ridley v. Taylor* [1965] 1 W.L.R. 611.
[14] *Re Lee's Application* (1963) 14 P. & C.R. 85.

(2) A sum to make up for any effect which the restriction had, at the time when the restriction was imposed, in reducing the consideration then received for the land affected by it."

Relevant matters

So far as heading (i) is concerned, the Lands Tribunal is obliged to take into account not only the reduction in the market value of the dominant land but also matters such as the loss of quiet during any building operations, loss of a view and the loss of the security of the covenant itself. One approach comparable to that adopted in *Wrotham Park Estate Co.* v. *Parkside Homes Ltd.*[15] has been to consider the amount which the parties would have achieved by reasonable negotiation.[16] The majority of reported decisions, however, concern applications under section 84(1)(*aa*). This incorporates the additional criteria under sub-paragraph (1A). The provision under heading (ii) is more straightforward arithmetically. Whilst it does not allow for the effects of inflation, it does provide a finite sum which is fairly easily ascertained, particularly if the covenant is only a decade or two old.[17]

Extinguishment

In addition to the provisions of section 84(1) of the 1925 Act, extinguishment may arise from express or implied release[18] by the dominant owner as well as union of ownership (merger) of the two properties.

Compulsory purchase   Finally, it should be borne in mind that when land is compulsorily purchased, or acquired under an agreement[19] by a statutory authority, the restrictive covenants affecting the land are not discharged, and they will revive if the land is subsequently sold.[20] A right to compensation lies under section 10(2) of the Compulsory Purchase Act 1965, upon the payment of which the covenants will be extinguished automatically.[21]

Compulsory Purchase Act 1965

---

[15] See n. 96 above.

[16] *Re S.J.C. Construction Co. Ltd.'s Application* (1975) 29 P. & C.R. 322.

[17] See *Re New Ideal Homes Ltd.'s Application* (1978) 36 P. & C.R. 476 for an example.

[18] As already seen, this will be a question of degree analogous to the doctrine of estoppel (see *Chatsworth Estates Co.* v. *Fewell* [1931] 1 Ch. 224).

[19] *Re 6, 8, 10 and 12 Elm Avenue, New Milton ex p. New Forest D.C.* [1984] 1 W.L.R. 1398.

[20] *Bird* v. *Eggleton* (1885) 29 Ch.D. 1012.

[21] *Long Eaton Recreation Ground Co.* v. *Midland Railway* [1902] 2 K.B. 574; *Re Sir John Simeon Isle of Wight R.D.C.* [1937] Ch. 525.

4 PARTY STRUCTURES, WALLS AND FENCES

Party structures

Definition   A party structure is any part of a building or other construction which divides two properties in different ownership. Whilst normally such an expression is limited to party walls and fences, it can, particularly in London,[1] extend to the horizontal boundary between two flats or maisonettes.[2] In the former respect, where ownership is in doubt, the provisions of section 38 of the Law of Property Act 1925 can be of considerable assistance in resolving disputes as to ownership, support or upkeep of the structure in question. Section 38 reads as follows:

L.P.A. 1925, s.38

"(1) Where under a disposition or other arrangement which, if a holding in undivided shares had been permissible, would have created a tenancy in common, a wall or other structure is or is expressed to be made a party wall or structure, that structure shall be and remain severed vertically as between the respective owners, and the owner of each part shall have such rights to support and user over the rest of the structure as may be requisite for conferring rights corresponding to those which would have subsisted if a valid tenancy in common had been created.

(2) Any person interested may, in case of dispute, apply to the court for an order declaring the rights and interests under this section of the persons interested in any such party structure, and the court may make such order as it thinks fit."

Maintenance and repair

In the absence of express provision either by deed or by statute,[3] no right of contribution can exist in favour of one owner carrying out repairs as against the other.

Weather-proofing

The case of *Phipps* v. *Pears*[4] still remains good law that there can be no easement of protection or shelter for a house. However, the case of *Bradburn* v. *Lindsay*[5] now suggests that a duty of care is owed in circumstances where an adjoining owner should reasonably have appreciated a danger arising from lack of repair (and dry rot). By the nature of its construction, it can be presumed that a lower flat or maisonette[6] does enjoy such protection from the upper storey as well as from the roof of the building in which it is situated.

Where part of the party structure projects over the boundary

---

[1] See London Building Acts (Amendment) Act 1939, s.4 for statutory definition of "party structures."
[2] See *Sturge* v. *Hackett* [1962] 1 W.L.R. 1257; *Campden Hill Towers Ltd.* v. *Gardner* [1977] Q.B. 823 and p. 8 above.
[3] See *e.g.* Part VI of the London Building Acts (Amendment) Act 1939.
[4] [1965] 1 Q.B. 76; but see *Marchant* v. *Capital & Counties* (1983) 267 E.G. 843.
[5] [1983] 2 All E.R. 408 following *Leakey* v. *National Trust* [1980] Q.B. 485.
[6] And, arguably, where flat held under a flying freehold, as *Bradburn* v. *Lindsay*, above.

Buildings projecting over boundary line (*e.g.* a gable end, length of guttering) then technically a trespass will have taken place of the adjoining owner's airspace.[7] However, the right to maintain such a projection may be, and usually is, acquired by an easement.[8]

Party walls

Definition The term "party wall" is used to describe the boundary wall dividing properties in different ownership. Such walls can be divided into four different categories:

1. Walls formerly owned as tenants in common Prior to the passing of section 38 of the Law of Property Act 1925, it was presumed that where the circumstances in which the wall was built and the amount of land contributed was unknown, each adjoining owner **Categories** held the wall equally as tenants in common. This presumption still continues save that section 38 now deems the wall to be severed vertically with cross-rights of support and user.

2. Walls divided vertically into two strips Occasionally these days, where it is clear that the centre of the wall runs along the boundary line so that the wall is divided effectively into two longitudinal strips, each half will be owned by the adjoining owner.[9] This will remain the case even though the wall may originally have been built at joint expense.[10] It is a question of fact whether the wall is exactly astride the boundary line. Minor inaccuracies will usually be ignored[11] following the *de minimis* principle. Strictly speaking, neither owner has a right of support but in practice a mutual right will be presumed or implied. Equally, there is no positive maintenance obligation. Accordingly, neither owner will be required to take any active steps to prevent the wall falling into disrepair unless some express, implied or customary agreement can be shown.[12] If an easement of support is acquired then the wall will fall into the fourth category, namely, a party wall subject to reciprocal easements.

3. Walls in single ownership Where the boundary wall is built entirely upon one owner's land it remains his exclusive property in the absence of any agreement to the contrary.[13] Long use of the wall by the adjoining owner may lead to the acquisition of easements by prescription but not normally title to the wall. Accordingly, subject to any right of support which may have

---

[7] *Kelsen* v. *Imperial Tobacco Co. Ltd.* [1957] 2 Q.B. 334; *Lemmon* v. *Webb* [1894] 3 Ch. 1 at 18; see also *Tollemache & Cobbold Breweries* v. *Reynolds* (1983) 268 E.G. 52.

[8] See *Harris* v. *De Pinna* (1885) 33 Ch.D. 238 at 250; *Lemmon* v. *Webb* [1894] 3 Ch. 1, and p. 58 above; pp. 94–95 below.

[9] See *Matts* v. *Hawkins* (1813) 5 Taunt. 20.

[10] See *Mayfair Property Co.* v. *Johnston* [1894] 1 Ch. 508.

[11] *Reading* v. *Barnard* (1827) Moo & M 71. and see *Jones* v. *Read* (1876) I.R. 10 C.L. 315 at 320.

[12] *Southwark and Vauxhall Water Co.* v. *Wandsworth Board of Works* [1898] 2 Ch. 603 at 612. See also *Sack* v. *Jones* [1925] Ch. 235.

[13] *Weston* v. *Arnold* (1873) 8 Ch.App. 1084; *Drury* v. *Army and Navy Stores Auxiliary Co. Operation Supply Ltd.* [1896] 2 Q.B. 271; *London and Gloucestershire Dairy Co.* v. *Morley* [1911] 2 K.B. 257.

been acquired during the intervening period, the owner is entitled to demolish the wall. Subject to statute,[14] the owner has seemingly no right to place the footings of the wall on to adjoining land without his neighbour's consent. Moreover, the owner's natural right of support will be limited to that arising from the soil only. In practice, an easement of support will usually have been acquired for the wall itself by grant or prescription.[15]

4. Walls subject to reciprocal easements   This is the most common form of party wall arrangement. The cross-rights granted under section 38 will permit the wall to be used for any purpose contemplated when the wall was built, *e.g.* the support of a roof.[16] It does not, however, create any positive obligation to keep either part of the wall in a state of repair. Accordingly, if the wall collapses because of the neglect of one owner, the adjoining owner has no right of action.[17] He is entitled, however, to enter his neighbour's land to carry out the repairs.[18] If the wall is damaged by a third party, each owner can only recover half the cost of its repair. However, neither owner can compel the other to contribute to the expense.[19]

Party wall agreements   Where a conveyance declares a wall to be a party wall, it often provides that each party shall pay one half of the cost of repairs to it. In law, such an obligation will amount to either an express or an implied covenant, the benefit of which will run with the land. In the rare event of one owner enjoying the right to have the wall kept in repair, it will be classed as an easement and pass under section 62 of the Law of Property Act 1925.[20]

Party structures in London

Introduction   The rights and duties of adjoining owners in the inner London boroughs[21] and the City of London are now codified under the London Building Acts (Amendment) Act 1939.[21] Provided that the provisions of the 1939 Act are complied with, the foregoing common law rights are of no application.[22] However, the 1939 Act does not alter or affect the legal title to a party structure for section 54 preserves all easements and rights arising under section 38 of the 1925 Act or otherwise.

London Building Acts (Amendment) Act 1939

Definitions   The following apply:

---

[14] *e.g.* London Building Acts (Amendment) Act 1939, s.45.
[15] See pp. 32, 46 and 47 above.
[16] *Jones* v. *Pritchard* [1908] 1 Ch. 630.
[17] *Sack* v. *Jones* [1925] Ch. 235.
[18] *Bond* v. *Nottingham Corporation* [1940] Ch. 429 at 439.
[19] *Leigh* v. *Dickeson* (1884) 12 Q.B.D. 194; on appeal (1884) 15 Q.B.D. 60; *Mayfair Property Co.* v. *Johnston* [1894] 1 Ch. 508 at 515.
[20] *Crow* v. *Wood* [1971] 1 Q.B. 77; and see below pp. 77 *et seq.*
[21] See also pp. 119–120 below.
[22] See *e.g. Gyle-Thompson* v. *Wall Street (Properties) Ltd.* [1974] 1 W.L.R. 123.

"Building owner"[23]   This means such one of the owners of adjoining land as is desirous of building or such one of the owners of building storeys or rooms separated from one another by a party wall or party structure as does or is desirous of doing a work affecting that party wall or party structure.

"Owner"[24]   This includes every person in possession or receipt either of the whole or of any part of the rent or profits of any land or tenement or in the occupation of any land or tenement otherwise than as a tenant from year to year or for any less term or as a tenant at will.

"Party fence wall"[25]   This means a wall (not being part of a building) which stands on lands of different owners and is used or constructed to be used for separating such adjoining lands but does not include a wall constructed on the land of one owner the artificially formed support of which projects into the land of another owner.

"Party structure"[25]   This means a party wall and also a floor partition or other structure separating buildings or parts of buildings approached solely by separate staircases or separate entrances from without.

"Party wall"   For the general purposes of the London Building Acts this means so much of a wall which forms part of a building as is used or constructed to be used for separating adjoining buildings belonging to different owners or occupied or constructed or adapted to be occupied by different persons together with the remainder (if any) of the wall vertically above such before-mentioned portion of wall.[25]

Section 44

For the purposes of Part VI of the 1939 Act (rights, etc., of building and adjoining owners) a special meaning is ascribed to "party wall" by section 44:

  (i) a wall which forms part of a building and stands on lands of different owners to a greater extent than the projection of any artificially formed support on which the wall rests; and
  (ii) so much of a wall not being a wall referred to in the foregoing paragraph (i) as separates buildings belonging to different owners.

New party structures   Under section 45 of the 1939 Act where the building owner wishes to build a party wall or party fence wall on a boundary of his land, hitherto unbuilt, he must serve written notice on the adjoining owner describing the intended wall. If the wall is to be erected astride a boundary line and the adjoining owner consents in writing, then the wall will be so constructed and the expenses of its construction can be shared by both owners in proportion to the use made or to be made of the

---

[23] s.5 of the 1939 Act. This definition includes a tenant for more than a year of part of a house (see *Fillingham* v. *Wood* [1891] 1 Ch. 51) and a long leaseholder who has sub-let for a term longer than from year to year (see *Hunt* v. *Harris* (1859) 19 C.B. (N.S.) 13).

[24] s.5 of the 1939 Act.

[25] s.4 of the 1939 Act.

wall and the cost of labour and materials prevailing when use is made by each owner respectively. The wall will then be treated as a party wall. On the other hand, if the building owner wishes to build the wall entirely on his own land or the adjoining owner objects or otherwise fails to give his written consent, then the wall must be built exclusively on his land. In this latter situation, the building owner is entitled at any time after the expiration of one month, but not exceeding six months from service of the notice, to build at his own expense projecting footings or foundations (but not special foundations)[26] below the ground level of the adjoining land. He must, however, make compensation to the adjoining owner or occupier for any damage done.

Existing party structures   Under section 46 of the 1939 Act[27] the building owner is given the following statutory rights to carry out work to existing party structures:

(a) A right to make good, underpin, thicken or repair or demolish and rebuild a party structure or party fence wall in any case where such work is necessary on account of defect or want of repair of the party structure or party fence wall;

(b) A right to demolish a timber or other partition which separates buildings belonging to different owners but is not in conformity with the London Building Acts or any byelaws made in pursuance of those Acts and to build

Statutory rights   instead a party wall in conformity therewith;

(c) A right in relation to a building having rooms or storeys belonging to different owners intermixed to demolish such of those rooms or storeys or any part thereof as are not in conformity with the London Building Acts or any byelaws made in pursuance of those Acts and to rebuild them in conformity therewith;

(d) A right (where buildings are connected by arches or structures over public ways or over passages belonging to other persons) to demolish such of those buildings, arches or structures or such parts thereto as are not in conformity with the London Building Acts or any byelaws made in pursuance of those Acts and to rebuild them in conformity therewith;

(e) A right to underpin, thicken or raise any party structure or party fence wall permitted by this Act to be underpinned thickened or raised or any external wall built against such a party structure or party fence wall subject to—

    (i) making good all damage occasioned thereby to the adjoining premises or to the internal finishings and decorations thereof; and

    (ii) carrying up to such height and in such materials as

---

[26] Under s.45(2), the written consent of the adjoining owner is expressly required. "Special foundations" means foundations in which an assemblage of steel beams or rods is employed for distributing any load (s.44).

[27] See *Gyle-Thompson* v. *Wall Street (Properties) Ltd.* [1974] 1 W.L.R. 123 (no right under paras. (a)–(k) to demolish a party wall and rebuild it to a reduced height). "Demolish" and "build" therefore mean reconstruction to the same level as before. See also *Burlington Property Co.* v. *Odeon Theatres* [1938] 3 All E.R. 469 (no award can be made in such a way to enable building owner to change the form of the party structure).

may be agreed between the building owner and the adjoining owner or in the event of difference determined in the manner provided in this Part of this Act, all flues and chimney stacks belonging to the adjoining owner on or against the party structure or external wall;

(f) A right to demolish a party structure which is of insufficient strength or height for the purposes of any intended building of the building owner and to rebuild it of sufficient strength or height for the said purposes subject to—

    (i) making good all damage occasioned thereby to the adjoining premises or to the internal finishings and decorations thereof; and

    (ii) carrying up to such height and in such materials as may be agreed between the building owner and the adjoining owner or in the event of difference determined in the manner provided in this Part of this Act, all flues and chimney stacks belonging to the adjoining owner on or against the party structure or external wall;

(g) A right to cut into a party structure subject to making good all damage occasioned thereby to the adjoining premises or to the internal finishings and decorations thereof;

(h) A right to cut away any footing or any projecting chimney breast, jamb or flue or other projection on or over the land of the building owner from a party wall, party fence wall, external wall or boundary wall in order to erect, raise or underpin an external wall against such party wall, party fence wall, external wall or boundary wall or for any other purpose subject to making good all damage occasioned thereby to the adjoining premises or to the internal finishings and decorations thereof;

(i) A right to cut away or demolish such parts of any wall or building of an adjoining owner overhanging the land of the building owner as may be necessary to enable a vertical wall to be erected against that wall or building subject to making good any damage occasioned thereby to the wall or building or to the internal finishings and decorations of the adjoining premises;

(j) A right to execute any other necessary works incidental to the connection of a party structure with the premises adjoining it;

(k) A right to raise a party fence wall, to raise and use as a party wall a party fence wall or to demolish a party fence wall and rebuild it as a party fence wall or as a party wall.

Party structure notices   Under section 47 of the 1939 Act, before the building owner can execute any of the foregoing works, he must serve written notice[28] on the adjoining owner specifying the proposed nature and particulars of the proposed works and the date when it will be begun. Party structure notices need only be accompanied by plans, sections and details of

Statutory rights

---

[28] By s.121 all notices must be in writing.

construction and loads where special foundations[29] are proposed. However, in practice, drawings or plans are usually attached for the purposes of clarification.

Time for service

The time for service[30] is as follows:

(1) A party fence wall or special foundations: At least one month before the stated date upon which the work is to be begun.
(2) A party structure: At least two months.

The party structure notice will not be effective unless the work to which the notice relates is begun within six months after the notice has been served and is prosecuted with due diligence.[31] However, such a notice is not required where the works in question arise out of a notice served under Part VII of the 1939 Act (*viz.* dangerous and neglected structures). The adjoining owners are also at liberty to agree such matters in writing without the need to comply with the foregoing procedure.[32]

Counter-notices

By section 48 the adjoining owner should serve a counter-notice in writing if he requires the building owner to carry out additional works. It should be accompanied by any plans, sections and particulars of the works to be executed by the building owner. He must comply with such requirements unless the execution of the additional works would be injurious to him or cause unnecessary inconvenience or delay.[33]

The time for service is as follows:

(1) Special foundations: Within 21 days after the service of the party structure notice.
(2) All other matters: Within one month.

Such works may include the building of chimneys, copings, breasts, jambs, flues, piers, recesses or other like works as may be reasonably required for the convenience of the adjoining owner. In the case of special foundations, a greater depth or strength may be insisted upon.

Foundations   Section 50 of the 1939 Act contains complicated provisions concerning the relation between foundations of the building in question and those of the adjoining owner. The building owner must serve written notice accompanied by all necessary plans, etc., within one month of the date of

Under-pinning

commencement of the works (a) if his proposed foundations are to be below the level of the adjoining owner's foundations where the buildings are 10 feet apart, or (b) where they are 20 feet apart, if the foundations would meet were a line to be drawn downwards at 45 degrees from the bottom of the adjoining owner's foundations. Within 14 days the adjoining owner may serve a counter-notice requiring or disputing the need for under-pinning, strengthening or safeguarding his foundations, in which event a dispute will be deemed to have arisen. The building owner is also obliged to compensate the adjoining owner or

---

[29] For which special consent is required from the adjoining owner (s.46(3)).
[30] Service is governed by s.124 requiring either post by pre-paid letter or delivery to the appropriate address (as if for the service of legal proceedings).
[31] s.47(3).
[32] s.47(4).
[33] s.48(4).

occupier for any inconvenience, loss or damage caused by such works.

Execution of works Section 51 states that the work must be carried out in accordance with the approved plans, byelaws and the like and in such manner or at such time as not to cause unnecessary inconvenience to the adjoining owner or occupier. At his own expense, the building owner must maintain a proper hoarding or shoring or temporary construction as is necessary for the protection of the land or building[34] and the security of the adjoining occupier. Where such works take place in a street or way less than 20 feet in width and involve excavations to a depth of 20 feet or more, then appropriate notices should be displayed at least four weeks beforehand.[35] A power of entry is provided under section 53(1) to the building owner, his servants, agents or workmen to enter the adjoining building during usual working hours for the purposes of carrying out the works. They may remove any furniture or fittings or take any other action necessary for that purpose upon the giving of 14 days' notice except in an emergency. If the adjoining premises are closed, then the building owner and his men may break open any fences or doors to enter the premises, provided that they are accompanied by a policeman.

Power of entry

Expenses Under section 56 of the 1939 Act, where works are carried out for the benefit of both owners (*e.g.* the repair of a defective party structure) then the cost can be shared between them in proportions fixed having regard to the use each makes of the party structure in question. This will also include any expenses incurred by the building owner when complying with a counter-notice under section 48. On the other hand, the building owner must bear the expense of any works carried out for his sole benefit. By section 57 the adjoining owner is entitled to serve written notice before the works are begun, requiring the building owner to give security by way of an agreed sum (or in default as determined by a county court judge) for the expenses, costs and compensation payable by the building owner. A like right is given to the building owner to seek such security from the adjoining owner in the circumstances indicated above.

Security

Disputes and awards Under section 49 of the 1939 Act, unless express consent is received in writing from the recipient to a party structure notice or counter-notice within 14 days, that person shall be deemed to have dissented and a difference shall be deemed to have arisen between the parties. To settle any difference, the parties are required by section 55 to consent in writing to the appointment of an "agreed surveyor," failing which they must each appoint their own surveyors to settle the difference by negotiation. They, in turn, can appoint a third

"Agreed surveyor"

---

[34] See p. 47 above for considerations. It is also still uncertain whether the words "lays open any part of the adjoining land or buildings" in s.51(2) include exposing a party wall. In practice, weather-proofing is likely to be carried out both to maintain good relations with the adjoining owner and to obviate a claim in nuisance (see *Bradburn* v. *Lindsay* [1983] 2 All E.R. 408 and *Tollemache & Cobbold Breweries* v. *Reynolds* (1983) 268 E.G. 52).

[35] s.52.

surveyor to act as an intermediary if an impasse is reached. The award of the surveyor or surveyors will then be declared conclusive and not open to challenge unless an appeal is made to the county court within 14 days of the delivery of such award.[36] The court is empowered to rescind or modify the award as it thinks fit. It should be noted that until the award has been made or finally determined, no work can commence.[37] The terms of the award as initially published will deal with how the work is to be supervised as well as the costs of the surveyors' determination.[38] The cost of any subsequent proceedings will be dealt with accordingly.[39]

Failure to comply   Section 148(2)(xix) of the 1939 Act prescribes that any failure to comply with an award will constitute an offence which will render the offender liable, upon summary conviction, to a fine of up to £200[40] and thereafter at the rate of £20[40a] per day until the prescribed work has been executed.

Old party wall awards   It should be borne in mind that whilst an award is conclusive at the time when it is made, it will not be binding upon subsequent parties (*e.g.* as to whether a wall is deemed to be a party wall) unless matters have been finally determined by a court of law. In such circumstances, the principle of *res judicata* may apply but only if the title of the wall is brought into question.[41] Otherwise, matters will turn upon the opinion of the surveyor and/or surveyors making the award. An old award will be of benefit to later surveyors as to what works took place at the time, *e.g.* at foundation level.

Fences

Definition   A fence is not only a form of barrier. It may consist of almost any kind of enclosure or division but a hedge, ditch, bank or wall[42] will be most commonly found to answer the term.[43] Under section 11 of the Animals Act 1971 fencing is defined as including the construction of any obstacle designed to prevent animals from straying.[44]

Duty to fence   The common law places no general obligation upon a landowner to fence his land either for his own or his neighbour's benefit.[45] Accordingly, evidence must be established

---

[36] s.55. A High Court hearing can be sought by an appellant if sufficient security is given, in which event the county court proceedings will be stayed. As the form of the proceedings is by way of arbitration, the High Court has, arguably, power to review matters by means of a direct reference under the Arbitration Acts 1950–1979.

[37] s.55(*k*).

[38] s.55(*c*).

[39] ss.55(*n*)(i) and 55(*o*)(v).

[40] The current "level 3" under the Criminal Justice Act 1982, ss.36 and 46.

[40a] See, currently, the Greater London Council (General Powers) (No. 2) Act 1978, s.7(4) and Sched. 2, Pt. II.

[41] Since title is not normally affected by an award, see the 1939 Act, s.54.

[42] But not the external walls of a building nor party walls.

[43] Woolrych, *Party Walls and Fences*, p. 281.

[44] The commonly used expression "stock-proof fence" is not defined by statute or at common law. In *Child* v. *Hearn* (1874) L.R.G. Exch. 176 at 182 where the obligation was to erect such a fence "that a pig not of a peculiarly wandering disposition, nor under excessive temptation will not get through it."

[45] See *e.g. Hilton* v. *Ankesson* (1872) 27 L.T. 519 and *British Railways Board* v. *Herrington* [1972] A.C. 877.

of a specific duty either from an agreement, prescription, implied grant or by statute.

Duties and obligations   Once a fence has been erected the landowner will be liable for its state if it constitutes a danger to adjoining owners[46] or users of the highway[47] as well as to visitors to his own land.[48]

Equally, such a duty will arise, both by statute[49] and at common law,[50] if there is some danger which has been artificially created (*e.g.* an excavation), particularly where it is near a street.[51] Specific provision has also been made for the fencing of hazards such as railways[52] and disused mines.[53] Dangers from natural features[54] (*e.g.* a river) will normally fall outside the landowner's duty, except where the hazard is a known allure to children.[55] A duty to fence may also arise in negligence for foreseeable escapes (*e.g.* in sporting activities)[56] depending upon the frequency of the risk and the cost of preventing its recurrence.

Artificially created hazards

Animals   Under the Animals Act 1971 a duty to fence may arise in practice to prevent liability for straying livestock since the owner is liable, generally, for any damage that the animals may cause on adjoining land[57] or the highway.[58] Equally, the livestock owner will not be liable if he can establish that his animals would not have strayed but for a breach of duty to fence by someone interested in the land.[59]

Right of entry   No general right exists to enter the adjoining land for the purpose of repairing a boundary fence, even though

---

[46] Actionable in nuisance (*e.g. Harrold* v. *Watney* [1898] 2 Q.B. 320—rotten fence adjoining highway).

[47] *e.g.* Highways Act 1980, s.164 (power to remove barbed wire); see also *Stewart* v. *Wright* (1893) 9 T.L.R. 480.

[48] Occupiers' Liability Act 1957, s.2(2) (common duty of care) and Defective Premises Act 1972, s.4 (landlord's obligations).

[49] Above; see also Occupiers' Liability Act 1984 (trespasses, etc.).

[50] *Att.-Gen.* v. *Roe* [1915] 1 Ch. 235; and *e.g. Stevenson* v. *Edinburgh Magistrates* [1934] A.C. 226 (gap in railings caused by motor accident).

[51] See Highways Act 1980, s.172 (hoardings to be set up during building). "Street" is defined by *ibid.* s.329 as including "any highway and any road, lane, footpath, square, court, alley or passage, whether a thoroughfare or not, and includes any part of a street." See also *ibid.* ss.139–140 for control of builders' skips.

[52] See the Railways Clauses Consolidation Act 1845, s.68 (obligation to fence in perpetuity now placed on British Rail).

[53] Mines and Quarries Act 1954, s.151 (including mines not worked for 12 months) see also Mines and Quarries (Tips) Act 1969, s.1.

[54] *Morrison* v. *London, Midland & Scottish Rly Co.* (1929) S.C. 1 and *Sutton* v. *Bootle Corporation* [1947] K.B. 359 at 368.

[55] See Occupiers' Liability Act 1957, s.2(3) (children naturally less careful than adults). See *Pannett* v. *McGuiness & Co. Ltd.* [1972] 2 Q.B. 599 and *Harris* v. *Birkenhead Corpn.* [1976] 1 W.L.R. 279 for former law relating to trespassing children in such circumstances.

[56] See *Castle* v. *St. Augustines Links* (1922) 38 T.L.R. 615 (golf ball); *Bolton* v. *Stone* [1951] 1 A.C. 850 and *Miller* v. *Jackson* [1977] Q.B. 966 (cricket ball); *Hilder* v. *Associated Portland Cement Manufacturers Ltd.* [1961] 3 All E.R. 709 (football).

[57] s.4(1).

[58] s.8(1). For unfenced land, see exemption under s.8(2) and below at p. 100.

[59] s.5(6).

such entry may be the only means of carrying out such work.[60] A right of entry will normally be implied, however, where the landowner is under an obligation to the adjoining owner to fence their common boundary and no other practicable means of carrying out such work exists.[61] Such a right will also be implied where the landlord is under an obligation to maintain the fences as part of his repairing obligations.[62]

Covenants to fence A covenant to fence or maintain fences of freehold land, being a positive covenant, can only be enforced by the parties to the conveyance because it will not run with the land so as to bind the covenantor's successors in title.[63] Various methods have been used to overcome this problem, *e.g.* by the creation of an estate rentcharge,[64] the resurrection of a right of re-entry in favour of the owner of the retained land[65] or the grant of a long lease at a peppercorn rent.[66] Damages for breach of covenant will be equivalent to the cost of carrying out the work to a reasonable standard[67] at a reasonable time.[68]

With leasehold land, under sections 141 and 142 of the Law of Property Act 1925, the benefits and burdens of a covenant to fence run with the reversion. Since the rule against perpetuities[69] does not apply to fencing covenants, there is no limit upon the effectiveness of such covenants. An implied obligation may also arise at common law, where there is a letting for a term of years, and by statute (*e.g.* under the Agriculture (Maintenance, Repair and Insurance of Fixed Equipment) Regulations 1973).[70]

Easements of fencing A landowner may acquire or become bound by an express grant of an easement or by prescription to maintain[71] a sufficient fence between his land and that of the adjoining owner. Since such a right does not come within the terms of the Prescription Act 1832, a case must be made out either under common law prescription[72] or under the doctrine of lost modern grant[73] unless it can be shown that the right has passed under section 62 of the Law of Property Act 1925.[74]

---

[60] *Kwiatkowski* v. *Cox* (1969) 213 E.G. 34; see also *John Trenberth Ltd.* v. *National Westminster Bank* (1979) 39 P. & C.R. 104.

[61] See *Ward* v. *Kirkland* [1967] Ch. 194; see also *Sutcliffe* v. *Holmes* [1947] K.B. 147 for position under Inclosure Acts.

[62] See *e.g.* Rent Act 1977, s.3(2); but it is unlikely that it would fall within a landlord's implied external repairing obligations under Landlord & Tenant Act 1985, s.11 (see *Hopwood* v. *Cannock Chase District Council* [1975] 1 W.L.R. 373).

[63] See *Jones* v. *Price* [1965] 2 Q.B. 618.

[64] Rentcharges Act 1977, ss.2, 8(4).

[65] See *Halsall* v. *Brizell* [1957] Ch. 169; *Shiloh Spinners Ltd.* v. *Harding* [1973] A.C. 691.

[66] *e.g.* for a term of 300 years or more without a proviso for re-entry.

[67] *Radford* v. *De Froberville (Lange third party)* [1977] 1 W.L.R. 1262 (in connection with a wall).

[68] *Dodd Properties (Kent) Ltd.* v. *Canterbury City Council* [1980] 1 W.L.R. 433.

[69] Perpetuities and Accumulations Act 1964, s.11.

[70] S.I. 1973 No. 1473, Sched., para. 5(1).

[71] The mere fact that the fence has been repaired for many years will not be evidence of a legal obligation to repair in itself (see *Jones* v. *Price* [1965] 2 Q.B. 618).

[72] See *Egerton* v. *Harding* [1975] Q.B. 62.

[73] See p. 37 above.

[74] See *Crow* v. *Wood* [1971] 1 Q.B. 77 ("quasi-easement" of fencing).

Ecclesiastical properties   In the absence of local custom, the duty to maintain the fences around a churchyard will lie with the parochial church council[75] or the cemetery company. So far as parsonage houses, rectories and vicarages are concerned, these will be the responsibility of the incumbent.[76]

[75] Parochial Church Council (Powers) Measure 1921, s.4; see also Burial Act 1855, s.18 and Cemeteries Clauses Act 1847, s.15.
[76] Repair of Benefice Buildings Measure 1972, ss.2–6; Endowments and Glebe Measure 1976, s.33.

5 REMEDIES

Causes of action

By way of a checklist, the following considerations should be borne in mind when litigation is contemplated:

Trespass

Defined A trespass to land is any unjustifiable intrusion onto another's soil or interference with his possession, whether the tortfeasor is aware of his act or not.[1] Whilst proof of actual damage is not required, the tortious act must constitute a direct and immediate injury to the land, *e.g.* the placing of a ladder against a neighbour's wall[2] or the act of walking on the land.[3]

Prospective parties   Any person who has the occupation or physical control of the land in question may sue and be sued.[3a] Where it is without buildings, possession will be established by acts of enjoyment (*e.g.* shooting over it or taking grass[4]) over at least part of the land.[5] Possession of an unoccupied building will be established by possession of the key or some other method of obtaining entry.[6] Proof of legal ownership will, prima facie, be sufficient to establish possession.[7] Where there is an alternative claimant to the ownership of the land in question, there must be clear evidence of dispossession against the true owner.[8] The same **Considerations** considerations apply where there is co-ownership of a party structure. If one owner destroys a party wall and does not rebuild it[9] or builds across the whole width of the existing wall,[10] then an action in trespass will lie. Where land is let other than by licence,[11] it will be the tenant who has the right to sue in trespass unless the landlord can establish that damage has been caused to the reversion,[12] *e.g.* where the demised premises are destroyed.

---

[1] *e.g. Conway* v. *George Wimpey & Co. Ltd. (No. 2)* [1951] 2 K.B. 266 at 273–274.

[2] *Westripp* v. *Baldock* [1939] 1 All E.R. 279.

[3] See generally *Hickman* v. *Maisey* [1900] 1 Q.B. 752.

[3a] Where title is not in issue, even where the acts complained of caused no harm, a landowner is entitled to an interlocutory injunction preventing trespass to his land as of right without consideration of the balance of convenience or adequacy of damages (see *Patel* v. *Smith (W. H.) (Eziot)* [1987] 1 W.L.R. 853).

[4] *Harper* v. *Charlesworth* (1825) 4 B. & C. 574.

[5] See *Jones* v. *Williams* (1837) 2 M. & W. 326 at 331 and *Matson* v. *Cook* (1838) 4 Bing.N.C. 392.

[6] *Jewish Maternity Society's Trustees* v. *Garfinkle* (1926) 95 L.J.K.B. 766.

[7] *Herbert* v. *Thomas* (1835) 1 Cr.M. & R. 861 at 864.

[8] *e.g. Fowley Marine (Emsworth) Ltd.* v. *Gafford* [1968] 2 Q.B. 618 (boat owners who moored in plaintiff's creek held not to have concurrent possession); see also p. 14 above for position where adverse possession claim is made.

[9] *Cubitt* v. *Porter* (1828) 8 B. & C. 257; *Standard Bank of British South America* v. *Stokes* (1878) 9 Ch.D. 68.

[10] *Stedman* v. *Smith* (1857) 8 E. & B. 1; *Watson* v. *Gray* (1880) 14 Ch.D. 192.

[11] See *Street* v. *Mountford* [1985] A.C. 809 for definition of exclusive possession; sub-tenants can sue but not lodgers or hotel guests. See *Hounslow L.B.C.* v. *Twickenham Garden Developments Ltd.* [1971] Ch. 233 for position of building contractor.

[12] *Mayfair Property Co.* v. *Johnston* [1894] 1 Ch. 508.

Defences   The following defences may apply:

Justification   This may arise by statute,[13] by operation of law, by way of an implied licence (*e.g.* to abate a nuisance or to recover goods taken by the wrongful act of the plaintiff) or under an existing right (*e.g.* to fish,[14] whether by custom or as a *profit à prendre*).

Express licence   Conversely, a licensee who exceeds the terms of his licence[15] or remains on the land after the licence has expired[16] or has not removed his goods within a reasonable time of its revocation[17] will have no defence.

Limitation   Under section 15(1) of the Limitation Act 1980, no action for recovery of land may be brought within 12 years of the act of possession.[18] For an ordinary action, the period otherwise remains six years.[19]

Prescription   This claim will amount to a defence after a full period of 20 years has elapsed.[20]

Measure of damages   Although no actual loss need be established, a prospective plaintiff will only recover substantive **Physical damage**   (as opposed to nominal) damages if physical damage can be shown. Usually, this will be assessed on the basis of the diminution in the value of the land.[21] However, if the plaintiff intends to make good the damage or defect,[22] then the measure will be the cost of repair and reinstatement, provided such expenditure is reasonable.[23] The relevant date of assessment will be the time when the works could be reasonable carried out.[24]

Nuisance

Defined   The tort of nuisance is any condition or activity which unduly interferes with the use or enjoyment of land resulting in consequential injury.[25]

Types of nuisance   The law recognises three kinds of private nuisance:

Continuing encroachment   *e.g.* from a cornice of a building or from overhanging branches or tree roots.

---

[13] *e.g.* in the exercise of a public right of way under the National Parks and Access to the Countryside Act 1949 and the Wildlife and Countryside Act 1981.

[14] See p. 28 and 41–42 above.

[15] *e.g. Willcox* v. *Kettell* [1937] 1 All E.R. 223 (extension of foundations beyond mere underpinning).

[16] *Robson* v. *Hallett* [1967] 2 Q.B. 939 (licensee allowed reasonable time to leave).

[17] *Minister of Health* v. *Bellotti* [1944] K.B. 298 at 308; *Thompson* v. *Park* [1944] K.B. 408.

[18] See pp. 14–16 above for further considerations.

[19] s.2 of the 1980 Act.

[20] See pp. 36–40 above.

[21] See *Jones* v. *Gooday* (1842) 8 M. & W. 736.

[22] *Hole & Son (Sayers Common)* v. *Harrisons of Thurnscoe* [1973] 1 Lloyd's Rep. 348; see also *Dodd Properties (Kent)* v. *Canterbury City Council* [1980] 1 W.L.R. 433.

[23] *Heath* v. *Keys* (1984) 134 New L.J. 888.

[24] See *Dodd Properties (Kent)* v. *Canterbury City Council* above.

[25] See *e.g. Read* v. *Lyons & Co. Ltd.* [1947] K.B. 216 at 236.

Acts or omissions causing physical damage   *e.g.* damp or subsidence.

Undue interference with comfort and enjoyment   *e.g.* smells, smoke,[26] unreasonable noise or interference with easements.

Criteria   The following considerations may apply:

Standard of comfort and convenience   This will be assessed objectively and will usually exclude abnormally sensitive activities (*e.g.* radio and television transmissions).[27]

Character of neighbourhood   *e.g.* what would be a nuisance in Belgrave Square would not necessarily be so in Bermondsey.[28]

Building operations   *Normal activities*   *e.g.* building operations. These will not, in themselves, amount to a nuisance, even though considerable inconvenience may be caused.[29] Allied to the reasonableness of the adjoining owner's activities will be his concurrent duty of care in most situations,[30] although negligence will not necessarily be a prerequisite for establishing nuisance.[31]

Duration of interference   Whilst this provides a helpful yardstick, substantial interference, even from a temporary source, can still amount to an actionable nuisance, *e.g.* excessive dust and noise.[32]

Deliberate acts   *e.g.* making telephone calls to disturb a person's sleep very late at night.[33]

Natural forms   The absence of human activity is no longer a defence to a nuisance arising from the natural condition of the land, *e.g.* landslip.[34]

Prospective parties   As with an action in trespass, any person who is in possession or occupation of the affected land may sue.
    The primary defendant will always be the actual wrongdoer[35] or, under the doctrine of vicarious liability, a person responsible for the acts of servants or agents, irrespective of whether he is in possession or occupation of the adjoining land. The landowner will be liable for the tortious acts of licensees if he has authorised the **Considerations**   commission of a nuisance (*e.g.* by allowing gypsies to camp on his land)[36] and for those of a trespasser only if the landowner continues

---

[26] See also Clean Air Acts 1956 and 1968 (as applied to London by the London Government Act 1963, s.40(1), (4)(*e*)).
[27] *Bridlington Relay Ltd.* v. *Yorkshire Electricity Board* [1965] Ch. 436.
[28] *Per* Thesiger L.J., *Sturges* v. *Bridgman* (1879) 11 Ch.D. 852 at 856.
[29] See *Harrison* v. *Southwark and Vauxhall Water Co.* [1891] 2 Ch. 409 at 413; *Phelps* v. *City of London Corpn.* [1916] 2 Ch. 255.
[30] See *Leakey* v. *National Trust* [1980] Q.B. 485.
[31] *The Wagon Mound (No. 2)* [1967] 1 A.C. 617.
[32] *Matania* v. *National Provincial Bank* [1936] 2 All E.R. 633.
[33] *Stoakes* v. *Brydges* (1958) 32 Austral.L.J. 205; see also *Hollywood Silver Fox Farm* v. *Emmett* [1936] 2 K.B. 468.
[34] See *Leakey* v. *National Trust* [1980] Q.B. 485; see also *Bradburn* v. *Lindsay* [1983] 2 All E.R. 408 (damp and dry rot).
[35] *Hall* v. *Beckenham Corpn.* [1949] 1 K.B. 716 (nuisance from noise caused by model aeroplanes in public park).
[36] *Att.-Gen.* v. *Stone* (1895) 12 T.L.R. 76; *Penge Motors* v. *Epsom & Ewell Borough Council* (1980) J.P.L. 396.

or adopts the nuisance but not if such activities take place without his knowledge or consent.[37] The same considerations apply where the original act of nuisance has been created by a predecessor in title.[38] The landowner will not be liable for the acts of an independent contractor unless some special risk or hazard is involved or there has been clear negligence in the choice of the contractor.[39]

Proof Where the nuisance causes physical damage to the land, then actual damage must be established.[40] On the other hand, where it consists of an encroachment damage will be presumed.[41] Where the nature of the nuisance is an interference with the comfort and enjoyment of the land or an easement, no injury to health or loss need be proved.[42] If negligence is a prerequisite for establishing nuisance then if the former claim fails on the grounds of foreseeability, the claim cannot still be pursued.[43]

Negligence

Defences The following defences may apply:

Act of God This arises only where the operation of natural forces is so unexpected that any consequent damage is regarded as being too remote, *e.g.* lightning[44] or flooding.[45] It will be a question of fact whether human foresight or prudence could have anticipated such an occurrence.[46]

Act of a trespasser Provided the occupier has no knowledge or means of knowledge of the nuisance created by a trespasser, then no liability will arise.[47]

Authorisation Other than express or implied consent from the plaintiff (which is then rescinded) this is likely to arise today only under statute.[48] The fact that the activity in question is useful and/or desirable in the public interest will not constitute a defence *per se* but may prevent the issue of an injunction.[49]

---

[37] *Sedleigh-Denfield* v. *O'Callaghan* [1940] A.C. 880; see also *Hilton* v. *James Smith & Sons (Norwood) Ltd.* (1979) 251 E.G. 1063.
[38] See *Rosewell* v. *Prior* (1701) 12 Mod. 635.
[39] See *Salsbury* v. *Woodland* [1970] 1 Q.B. 324 but for a broader approach see *Matania* v. *National Provincial Bank* above and *Spicer* v. *Smee* [1946] 1 All E.R. 489.
[40] See *Sedleigh-Denfield* v. *O'Callaghan* [1940] A.C. 880 at 896, 919–920 although a *quia timet* injunction can be obtained if imminent impending danger is faced.
[41] See *Fay* v. *Prentice* (1845) 1 C.B. 828.
[42] *Crump* v. *Lambert* (1867) L.R. 3 Eq. 409; and *Halsey* v. *Esso Petroleum Co.* [1961] 1 W.L.R. 683.
[43] *The Wagon Mound (No. 2)* [1967] 1 A.C. 617.
[44] See *Goldman* v. *Hargrave* [1967] 1 A.C. 645 (fire started by lightning striking tree).
[45] See *Leakey* v. *National Trust* [1980] Q.B. 485 as to reasonable foreseeability of risk.
[46] *e.g.* *Greenock Corpn.* v. *Caledonian Rly* [1917] A.C. 556 and *Greenwood Tileries Ltd.* v. *Clapson* [1937] 1 All E.R. 765.
[47] *e.g.* where railing broken outside a vacant house causing child to fall through (*Barker* v. *Herbert* [1911] 2 K.B. 633).
[48] See *Allen* v. *Gulf Oil Refining Ltd.* [1981] 2 W.L.R. 188 (nuisances from oil refinery deemed to be authorised under Private Act of Parliament). See also S.I. 1970 No. 289 for exemption of military aircraft under the provisions of the Civil Aviation Act 1982.
[49] See *Miller* v. *Jackson* [1977] Q.B. 966 (cricket club).

Apportionment

Contributory negligence   This will be subject to the apportionment provisions of the Law Reform (Contributory Negligence) Act 1945. The fact that a plaintiff purchases the land with the nuisance already in existence does not prevent him from recovering damages or an injunction.[50] Even if the activity causing the nuisance is carried out with all due care and skill, this will not afford a defence once nuisance is established.[51]

Ignorance of the nuisance   The relevant test is foreseeability of risk.[52] A higher duty is placed upon the owners of buildings adjoining the highway.[53]

Inevitable accident   This will only be a defence to a claim in nuisance where liability depends upon a finding in negligence, *e.g.* in a highway case.

Necessity   Examples of this defence are preventing the spread of a fire by spraying water or destroying heather.[54]

Prescription   This defence can be raised where the right to commit the nuisance is capable of being an easement, *e.g.* to discharge rainwater from eaves[55] or surface water onto adjoining land[56] but not for the roots or branches of a tree to encroach[57] nor nuisance arising from smoke, smells, noise or vibration where the gravity of the inconvenience is variable.[58]

Measure of damages   The normal measure, where physical damage is caused or continuing encroachment occurs, is the difference in the value of the affected property before and after the act of nuisance unless the cost of repairs can be justified.[59] Interference with the enjoyment of the property is now likely to be assessed by analogy with personal injury cases.[60]

Consequential damages

Consequential damages for injury to chattels and health may also be recovered in both sets of circumstances.[61]

Abatement   The right of abatement (self-help) will arise if the landowner would equally be entitled to a mandatory injunction if he were to go to court.[62] For this purpose, he is entitled lawfully to enter the wrongdoer's land and to remove the cause of the nuisance. The act of abatement must, however, be carried out

[50] *St. Helen's Smelting Co.* v. *Tipping* (1865) 11 H.L.Cas. 642.
[51] *Rapier* v. *London Tramways Co.* [1893] 2 Ch. 588; *Farrell* v. *John Mowlem & Co. Ltd.* [1954] 1 Lloyd's Rep. 437 at 440.
[52] *e.g. Cunliffe* v. *Bankes* [1945] 1 All E.R. 459 and *British Road Services* v. *Slater* [1964] 1 W.L.R. 498 for liability of owners of trees and adjoining highway.
[53] See *Wringe* v. *Cohen* [1940] 1 K.B. 229.
[54] *Cope* v. *Sharp (No. 2)* [1912] 1 K.B. 496; see also special provisions as to Fire below.
[55] *e.g. Harvey* v. *Walters* (1872–73) L.R. 8 C.P. 162.
[56] *Att.-Gen.* v. *Copeland* [1902] 1 K.B. 690.
[57] *Lemmon* v. *Webb* [1895] A.C. 1; *Morgan* v. *Khyatt* [1964] 1 W.L.R. 475.
[58] See *Crump* v. *Lambert* (1867) L.R. 3 Eq. 409 (smoke and noise); *Sturges* v. *Bridgman* (1879) 11 Ch.D. 852 (vibration).
[59] See p. 87 above.
[60] See *Bone* v. *Seale* [1975] 1 W.L.R. 797 (smell from pig farm equated with loss of sense of smell).
[61] *Halsey* v. *Esso Petroleum Co. Ltd.* [1961] 1 W.L.R. 683.
[62] *Lane* v. *Capsey* [1891] 3 Ch. 411; see also *Redland Bricks Ltd.* v. *Morris* [1970] A.C. 652 for principles applying to mandatory injunctions. See also R.S.C. Ord. 45, r. 8 for plaintiff's right to carry out works prescribed by mandatory injunction and to recover expenses where defendant disobeys order.

Notice peacefully and on notice[63] except, perhaps, in the case of an emergency, and with as little damage as possible.[64] However, actual damage need not occur before the right to abate can be exercised, *e.g.* where roots or branches overhang.[65] Whilst the right to abate will exist in such circumstances, no action will lie unless physical damage has been caused.[66] The act of abatement will, generally, preclude a subsequent application for a mandatory injunction[67] but not a claim for substantive damages before the abatement.[68]

Rylands v. *Fletcher*

Defined The rule in *Rylands* v. *Fletcher*[69] imposes strict liability for all damage consequent upon the escape of anything which is a "non-natural use" of the land. These have been held to include the bulk storage of water,[70] gas and electricity[71] (but not ordinary domestic supplies[72]), sewage,[73] motor vehicles (whether containing petrol or not,[74]) a blowlamp,[75] paraffin[76] and poison.[77] Whilst the rule has also been held to apply to vibrations set up by pile-driving[78] and to the grant of licenses to caravan dwellers to use a field,[79] it is now doubtful whether they would be similarly considered in view of alternative remedies in nuisance[80] or negligence.[81]

Extent of liability In Blackburn J.'s statement of the rule "once there has been an escape, those damnified may claim. They need not be the occupiers of adjoining land or indeed any land." Provided that causation can be established, there would appear to

No limit be no limit, including claims for personal injuries.[82]

---

[63] *Lagan Navigation Co.* v. *Lambeg Bleaching, Dyeing and Finishing Co. Ltd.* [1927] A.C. 226 at 244. Notice not required for purposes of removing overhanging branches (*Lemmon* v. *Webb* [1895] A.C. 1) and possibly roots (*Butler* v. *Standard Telephones and Cables Limited* [1940] 1 K.B. 399) but not to pick or appropriate the fruit (*Mills* v. *Brooker* [1919] 1 K.B. 555).

[64] See *Lagan Navigation Co.* v. *Lambeg, etc. Co. Ltd.* above.

[65] See *Lemmon* v. *Webb* above.

[66] *Smith* v. *Giddy* [1904] 2 K.B. 448.

[67] See *Lane* v. *Capsey* [1891] 3 Ch. 411 at 416.

[68] *Kendrick* v. *Bartland* (1679) 2 Mod.Rep. 253.

[69] (1868) L.R. 3 H.L. 330.

[70] See pp. 111–112 below.

[71] See pp. 105–106 below.

[72] *Collingwood* v. *Home & Colonial Stores Ltd.* [1936] 3 All E.R. 200.

[73] *Charing Cross Electricity Supply Co.* v. *Hydraulic Power Co.* [1914] 3 K.B. 772 and *Smeaton* v. *Ilford Corporation* [1954] Ch. 450.

[74] *Musgrove* v. *Pandelis* [1919] 2 K.B. 43; *Perry* v. *Kendricks Transport Co.* [1956] 1 W.L.R. 85.

[75] *Balfour* v. *Barty-King* [1957] 1 Q.B. 496.

[76] *Mulholland and Tedd Ltd.* v. *Baker* [1939] 3 All E.R. 253.

[77] *West* v. *Bristol Tramways Co.* [1908] 2 K.B. 14; see also *Halsey* v. *Esso Petroleum Co. Ltd.* [1961] 1 W.L.R. 683 (smuts and oily drops).

[78] *Hoare & Co.* v. *McAlpine* [1923] 1 Ch. 167 but disapproved in *Barrette* v. *Franki Compressed Pile Co. of Canada* [1955] 2 D.L.R. 665 (vibrations actionable in nuisance only).

[79] *Att.-Gen.* v. *Corke* [1933] Ch. 89.

[80] See *Smith* v. *Scott* [1973] Ch. 314.

[81] *Home Office* v. *Dorset Yacht Co.* [1970] A.C. 1004.

[82] See *Miles* v. *Forest Rock Granite Co.* (1918) 34 T.L.R. 500 and *Halle* v. *Jennings Bros.* [1938] 1 All E.R. 579; but also *Read* v. *Lyons, J. & Co. Ltd.* [1947] A.C. 156 at 159, 163 and *Perry* v. *Kendricks Transport Co.* [1956] 1 W.L.R. 85.

Defences   These can be listed[82a] as follows:

(1) Act of God;
(2) Act or default of the plaintiff;
(3) Consent of the plaintiff;
(4) Independent act of a third party;
(5) Statutory authority.

Negligence

Defined   In essence the tort of negligence is committed when damage, which is not too remote, is caused by the breach of a duty of care owed by the defendant to the plaintiff.[83]

Proof   To found a claim, the following must be established:

(1) the existence in law of a duty of care;
(2) careless behaviour on the part of the defendant;
(3) foreseeability that such behaviour would inflict harm to the plaintiff;
(4) a causal link between the defendant's behaviour and the damage;
(5) the extent of the damage attributable to the defendant;
(6) the monetary estimate of such damage.

Defences   The various defences available in tort have already been considered above. For completeness, regard should also be paid to the pleas of *volenti non fit injuria* (willing acceptance of a risk) and *novus actus interveniens*.

Occupiers' Liability Act 1957

Scope   Section 2 of the Act imposes upon every occupier[84] of premises a "common duty of care" to ensure that every visitor to those premises will be reasonably safe in using those premises for the purposes for which the visitor[85] is invited or permitted to be there.

Warnings and knowledge of risk   An occupier cannot exclude[86] his liability and can only warn if the warning is enough in all the circumstances to enable the visitor to be reasonably safe.[87] The defence of *volenti* is, however, specifically preserved by section 2(5) of the Act. Contributory negligence may also be established.

[82a] See pp. 89–90 above.

[83] See *The Wagon Mound (No. 1)* [1961] A.C. 338 at 425.

[84] "Occupier" is not defined but connotes a sufficient degree of control (see *e.g.* *AMF International Ltd.* v. *Magnet Bowling Ltd.* [1968] 1 W.L.R. 1028 where both the building's owners and their contractors were held to be occupiers. An absentee landlord, therefore, falls outside the scope of the 1957 Act unless he is in breach of his repairing obligations (see s.4 of the Defective Premises Act 1972).

[85] s.1(2) includes invitees and licensees with implied or limited permission (*e.g.* to carry out works of construction or maintenance). An occupier must be prepared for children to be less careful than adults s.2(3)(*a*) (see p. 103 below).

[86] s.2 of the Unfair Contract Terms Act 1977.

[87] s.2(4).

Occupiers' Liability Act 1984

Scope The purpose of the 1984 Act is to define an occupier's duty towards trespassers[88] for personal injury in place of the common law rules,[89] save as to an occupier's liability for damage to a trespasser's property.[90] The relevant parts of section 1 provide as follows:

"(3) An occupier of premises owes a duty to another (not being his visitor) in respect of any such risk as is referred to in subsection (1) above if—

   (*a*) he is aware of the danger or has reasonable grounds to
Statutory duty   believe that it exists;

   (*b*) he knows or has reasonable grounds to believe that the other is in the vicinity of the danger concerned or that he may come into the vicinity of the danger (in either case, whether the other has lawful authority for being in that vicinity or not); and

   (*c*) the risk is one against which, in all the circumstances of the case, he may reasonably be expected to offer the other some protection.

(4) Where, by virtue of this section, an occupier of premises owes a duty to another in respect of such a risk, the dutry is to take such care as is reasonable in all the circumstances of the case to se that he does not suffer injury on the premises by reason of the danger concerned.

(5) Any duty owed by virtue of this section in respect of a risk may, in an appropriate case, be discharged by taking such steps as are reasonable in all the circumstances of the case to give warning of the danger concerned or to discourage persons from incurring the risk.

(6) No duty is owed by virtue of this section to any person in respect of risks willingly accepted as his by that person (the question whether a risk was so accepted to be decided on the same principles as in other cases in which one person owes a duty of care to another).

(7) No duty is owed by virtue of this section to persons using the highway, and this section does not affect any duty owed to such persons.

(8) Where a person owes a duty by virtue of this section, he does not, by reason of any breach of the duty, incur any liability in respect of any loss of or damage to property."

It should also be noted that under section 2 occupiers of business premises may exempt themselves from the provisions of
U.C.T.A. 1977 the Unfair Contract Terms Act 1977[91] where access is granted

[88] The wider term used in s.1(3), "*viz.* a person (not being his visitor)" will also embrace persons using private and public rights of way and entrance under the National Parks and Access to the Countryside Act 1949.
[89] *viz.* "the duty of ordinary humanity" (see *British Railways Board* v. *Herrington* [1972] A.C. 877).
[90] s.1(8). In *Tutton* v. *A. D. Walter Ltd.* [1986] Q.B. 61, a farmer was held liable for negligently killing his neighbour's bees. Although the judge thought the bees were not trespassing, he had no doubt that the farmer was liable under the principles in *British Railways Board* v. *Herrington* above.
[91] *viz.* s.1(3) no exclusion of liability where premises used for business purposes.

only for educational or recreational purposes[92] over land needed for business purposes, *e.g.* a commercial forest or arable farmland.

Statutory rights of redress and judicial review

Complaint to authority

Because of the extensive overlap today between statutory regulation and private law remedies, it is important to bear in mind that in some cases pressure can be brought to bear more speedily and effectively upon a neighbour by complaint being made direct to an authority, the local council or otherwise, as may be the case. This avenue of relief may be of particular help where a private law remedy cannot be pursued[93] or where an interlocutory injunction would be inappropriate on the balance of convenience test.[94] Because of its public law responsibilities, the relevant authority will normally be obliged at least to investigate the complaint. Unfortunately, if the authority declines to take steps (*e.g.* for reasons of policy or finance) then the injured party will only be able to pursue the limited remedy of judicial review.[95]

Specific circumstances

Airspace

A landowner's rights to this area above his land are restricted by the height necessary for the ordinary use and enjoyment of the land and the structures on it and not to the limits of the atmosphere.[96] Within this limit, the owner is entitled to exclude

---

[92] *e.g.* under the National Parks and Access to the Countryside Act 1949 (see further p. 52 above).

[93] *e.g.* where the removal of a builder's skip on the highway is required (see Highways Act 1980, s.140).

[94] *i.e.* where adequate compensation can be provided in damages (see *American Cyanamid Co.* v. *Ethicon Ltd.* [1975] A.C. 396).

[95] This will usually be on *Wednesbury* principles, *i.e.* that no reasonable authority would have reached the decision in question (see *Associated Provincial Picture Houses Ltd.* v. *Wednesbury Corporation* [1948] 1 K.B. 223). The relief available under R.S.C. Ord. 53, r. 1 will, in such circumstances, be limited to an order of *certiorari* quashing the original decision with a direction to reconsider and to make a fresh resolution in the light of the court's findings (R.S.C. Ord. 53, r. 9(4)) or an order of *mandamus* requiring the authority to make a decision and/or take appropriate steps in the exercise of its powers once a decision has been made. Because of the limited scope of the court's powers it is unlikely that this form of redress will be available save in exceptional circumstances. Speed is essential: R.S.C. Ord. 53, r. 4(1) states that the application for leave (which is made *ex parte*) to apply for judicial review shall be made promptly, and in any event, within three months from the date when the grounds for the application first arose unless the court considers that there is good reason for extending time. If leave is granted then the merits are argued at a subsequent *inter partes* hearing. All evidence is on affidavit (Ord. 53, r. 6); but discovery, interrogatories and cross-examination can be sought with leave of the court (Ord. 53, r. 8). See also *O' Reilly* v. *Mackman* [1983] 2 A.C. 237.

[96] *Bernstein of Leigh (Baron)* v. *Skyview & General Ltd.* [1978] Q.B. 479.

Trespass trespasses by, for example, trees, cranes,[97] eaves,[98] telephone wires[99] or signboards.[1]

Statutory dispensations A wide dispensation is granted to all types of civilian aircraft[2] (including helicopters and hovercraft[3]) under the Civil Aviation Act 1982. By section 76(10) "no action shall lie in respect of trespass by reason only of the flight of aircraft over any property at a height above the ground which, having regard to wind, weather and all the circumstances of the **Ordinary incidents** case, is reasonable, or the ordinary incidents of such flight, so **of flight** long as the provisions of any Air Navigation Order[4] or any Orders under section 62 above[5] have been duly complied with and there has been no breach of section 81 below."[6] Noise and vibration seemingly come within the phrase "ordinary incidents"[7] but not repeated passages for advertising purposes (whether smoke is used or not) nor stunting and aerobatics (except in connection with a properly authorised display).

However, section 76(2) provides that "where material damage is caused to any person or property on land or water by, or by a person in or an article or person falling from, an aircraft while in flight, taking off or landing, then unless the loss or damage was caused or contributed to by the negligence of the **Strict liability** person by whom it was suffered, damages in respect of the loss or damaged shall be recoverable without proof of negligence or intention or other cause of action as if the loss or damage had been caused by the wilful act, neglect or default of the owner of the aircraft."

In order to succeed in such circumstances, the landowner must establish the causal link between the material loss and damage and the incidents under the section. This may prove difficult.[8] Cumulative damage caused by a number of aircraft is also actionable under this sub-section but proof of causation will be even more demanding.[9]

---

[97] *Woollerton & Wilson Ltd.* v. *Richard Costain Ltd.* [1970] 1 W.L.R. 411.

[98] *Tollemache & Cobbold Breweries* v. *Reynolds* (1983) 268 E.G. 52.

[99] *Wandsworth District Board of Works* v. *United Telephone Co. Ltd.* (1884) 13 Q.B.D. 904.

[1] *Kelsen* v. *Imperial Tobacco Co. (of Great Britain & Ireland) Ltd.* [1957] 2 Q.B. 334. For further consideration of this subject (including damages) see the article by E. McKendrick (1988) 138 New L.J. 23.

[2] Military aircraft are exempt by s.101 of the 1982 Act and Civil Aviation (Crown Aircraft) Order 1970 (S.I. 1970 No. 289). However, a statutory scheme of compensation is administered by the Ministry of Defence under the Land Compensation Act 1973.

[3] s.100 of the 1982 Act and the Hovercraft Act 1968.

[4] *e.g.* Air Navigation (Noise Certification) Order 1984 (S.I. 1984 No. 368). See also controls on aerial spraying provided by the Control of Pesticides Regulations 1986 (S.I. 1986 No. 1510).

[5] *i.e.* control of aviation in time of war or emergency.

[6] *i.e.* dangerous flying.

[7] See *Steel-Maitland* v. *British Airways Board* (1981) S.T.L. 110 (damage caused by vibration and droplets of aviation spirit actionable by castle owner near Edinburgh Airport).

[8] See *e.g. Greenfield* v. *Law* [1955] 2 Lloyd's Rep. 696 (plaintiff injured falling from horse which had allegedly bolted as a result of fright at the sound of a low-flying aircraft. Action not successful).

[9] See *Steel-Maitland* v. *British Airways Board* above.

Advertising   It is worthy of note that section 82(1) prohibits, by way of criminal sanction, the emitting or displaying of any aerial advertising and propaganda by any aircraft while in the air, except in certain prescribed circumstances.[10]

Animals

Definitions   Under the Animals Act 1971, no statutory definition is given of the term "animals"[11] although a distinction is drawn between animals which belong to a dangerous species (*ferae naturae*) and other animals (*mansuetae naturae*). The following definitions are, however, to be found in section 15 of the Protection of Animals Act 1911:

(1) The expression "animal" means any domestic or captive animal;

(2) The expression "domestic animal" means any horse, ass, mule, bull, sheep, pig, goat, dog, cat, or fowl, or any other animal of whatsoever kind or species, and whether a quadruped or not which is tame or which has been or is being sufficiently tamed to serve some purpose for the use of man;

Definitions

(3) The expression "captive animal" means any animal (not being a domestic animal) of whatsoever kind or species, and whether a quadruped or not, including any bird, fish, or reptile, which is in captivity, or confinement, or which is maimed, pinioned, or subjected to any appliance or contrivance for the purpose of hindering or preventing its escape from captivity[12] or confinement;

(4) The expression "horse" includes any mare, gelding, pony, foal, colt, filly, or stallion; and the expression "bull" includes any cow, bullock, heifer, calf, steer, or ox, and the expression "sheep" includes any lamb, ewe, or ram; and the expression "pig" includes any boar, hog, or sow; and the expression "goat" includes a kid; and the expression "dog" includes any bitch, sapling, or puppy; and the expression "cat" includes a kitten; and the expression "fowl" includes any cock, hen, chicken, capon, turkey, goose, gander, duck, drake, guinea-fowl, peacock, peahen, swan, or pigeon.

Proprietary rights   A landowner has only qualified ownership of wild animals whilst they are on his land. A person who takes, tames or reclaims a wild animal is entitled to claim it as his property until it regains its natural liberty.[13] He also has a proprietary right to the young of such animals born on his land until they can run or fly away.[14] An action in trespass or

---

[10] See Civil Aviation (Aerial Advertising) Regulations 1983 (S.I. 1983 No. 1885).
[11] See n. 32 below for definitions of "livestock" and "poultry" under s.11 of the 1971 Act.
[12] See *Rowley* v. *Murphy* [1964] 2 Q.B. 43 (mere temporary inability to get away is not a state of captivity).
[13] *Grymes* v. *Shack* (1610) Cro.Jac. 662; *e.g.* wild game birds kept in an enclosure.
[14] *Blades* v. *Higgs* (1865) 29 J.P. 390.

Wild animals

conversion can therefore be maintained against poachers. The landowner is equally entitled to hunt, take and kill[15] wild animals so long as they are within the boundaries of his land including the airspace above. Once the animal is dead it becomes the absolute property of the landowner on whose land it lived.[16] No liability can attach to a landowner as a result of wild animals causing damage to an adjoining property[17] unless an unreasonable number are kept.[18] Equally, if the landowner reclaims wild animals and they trespass, he will be liable.[19]

Domestic animals

Domestic animals are automatically the property of the landowner.

Dangerous animals

Dangerous animals A "dangerous species" is defined by section 6(2) of the Animals Act 1971 as a species:

"(*a*) which is not commonly domesticated in the British Islands; and
(*b*) whose fully grown animals normally have such characteristics that they are likely, unless restrained, to cause severe damage or that any damage they may cause is likely to be severe."

Strict liability

Examples include an elephant,[20] a lion[21] and certain types of monkey.[22]

Section 2(1) imposes strict liability on the keeper[23] of the animal for "any damage." Accordingly, all that needs to be established is a causal link between the damage and the animal in question.

Other animals Section 2(2) of the 1971 Act also provides:

"Where damage is caused by an animal which does not belong to a dangerous species, a keeper of the animal is liable for the damage, except as otherwise provided by this Act, if—

[15] For statutory controls see *e.g.* Protection of Animals Act 1911, Animals (Cruel Poisons) Act 1962 and Regulations 1963 (S.I. 1963 No. 1278); Pests Act 1954; Small Ground Vermin Traps Order 1958 (S.I. 1958 No. 1958); Spring Traps Approval Order 1975 (S.I. 1975 No. 1647); Deer Act 1963; Badgers Act 1973; Bees Act 1980; Wildlife and Countryside Act 1981; Animal Health Act 1981.
[16] *Fitzgerald* v. *Firbank* [1897] 2 Ch. 96. See also Game Act 1831 and Game Licences Act 1860 for licensing provisions.
[17] *Stearn* v. *Prentice Bros.* [1919] 1 K.B. 394 (rats escaping and damaging plaintiff's corn).
[18] *Farrer* v. *Nelson* (1885) 15 Q.B.D. 258 at 260; see also *Seligman* v. *Docker* [1949] Ch. 53 (presence of large number of pheasants).
[19] See *e.g. Brady* v. *Warren* (1900) 2 I.R. 632 where landowner held liable for damage done by deer which had escaped from his park six years previously.
[20] *Behrens* v. *Bertram Mills Circus* [1957] 2 Q.B. 1.
[21] *Murphy* v. *Zoological Society of London* [1962] C.L.Y. 68.
[22] *Brook* v. *Cook* (1961) 105 S.J. 684. See also the Dangerous Wild Animals Act 1976 for the licensing of the keepers of such animals, and the Zoo Licensing Act 1981.
[23] A person is a "keeper if (a) he owns the animal or has it in his possession; or (b) he is the head of a household of which a member under the age of 16 owns the animal or has it in his possession; and if at any time an animal ceases to be owned by or to be in the possession of any person who immediately before that time was a keeper thereof . . . continues to be a keeper of the animal until another person becomes a keeper thereof . . . " (s.6(3)).

(a) the damage is of a kind which the animal, unless restrained, was likely to cause or which, if caused by the animal, was likely to be severe; and

Other animals

(b) the likelihood of the damage or of its being severe was due to characteristics of the animal which are not normally found in animals of the same species or are not normally so found except at particular times or in particular circumstances; and

(c) those characteristics were known to that keeper or were at any time known to a person who at that time had charge of the animal as that keeper's servant or, where that keeper is the head of a household, were known to another keeper of the animal who is a member of that household and under the age of sixteen."

The majority of animals, therefore, come within this provision except for cats.[24] Strict libility for damage by dogs is restricted to killing or injuring livestock.[25]

Requirement of knowledge   It is a prerequisite to establishing liability that the keeper has knowledge[26] of the animal's characteristics and propensity to cause damage.[27] Such knowledge, however, must be actual rather than constructive to impose strict liability. Constructive knowledge would still, however, be relevant if a claim were to be made in negligence.

Defences   The following statutory defences are provided by section 5:

(1) where any damage is due wholly to the fault of the person suffering it[28];
(2) where the injured party has voluntarily accepted the risk[29]; and
(3) where the injured party is a trespasser if it is proved either (a) that the animal was not kept there for the protection of persons or property or (b) if so kept, that keeping it there for that purpose was not unreasonable (section 2).

Contributory negligence

Contributory negligence is also retained under section 10. Leave and licence of the plaintiff, at common law, will also provide a good defence.[30]

---

[24] See *Buckle* v. *Holmes* [1926] 2 K.B. 125 for exclusion at common law.
[25] See s.3 below.
[26] See *Glanville* v. *Sutton & Co. Ltd.* [1928] 1 K.B. 571; *Brock* v. *Richards* [1951] 1 K.B. 529; *Wallace* v. *Newton* [1982] 1 W.L.R. 375 and *Cummings* v. *Grainger* [1977] Q.B. 397.
[27] "Damage" includes the death of, or injury to, any person (including any disease and any impairment of physical or mental condition).
[28] See *Cummings* v. *Grainger*, above (knowledge of existence of ferocious dog and warning notices on premises sufficient—plaintiff also a trespasser).
[29] See *Wellaway* v. *Courtier* [1918] 1 K.B. 200 at 203; *Park* v. *J. Jobson & Son* [1945] 1 All E.R. 222; see also *League Against Cruel Sports Ltd.* v. *Scott* [1985] 3 W.L.R. 400.
[30] See p. 87 above (defence of justification).

Dogs Section 3 of the 1971 Act imposes strict liability[31] where a dog causes damage by killing or injuring livestock.[32] Where several dogs with different keepers are involved, each keeper can be sued[33] with liability being apportioned under the Civil Liability (Contribution) Act 1978.

Dogs

Defences These are as follows:

(1) where any damage is due wholly to the fault of the person suffering it (section 5(1)).
(2) where the dog either belonged to the occupier or its presence on the land was authorised by the occupier (section 5(4)).
(3) where the plaintiff was contributorily negligent (section 10).

In addition, where the adjoining owner has killed or caused injury to the dog, he has a statutory defence under section 9 if he can prove:

(1) that he acted for the protection[34] of the livestock and was entitled[35] so to act; and
(2) that he had given notice to the police within 48 hours of the killing or injury of such an event.

Straying livestock Section 4 of the 1971 Act provides as follows:

Straying livestock

"(1) Where livestock belonging to any person strays on to land in the ownership or occupation of another and—
   (*a*) damage is done by the livestock to the land or to any property on it which is in the ownership of possession of the other person; or
   (*b*) any expenses are reasonably incurred by that other person in keeping the livestock while it cannot be restored to the person to whom it belongs or while it is detained in pursuance of section 7 of this Act, or in ascertaining to whom it belongs;
the person to whom the livestock belongs is liable for the damage or expenses, except as otherwise provided by this Act.

Strict liability

---

[31] Criminal liability is to be found under the Dogs (Protection of Livestock) Act 1953. See also licensing provisions of the Guard Dogs Act 1975.

[32] Under s.11 "livestock" means cattle, horses, asses, mules, hinnies (the offspring of she-asses by stallions), sheep, pigs, goats and deer (not in a wild state) and while in captivity, pheasants, partridges and grouse. "Poultry" means the domestic varieties of fowls, turkeys, geese, ducks, guinea-fowls, pigeons, peacocks and quails.

[33] *Arnell* v. *Paterson* [1931] A.C. 560.

[34] s.9(3) states that a person shall be deemed to act for the protection of any livestock if, and only if, either (a) the dog is worrying or is about to worry the livestock and there are no other reasonable means of ending or preventing the worrying; or (b) the dog has been worrying livestock, has not left the vicinity and is not under the control of any person and there are no practicable means of ascertaining to whom it belongs. It is sufficient if he believed, and had reasonable grounds for that belief (s.5(47)).

[35] "Entitled" (to protect) means if, and only if: (a) the livestock on the land on which it is belong to him or to any person under whose express or implied authority he is acting, and (b) the circumstances are not such that liability for killing or causing injury would be excluded by s.5(4) (s.9(2)).

(2) For the purposes of this section any livestock belongs to the person in whose possession it is.''

Within the definition of "livestock"[36] come most ordinary farm animals. Pure financial loss and personal injury arising from their activities are excluded since the terms of section 4(1)(*a*) are limited to damage to land. However, not only the tenant but also the landlord of the affected land may sue since the wording of the section covers not only occupiers but also owners.

Detention and sale   Under section 7 of the 1971 Act, which abolishes the old right of distress damage feasant,[37] an occupier of land may detain any livestock which has strayed onto his land and which is not then under the control of any person. The right to detain ceases within 48 hours unless notice has been given to the police and, if known, to the person to whom the livestock belong. It will also cease if sufficient money is tendered to satisfy any claim which the landowner may have for damage and expenses in respect of the straying livestock, or if he has no such claim where the livestock is claimed by a person entitled to its possession. Where the livestock has been detained for a period of not less than 14 days, the person detaining it, so long as he has complied with the foregoing requirements, may sell it at market or by public auction unless proceedings are then pending for the return of the livestock or for any claim for damages done by it or expenses incurred in detaining it. Where the net proceeds of sale exceed the amount of any claim, the excess is recoverable by the person who would be entitled to the livestock but for the sale. During the period of detention, the person detaining the livestock is liable for any damage caused to it by failure to treat it with reasonable care and supply it with adequate food and water.

Right to detain

Defences   These are provided for as follows:

(1) Where any damage is due wholly to the fault of the person suffering it (section 5(10));
(2) Where the livestock has strayed from the highway and its presence was a lawful use of the highway (section 5(5));
(3) Where there has been a failure to fence[38] on the part of the injured party (section 5(6));
(4) Where the plaintiff has been contributorily negligent (section 10).

Straying livestock on highway   In addition to the foregoing provisions concerning strict liability in trespass by straying livestock, section 8(2) of the 1971 Act now places a statutory duty of care on a landowner to prevent his animals[39] from straying *onto* the highway. The common law principles in negligence relating to the straying of livestock *off* the highway[40] or being driven along the highway[41] remain unaffected. Section 8(2) also creates a

Statutory duty of care

---

[36] See n. 32 above.
[37] See also s.1(1)(*c*) which also abolishes the rules of common law imposing liability for cattle trespass.
[38] See *Egerton* v. *Harding* [1975] Q.B. 62 and pp. 82–85 above.
[39] "Animals" is not defined under the Act.
[40] The driving of livestock from the highway onto adjoining land would be a trespass.
[41] See *Deen* v. *Davies* [1935] 2 K.B. 282.

statutory defence in relation to unfenced land where it can be established that the land is common land or is land situated in an area where fencing is not customary, or is a town or village green and the person who placed the animals[42] on the land had a right so to do.

Negligence   Generally, where an animal is brought onto the highway or upon the land of another person (with his licence) the keeper must use all reasonable care to prevent damage.[43] Such liability extends to the spread of disease and infection.[44]

Common law   In addition to strict liability under the Act of 1971, a right of action may need to be pursued at common law, *e.g.* in trespass where staghounds simply stray onto land over which hunting is prohibited by the owner[45] or where wild animals are kept on the land and escape.[46] This will amount to a nuisance, as will the noise caused by, for example, the keeping of large numbers of cockerels on a poultry farm.[47] The smells resulting from such husbandry may also amount to a nuisance (*e.g.* from horses[48] and pigs[49]). Such matters will invariably turn upon excessive user.[50]

Trespass and nuisance (margin)

The Crown (margin)   The Animals Act 1971 binds the Crown but proceedings are not authorised against the Queen in her private capacity.

Building operations

Nuisance (margin)   The extent to which building operations will constitute a nuisance will usually turn upon the following matters:

(1) The nature of the operations (*e.g.* demolition is bound to result in noise and duty).[51]

[42] See *Davies* v. *Davies* [1975] Q.B. 172 (right to grant a sub-licence to another) and *Rees* v. *Morgan* (1976) 120 S.J. 148 (once an animal strays beyond the point where the common land adjoins the highway the owner of the livestock will be liable).

[43] *e.g. Gomberg* v. *Smith* [1963] 1 Q.B. 25 (improper tethering of a St. Bernard dog); *Turnbull* v. *Wieland* (1916) 33 T.L.R. 143 (insufficient control of cows).

[44] *Theyer* v. *Purnell* [1918] 2 K.B. 333 (mingling of diseased animals with others); *Weller & Co.* v. *Foot and Mouth Disease Research Institute* [1966] 1 Q.B. 569.

[45] See *League Against Cruel Sports Ltd.* v. *Scott* [1985] 3 W.L.R. 400.

[46] *e.g. Farrer* v. *Nelson* (1885) 15 Q.B.D. 258 at 260 (nuisance by unreasonable number of pheasants brought onto the land).

[47] *Leeman* v. *Montague* [1936] 2 All E.R. 1677.

[48] *Ball* v. *Ray* (1873) L.R. 8 Ch. 467; *Rapier* v. *London Tramways Co.* [1893] 2 Ch. 588.

[49] *Bone* v. *Seale* [1975] 1 W.L.R. 797.

[50] *Bland* v. *Yates* (1914) 58 S.J. 612 (market gardener keeping very large quantity of manure leading to excessive breeding of flies); *Stearn* v. *Prentice* [1919] 1 K.B. 394 (heap of bone manure attracting rats not excessive).

[51] *Andreae* v. *Selfridge & Co. Ltd.* [1938] Ch. 1; *Matania* v. *National Provincial Bank Ltd.* [1936] 2 All E.R. 202. For terms of possible injunctions see the Appendix (Precedents HC6 and CC4) and also *e.g. Boynton* v. *Helena Rubenstein and Hall, Beddall and Co.* (1960) 176 E.G. 443 (contractors restrained from using hoist except between 9 a.m. and 6 p.m.; engine to be switched off when not in use; brake mechanism to be operated to minimise noise and inconvenience).

(2) The methods of work adopted.[52]

(3) The extent to which the contractor and the landowner have taken steps to ensure that no undue inconvenience is being caused to neighbours (*viz*. what steps have been taken to reduce annoyance).[53]

(4) The time scale of the works.[54]

Damages will accordingly only be awarded in respect of what is excessive.[55]

Negligence   The landowner may also be negligent:

(1) as to his choice of contractor[56]; and/or

(2) in the steps that he has taken to supervise the contractor and to avoid causing annoyance[57] in addition to the liability of the contractor[58] himself.

Children

Personal liability   The fact that a child is a minor in law is not a defence to an action in tort. Accordingly, apart from his appearing by his *guardian ad litem*, the child may be sued as if he were of full age.[59] However, his age may be highly relevant[60]; equally, the degree to which he will not normally be expected to foresee injury.[61]

Parental liability   A parent will not be liable for the negligence of his child unless the child was acting as his servant or agent at

---

[52] *Andreae* v. *Selfridge & Co.Ltd.* above; also *Hoare & Co.* v. *McAlpine* [1923] 1 Ch. 167 (strict liability for vibrations set up by pile driving) but disapproved in *Barette* v. *Franki Compressed Pile Co. of Canada* [1955] 2 D.L.R. 665 (vibrations a nuisance). See also *Gosnell* v. *Aerated Bread Co. Ltd.* (1894) 10 T.L.R. 661 (application for injunction to restrain internal structural alterations between 10 a.m. and 6 p.m. refused); *Clark* v. *Lloyds Bank Ltd.* (1910) 79 L.J.Ch. 645 (hotel owner refused injunction in respect of demolition work conducted in reasonable manner, starting at 6.30 a.m.); and *De Keyser's Royal Hotel Ltd.* v. *Spicer Bros. Ltd. and Minter* [1914] 30 T.L.R. 257 (nocturnal pile driving an actionable nuisance).

[53] These duties cannot be delegated to an independent contractor (see *Matania* v. *National Provincial Bank* above); likewise where obligation arises under statute, *e.g. Gray* v. *Pullen* (1864) 5 B. & S. 970 (failure to reinstate road after drain-laying). See also *H & N Emanuel Ltd.* v. *GLC* [1971] 2 All E.R. 865 (owner liable for negligence of contractor resulting in spread of fire) and Control of Pollution Act 1974, ss.35, 60 and 61 (control of noise on construction sites). But note that in *Lloyds Bank* v. *Guardian Assurance and Trollope & Colls* (1987) 35 Build.L.R. 34, the Court of Appeal held that the jurisdiction of the court to grant an interlocutory injunction was not affected by a local authority's s.60 notice restricting working hours to a lesser extent than the injunction.

[54] *Matania* v. *National Provincial Bank Ltd.* above; see also *Metropolitan Properties Ltd.* v. *Jones* [1939] 2 All E.R. 202 (noise lasting three weeks).

[55] See *Andreae* v. *Selfridge & Co. Ltd.* [1938] Ch. 1.

[56] See Occupiers' Liability Act 1957, s.2(4)(*b*) and for concurrent liability of owner and contractor see, *e.g. AMF International Ltd.* v. *Magnet Bowling Ltd.* [1968] 1 W.L.R. 1928.

[57] *H & N Emanuel Ltd.* v. *GLC* above.

[58] See *e.g. AMF International Ltd.* v. *Magnet Bowling Ltd.* above.

[59] *Gorely* v. *Codd* [1967] 1 W.L.R. 19.

[60] See *e.g. Kerry* v. *Carter* [1969] 3 All E.R. 723 at 727. Note also that the age of criminal responsibility is still fixed at 10 years by Children and Young Persons Act 1933, s.50 (as amended by s.16(1) of the Children and Young Persons Act 1963).

[61] *e.g. Tillander* v. *Gosselin* [1966] 60 D.L.R. (2d) 18 (child under three years not held liable in negligence or trespass).

the material time.[62] However, the parent will be negligent himself if it can be established that he has failed to exercise such control over the child as a prudent parent would exercise.[63] Once again the age of the child will be material.[64]

Landowner's duties   Section 2(3) of the Occupiers' Liability Act 1957 provides that in assessing the common duty of care, an occupier must be prepared for children to be less careful than **Allurements** adults.[65] Accordingly, he must guard against "allurements",[66] *e.g.* a grass bank with tins and broken glass at the bottom[67] or a tree close to a live electric cable.[68] Similar practical considerations also apply to child trespassers although the common law considerations have now been replaced by the Occupiers' Liability Act 1984.[69]

Easements and *profits à prendre*

An action for the protection of easements and *profits à prendre* will **Trespass and** invariably lie in trespass and/or nuisance.[70] Where there is an **nuisance** apprehension of injury, an injunction in a *quia timet* action may be obtained.
Quia timet   The law recognises two types of situation in this regard:
injunctions

(1) where the defendant is threatening to do works which will cause irreparable harm to the plaintiff's land (*e.g.* loss of light from the erection of a building[71]);
(2) where the plaintiff alleges that the defendant's earlier actions may lead to future damage and positive works are required to remedy the situation (*e.g.* continuing landslips despite defendant's remedial works).[72]

Explosives

A landowner who stores[73] or manufactures[74] explosives on his land will be under the strict liability imposed by the rule in *Rylands* v. *Fletcher*.

[62] *North* v. *Wood* [1914] 1 K.B. 629; *Donaldson* v. *McNiven* [1952] 2 All E.R. 691; *Gorely* v. *Codd* above.
[63] This has been held to be as stringent as that of a schoolmaster, which is said to be that of a "careful father" (see *Williams* v. *Eady* (1893) 10 T.L.R. 41); see also *Rickets* v. *Erith Borough Council* [1943] 2 All E.R. 629 and *Jauffur* v. *Akhbar* [1984] C.L.Y. 2332 (failure to supervise use of candles by 14 year-old boy).
[64] See *Kerry* v. *Carter* above (lack of experience of boy aged 17½ with circular saw).
[65] *e.g.* where a small child fell through gap in railings too small for an adult (*Moloney* v. *Lambeth Borough Council* (1966) 64 L.G.R. 440).
[66] See *Phipps* v. *Rochester Corpn.* [1955] 1 Q.B. 450 for review of principal cases.
[67] *Williams* v. *Cardiff Corpn.* [1950] 1 All E.R. 250.
[68] *Buckland* v. *Guildford Gas Light and Coke Co.* [1949] 1 K.B. 410.
[69] See pp. 93–94 above.
[70] For particular considerations, see pp. 86–87 and 87–91. For terms of injunctions and declarations see Appendix (Precedents HC5 and CC1).
[71] *Litchfield-Speer* v. *Queen Anne's Gate Syndicate* [1919] 1 Ch. 407.
[72] *Redland Bricks Ltd.* v. *Morris* [1970] A.C. 652.
[73] *Miles* v. *Forest Rock Granite Co.* (1918) 34 T.L.R. 500.
[74] *Rainham Chemical Works* v. *Belvedere Fish Guano Co.* [1921] 2 A.C. 465.

Fire

Fires Prevention (Metropolis) Act 1774   Section 86 of the Fires
Prevention (Metropolis) Act 1774 provides that

Accident

> "no action, suit or process whatever shall be had,
> maintained or prosecuted against any person in whose
> house, chamber, stable, barn or other building, or on whose
> estate[75] any fire shall accidentally[76] begin."

Conversely, if the fire is started either intentionally or as a
result of negligence, then the landowner will be liable not only for
his own acts or omissions but also for those of his servants or
agents.[77] As a statutory defence, the defendant does not, though,
have to disprove negligence, the onus being upon the plaintiff to
establish the cause of the fire.[78]

Where the source of the fire is a domestic grate, the lighting
of it will be an intentional act. Accordingly, the plaintiff will have
to establish negligence, *e.g.* in the making of the fire or by leaving
the grate unguarded, to prevent the defendant from relying upon
the provisions of the 1774 Act.[79]

Rylands v. Fletcher   A concurrent liability may also arise under
the rule in *Rylands* v. *Fletcher*. The storage of inflammable
materials[80] and the carrying out of dangerous operations[81] will
usually amount to a non-natural use of land. On the other hand,
the mere lighting of a fire (*e.g.* to burn paper) will not in itself be
a non-natural use of land[82] but, for the reasons stated above,
liability may still be established under the 1774 Act.

Negligence   The common law duty of care will also apply in all
the foregoing situations and will provide a remedy where the
rules of strict liability cannot be applied, *e.g.* where fire
Common law duty   accidentally begins but spreads as a result of the defendant's
of care   negligence[83] or where sparks are blown onto neighbouring
premises,[84] subject to the foreseeability test.[84a] Negligence will
not have to be proved if the source of the fire is inherently

---

[75] *i.e.* real property.
[76] *i.e.* "a fire produced by mere chance or incapable of being traced to any cause"
(see *Filliter* v. *Phippard* (1847) 11 Q.B. 347) (defendant liable where fire started
for purpose of burning weeds); *Collingwood* v. *Home & Colonial Stores* [1936] 3
All E.R. 200 (defendant not liable where fire caused by defect in electrical
wiring).
[77] *Black* v. *Christchurch Finance Co.* [1894] A.C. 48; *Balfour* v. *Barty-King* [1957]
1 Q.B. 496; *H & N Emanuel Ltd.* v. *GLC* [1971] 2 All E.R. 865.
[78] *Mason* v. *Levy Auto Parts of England Ltd.* [1967] 2 Q.B. 530 at 538.
[79] *e.g. Sochacki* v. *Sas* [1947] 1 All E.R. 344.
[80] See *Mason* v. *Levy Auto Parts* above.
[81] Here duty is not absolute and negligence may also have to be established (see
Honeywill and Stein Ltd. v. *Larkin Bros. Ltd.* [1934] 1 K.B. 191.
[82] See *J. Doltis Ltd.* v. *Isaac Braithwaite & Sons (Engineers) Ltd.* [1957] 1 Lloyd's
Rep. 522.
[83] See *Musgrove* v. *Pandelis* [1919] 2 K.B. 43; *Sturge* v. *Hackett* [1962] 1 W.L.R.
1257.
[84] *H & N Emanuel Ltd.* v. *GLC* [1971] 2 All E.R. 865.
[84a] See *Smith* v. *Littlewoods Organisation* [1987] 2 W.L.R. 480: owners of disused
cinema held not liable in negligence to owners of adjoining premises where
vandals started fire in the cinema as it was not highly probable or very likely, as
opposed to a mere possibility, the vandals would set fire to the cinema.

dangerous, *e.g.* sparks from a traction engine on the highway[85] (a burning car or tractor today).

Gas and electricity

Negligence

Strict liability   Since gas and electricity are inherently dangerous, the rule in *Rylands* v. *Fletcher* will prima facie apply.[86] However, negligence will also have to be shown in the ordinary domestic situation since the other occupiers of a property impliedly consent to such a use of the land.[87]

Statutory liability

Gas   The majority of gas supplies are provided by the British Gas Corporation ("British Gas") under its statutory powers contained in the Gas Act 1972. Liability here can only be established if negligence is proved.[88] An exception is made, however, where gas is stored underground under the Gas Act 1965[89] where liability will be strict.

Nuisance

   Liability for nuisance, at common law, is preserved by the Gas Act 1972.[90] When this remedy is pursued, it is not necessary to establish that an escape of gas has continued for a substantial period of time.[91]

Statutory liability

Electricity   The supply of electricity is regulated by the Electricity Act 1947 which nationalised the electricity supply industry and set up the Area Boards, and by the Electricity Act 1957, the Central Electricity Generating Board and the Electricity Council. The Energy Act 1983 makes provision for the manufacture and supply by private generators.[92] In the exercise of the statutory obligations under the Electricity (Supply) Acts 1882 to 1936,[92a] an electricity board (undertaking) is answerable for all accidents, damages and injuries happening through the act or default of the board or of any person in its employment.[93] Once again, it is doubtful whether liability can be established without proof of negligence.[94]

   The Electricity Lighting (Clauses) Act 1899[95] also preserves the right to sue an electricity board (undertaking) in nuisance. Defective wiring, if detectable, will also be actionable against the landowner even though it may have been caused by the negligence of an independent contractor.[96]

---

[85] *Powell* v. *Fall* (1880) 5 Q.B.D. 597; *C* v. *James* (1908) 24 T.L.R. 868.

[86] *e.g.* where a calor gas tank explodes or an external electricity cable short-circuits.

[87] *Glennister* v. *London & Eastern Gas Board* [1951] 2 Lloyd's Rep. 115 (but arguably not an entirely separate building) (*Anderson* v. *Oppenheimer* (1880) 5 Q.B.D. 602 at 608). See also *Collingwood* v. *Home & Colonial Stores Ltd.* [1936] 3 All E.R. 700 (use of electricity in house not a non-natural user).

[88] See *Dunne* v. *North Western Gas Board* [1964] 2 Q.B. 806; *Pearson* v. *North Western Gas Board* [1968] 2 All E.R. 669 (frost fracture not due to negligence).

[89] s.14.

[90] Sched. 4, para. 33.

[91] *Midwood* v. *Manchester Corporation* [1905] 2 K.B. 597; *Charing Cross Electricity Supply Co.* v. *Hydraulic Power Co.* [1914] 3 K.B. 772.

[92] s.5.

[92a] A collective title; for the separate Acts see the Table of Statutes.

[93] Electric Lighting (Clauses) Act 1899, Sched., para. 77.

[94] *Dumphy* v. *Montreal Light, Heat & Power Co.* [1907] A.C. 454; see also *Buckland* v. *Guildford Gas Light and Coke Co.* [1949] 1 K.B. 410.

[95] s.81; see also *Manchester Corporation* v. *Farnworth* [1930] A.C. 171.

[96] *Spicer* v. *Smee* [1946] 1 All E.R. 498.

Negligence   A concurrent liability will exist in negligence for any act or omission resulting in an escape, whether this is at the time of installation[97] or repair[98] or subsequently (*e.g.* by interference from building operations[99]). It should also be borne in mind that whilst the meter remains the property of the statutory undertaking,[1] the land owner will be under a duty of care to ensure that the pipes and wires within his property are kept in proper order.[2]

Pipes and wires

Landlord and tenant

Tenant's liability   As the occupier of land, a tenant will be liable to a neighbour for acts of nuisance, trespass and the like as the actual wrongdoer. He will not escape liability, even though his landlord may be liable.[3]

Landlord's liability   A landlord will personally be liable if he has let the premises with a nuisance on them,[4] or for purposes which "naturally and necessarily" (or almost inevitably) would amount to a nuisance,[5] where he specifically authorises the commission of the nuisance[6] or where he has retained substantial control over what the tenant does and culpably fails to exercise such control.[7] A landlord cannot, however, be made responsible for the acts of his tenants[8]; but it is now arguable that he could be held liable in negligence for his choice of tenant[9] (*e.g.* "Hell's Angels").

Nuisance

Mines and minerals

Definitions   Section 205(1)(ix) of the Law of Property Act 1925 defines "mines and minerals" as including "any strata or seam of minerals or substances in or under any land and powers of

---

[97] See Defective Premises Act 1972, s.3. See also *e.g. Attia* v. *British Gas* [1987] 3 All E.R. 455 (though the preliminary point of law concerned recovery for nervous shock).

[98] *Ibid.* s.4 (landlord's repairing obligations); *Parry* v. *Smith* (1879) 4 C.P.D. 325 (negligent fitting).

[99] *Driscoll* v. *Poplar Board of Works* (1897) 14 T.L.R. 99 (gas pipe fractured by steam roller); *SCM (United Kingdom) Ltd.* v. *W. J. Whittall & Son Ltd.* [1971] 1 Q.B. 137 (contractor severing electricity cable).

[1] Gas Act 1972, Sched. 4, para. 7; Electric Lighting (Clauses) Act 1899, Sched., para. 56; Electricity Supply (Meters) Act 1936, s.2.

[2] *Spicer* v. *Smee* above; Landlord and Tenant Act 1985, s.11; see also Sched. 4, para. 8 to the 1972 Act and Sched., para. 54 to the 1899 Act.

[3] *Wilchick* v. *Marks and Silverstone* [1934] 2 K.B. 56 at 58; *St. Anne's Well Brewery Co.* v. *Roberts* (1929) 140 L.T. 1 at 8.

[4] *R.* v. *Pedly* (1834) 1 A. & E. 822; for liability of successors in title, see *Sampson* v. *Hodson-Pressinger* [1981] 3 All E.R. 710.

[5] *Harris* v. *James* (1876) 45 L.J.Q. 545 (burning lime); *Tetley* v. *Chitty* [1986] 1 All E.R. 663 (land let by local authority for go-karting).

[6] See *Jenkins* v. *Jackson* (1888) 40 Ch.D. 71.

[7] *Hilton* v. *James Smith (Norwood) Ltd.* (1979) 251 E.G. 1063 (failure to keep right of passage open for tenant due to parked cars of other tenants); see also *Page Motors* v. *Epsom & Ewell Borough Council* (1980) 78 L.G.R. 505 (local authority's failure to evict gypsies).

[8] *Smith* v. *Scott* [1973] Ch. 314.

[9] See *Tetley* v. *Chitty* [1986] 1 All E.R. 663 at 671 on basis of foreseeability. In *Smith* v. *Scott* (above) the local authority were held not liable for nuisances committed by undesirable council tenants arguably on the grounds of public policy).

working and getting the same, but not an individed share thereof."[10]

At common law, the phrase "mines and minerals" has been held capable of bearing a wide variety of meanings. Unless such meaning is clear from the relevant grant, it must be considered in the light of the use of such a term in the mining world, the commercial world and by landowners at the time of grants.[11]

Property rights   Unless an exception is expressly made, the rights to mines and minerals pass with freehold land without mention, unless the land has been purchased by a company or public authority under certain statutory powers. A lease does not pass to the lessee the right automatically to work mines and **Special power**   minerals on the land[12] so a special power will be required. Where the grant is not exclusive, the owner of the surface still has a right to work the land for minerals so long as he does not disturb a grantee (*e.g.* a licensee) in any working which he is carrying on at the time.[13]

Where an exception[14] is made of such rights, the following terms are likely to be used:

Mines   A reservation of the stratum so that the owner can use it for any purpose that he thinks fit.[15]

Minerals   A provision that only the minerals can be taken.

Mines and minerals   A reservation of all the powers necessary for working the minerals so long as the surface is not damaged.[16] An exception excluding the right of support may also be made when the ownership of the underlying minerals is severed from the surface. In such circumstances, an unequivocal intention must be established either by the use of express words or by necessary implication.[17]

Coal   Under the Coal Acts 1938 to 1943 and the Coal Industry **Statutory**   Nationalisation Act 1946, all interests in coal (including mines) **restrictions**   are now vested in the National Coal Board ("British Coal") including the rights to withdraw support.[18]

Gold and silver   At common law, as modified by statute, the Crown is entitled to all gold and silver in mines.[19]

---

[10] See also s.3(xiv) of the Land Registration Act 1925 for same definition.
[11] *Lonsdale (Earl of)* v. *Att.-Gen.* [1982] 1 W.L.R. 887 at 928 where Slade J. held that the term "mines and minerals" in an 1880 conveyance and a 1935 deed of exchange did not carry oil or natural gas.
[12] *Astry* v. *Ballard* (1677) 2 Lev. 185.
[13] *Duke of Sutherland* v. *Heathcote* [1892] 1 Ch. 475.
[14] See pp. 3–4 above.
[15] *e.g. Duke of Hamilton* v. *Graham* (1871) L.R. 2 Sc. & Div. 166 where a roadway was made through the stratum for the conveyance of minerals from adjoining mines.
[16] *Mundy* v. *Duke of Rutland* (1883) 23 Ch.D. 81.
[17] *Butterknowle Colliery Co.* v. *Bishop Auckland Cooperative Society* [1906] A.C. 305; *Warwickshire Coal Co.* v. *Coventry Corporation* [1934] 1 Ch. 488.
[18] See Coal Industry Act 1975, ss.2 and 3 and Sched. 1.
[19] *The Case of Mines* (1567) 1 Plowd. 313; Royal Mines Acts 1688, 1693; and *Att.-Gen.* v. *Morgan* [1891] 1 Ch. 432.

Oil and natural gas   These also vest in the Crown[20] which then has the power to grant licences to commercial organisations for the purposes of exploration and extraction.

Withdrawal of support   The withdrawal of support only becomes actionable in nuisance when subsidence occurs and actual damage is caused.[21] Repairs or payments when structural damage is caused may also be claimed under the Coal Industry Act 1975[22] against British Coal. Interference with the working of the minerals (*e.g.* by an escape of water or pollutants) can be pursued in nuisance or under the rule in *Rylands* v. *Fletcher*.

Noise

Nuisance   An action will usually lie in nuisance although the question of negligence may also be pertinent.[23] Relevant considerations are as follows:

Considerations
(1) What is the source of the noise?[24]
(2) Is it an unreasonable use of the neighbouring property?[25]
(3) What is the nature and character of the surrounding area?[26]
(4) For how long has it lasted?[27]

Control of Pollution Act 1974   Regard must now be paid to the provisions of the Control of Pollution Act 1974. Under section 58, the local authority may serve notice requiring a landowner to abate, prohibit or restrict the occurrence or recurrence of noise where it is satisfied that it amounts to a nuisance.[28] The local authority can also require the execution of works and other steps to secure compliance with the notice. Contravention thereafter without reasonable excuse[29] will lead to criminal prosecution in the magistrates' court. Certain statutory defences exist including the following:

(1) That the alleged offence was covered by a notice under section 60 concerning the control of noise on construction

---

[20] See Petroleum (Production) Act 1934, ss.1(1), (2) and *Lonsdale (Earl of)* v. *Att.-Gen.* [1982] 1 W.L.R. 887.

[21] *Greenwell* v. *Low Beechburn Coal Co.* [1897] 2 Q.B. 165; *Hall* v. *Norfolk* [1900] 2 Ch. 493. See further *subsidence* below p. 109.

[22] s.2 and Sched. 1.

[23] See *Tetley* v. *Chitty* [1986] 1 All E.R. 663 at 671. For the terms of an injunction see Appendix (Precedent HC7).

[24] *e.g. Dunton* v. *Dover District Council* (1978) 76 L.G.R. 87 (playground noise).

[25] *e.g. Andreae* v. *Selfridge & Co. Ltd.* [1938] Ch. 1; *Leeman* v. *Montague* [1936] 2 All E.R. 1677. However, the noise need not be injurious to health to be actionable: see *e.g. Vanderpant* v. *Mayfair Hotel Co. Ltd.* [1930] 1 Ch. 138 (building) and *Hampstead and Suburban Properties Ltd.* v. *Diomedous* [1969] 1 Ch. 248 (loud music).

[26] *Sturges* v. *Bridgman* (1819) 11 Ch.D. 852 and *Rushmer* v. *Polsne and Alfieri Ltd.* (1907) 51 S.J. 324 (noise from printing press unreasonable having regard to background noise in the locality).

[27] *e.g. Leeman* v. *Montagu* [1936] 2 All E.R. 1677 and *Metropolitan Properties Ltd.* v. *Jones* [1939] 2 All E.R. 202.

[28] This will usually require noise levels to be monitored by the Environmental Health Department. The local authority will also have to establish the source of the nuisance.

[29] What is a "reasonable excuse" is a question of fact (see *Leck* v. *Epsom Rural District Council* [1922] 1 K.B. 383). Arguably ignorance of the statutory provisions provides no reasonable excuse (*Aldridge* v. *Warwickshire Coal Co. Ltd.* (1925) 133 L.T. 439).

sites) or consent given under section 61 (prior consent for work on construction sites) or section 65 (noise exceeding registered level).

(2) That the level of noise was below certain levels fixed under sections 66 and 67.

The landowner may himself take proceedings under section 59 of the 1974 Act in his capacity as occupier of the premises. This procedure will be of benefit where the aggrieved party cannot afford to pursue civil remedies (*e.g.* through his inability to obtain legal aid or where the local authority decline to intervene.

Private prosecution
Proceedings should be brought against the person responsible for the nuisance or, if that person cannot be found, against the owner or occupier of the premises from which the noise is emitted or would be emitted.[30] At the hearing, if the magistrates' court is satisfied that the alleged nuisance exists, or that although abated it is likely to recur on the same premises, it will make an order:

(1) requiring the defendant to abate the nuisance, within a time specified in the order and to execute any works necessary for that purpose; and/or

(2) prohibiting a recurrence of the nuisance, and requiring the defendant, within a time specified in the order, to execute any works necessary to prevent the recurrence.[31]

Statutory defence
Where the noise arises as a result of a trade or business, a statutory defence is provided, namely, that the best practicable means have been used for preventing or for counteracting the effect of the noise.[32] The court may also, after giving the local authority in whose area the nuisance has occurred an opportunity of being heard, direct the authority to do anything which the person convicted was required to do by the order to which the conviction relates.[33]

Pollution

Civil liability for damage caused by the deposit of poisonous, noxious or polluting waste on land resulting in an offence under section 3(3) of the Control of Pollution Act 1974 is retained under section 88 of that Act.

An action will usually lie in nuisance.[34]

Subsidence

Nuisance An action in nuisance will only arise where subsidence occurs.[35] Accordingly, for purposes of section 2 of the Limitation Act 1980, the right of action occurs when the actual damage is occasioned.[36] A fresh cause of action arises each time further subsidence occurs although no new excavation has been

---

[30] s.59(3).
[31] s.59(2).
[32] s.59(5).
[33] s.59(6).
[34] See pp. 87–91 above.
[35] *Greenwell* v. *Low Beechburn Coal Co.* [1897] 2 Q.B. 165; *Hall* v. *Norfolk* [1900] 2 Ch. 493.
[36] *Backhouse* v. *Bonomi* (1861) 9 H.L.C. 503. For the terms of an injunction see Appendix (Precedents HC4 and CC5).

Injunction   carried out in the interim.[37] The threat of subsidence can also lead to the grant of a *quia timet* injunction.[38]

Negligence   Following the decision of the Court of Appeal in *Leakey* v. *National Trust*,[39] a concurrent and, arguably, a separate cause of action can arise in negligence when the defendant fails to take steps to prevent or minimise the risk of known or foreseeable damage or injury to a neighbour.

Trees

Nuisance   The encroachment of branches or roots of trees from neighbouring land is a nuisance.[40] However, no action will lie unless actual damage is done by the offending branches[41] or roots.[42] In the latter respect, it will be sufficient to establish that the roots are abstracting water from the soil making it less suitable than it was previously.[43]

There is a right to cut overhanging branches without notice,[44] though this must be carried out without trespassing on

Right of removal   the adjoining land.[44] The right of removal extends as far as the point where the offending branch overhangs the boundary line.[45] The landowner is not entitled, though, to appropriate any fruit growing on a severed branch or the wood,[46] contrary to popular belief. These considerations apply equally to encroaching roots. An injunction may also be obtained to restrain the defendant from causing or permitting the roots to encroach.[47]

Negligence   Since *Leakey* v. *National Trust*,[48] two reported decisions, albeit in the context of claims against the local highway authority, have established that an equal liability for failure to foresee the likelihood of damage from the roots[49] will lie in negligence. A quantification of loss will not only cover the cost of remedial works but also a sum in respect of the disturbance and

---

[37] *Darley Main Colliery* v. *Mitchell* (1866) 11 App.Cas. 127.
[38] See p. 103 above.
[39] [1980] Q.B. 485; see also *Bradburn* v. *Lindsay* [1983] 2 All E.R. 408.
[40] *Lemmon* v. *Webb* [1895] A.C. 1; *Davey* v. *Harrow Corporation* [1958] 1 Q.B. 60.
[41] See *e.g. Smith* v. *Giddy* [1904] 2 K.B. 448 (interference with growth of fruit trees); *Crowhurst* v. *Amersham Burial Ground* (1878) 4 Ex.D 5 (poisoning earth).
[42] *Butler* v. *Standard Telephones and Cables Ltd.* [1940] 1 K.B. 399; *McCombe* v. *Read* [1955] 2 Q.B. 429 (roots of poplar trees causing continuing nuisance).
[43] See *King* v. *Taylor* (1976) 238 E.G. 265.
[44] *Lemmon* v. *Webb* above.
[45] *Lemmon* v. *Webb* above and *Smith* v. *Giddy* above. Power is also given to any authorised undertaker to lop trees and hedges obstructing lines under the Electricity (Supply) Act 1926, s.43.
[46] *Mills* v. *Brooker* [1919] 1 K.B. 555.
[47] *McCombe* v. *Read* [1955] 2 Q.B. 429.
[48] [1980] Q.B. 485.
[49] In *Solloway* v. *Hampshire County Council* (1981) 79 L.G.R. 449 the risk of damage from the roots of a tree on the highway was held to be too vague and too remote and the cost of rectification disproportionate to found liability; but in *Russell* v. *Barnet London Borough Council* (1985) 83 L.G.R. 152 where the encroachment was reasonably foreseeable and the authority had the financial resources to take appropriate precautions. See also *Greenwood* v. *Portwood* [1985] C.L.Y. 2500 (no real risk reasonably apparent to defendant to put him on notice where cracking caused half by plaintiff's hedge and defendant's trees not suspected as root damage until experts were consulted).

loss of amenity both while the plaintiff awaited the structural repairs and while they are being carried out.[50]

Trespassers

Particular aspects of this subject have already been covered in discussion of the Occupiers' Liability Acts and Children above.

Water

Flow   Any interference by a neighbour with the flow by way of diversion[51] or interference with the purity of water[52] or rights of access[53] to and from land abutting water is actionable without proof of special damage in trespass. An action may also be sustained in nuisance[54] and the Control of Pollution Act 1974[55]
Statutory control   now governs statutory control over such matters. As with other situations, private and public law remedies overlap. Time and cost as well as benefit will be gained by persuading the relevant authority to take proceedings.

Liability for damage   This will depend upon the type of watercourse or the source of escaping water:

Natural watercourses   No liability arises if an escape of water occurs (whether by flooding or seepage) if it arises as a result of the ordinary and proper use of the land.[56] However, the neighbour may be liable if the escape occurs in circumstances amounting to a misuse[57] or from negligence.[58]

Artificial watercourses   Liability arises in such circumstances under the rule in *Rylands* v. *Fletcher* unless one of the exceptions can be established.[59]

Roof drainage   It is an actionable nuisance for water to fall from eaves and gutters onto neighbouring land or property.[60] A claim

---

[50] See *e.g. Bridges* v. *Harrow London Borough Council* (1981) 260 E.G. 284. For suggested quantification of losses, see Appendix (Precedent HC2).
[51] *Earl of Norbury* v. *Kitchin* (1866) 15 L.T. 501. Actual damage must be established if the quality of the flow is affected.
[52] *Jones* v. *Llanrwst Urban District Council* [1911] 1 Ch. 393.
[53] *Lyon* v. *Fishmongers' Co.* (1876) 1 App.Cas. 662; *Att.-Gen. of Straits Settlement* v. *Wemyss* (1888) 13 App.Cas. 192 (on the surface or underground).
[54] *e.g. Pride of Derby and Derby Angling Association* v. *British Celanese* [1953] Ch. 149.
[55] Pt. II (ss.31–56).
[56] See *Rylands* v. *Fletcher* (1868) L.R. 3 H.L. 330 (reservoir a non-natural use) but see *Rouse* v. *Gravelworks* [1940] 1 K.B. 489 (owner held not liable for water from disused gravel pit eroding support to adjoining land).
[57] *e.g.* due to diversion or silting up of stream (*Fletcher* v. *Smith* (1877) 2 App.Cas. 781).
[58] *Leakey* v. *National Trust* [1980] Q.B. 485.
[59] See pp. 91–92 above.
[60] *e.g. Thaker* v. *Newman* (1839) 11 Ad. & El. 40.

in negligence may also lie.[61] No action will lie, however, under the rule in *Rylands* v. *Fletcher*, for damage caused from the escape of roof water from a tank in circumstances beyond the control of the owner or if the injured party has consented to such an arrangement[62] but an action can usually be sustained in negligence.[63]

Strict liability

Internal water supply systems   The owner or occupant will only be liable if negligence can be established.[64] In addition, the Water Act 1981[65] imposes on all statutory undertakers strict liability for damage from an escape of water from a communication pipe or mains.[66]

In addition to his personal liability the occupier will be liable for the acts of a servant acting within the scope of his employment[67]; this does not apply to the acts of an independent contractor.[68]

Weeds

Statutory liability   Under the Weeds Act 1959, it is an offence[69] to allow certain types of injurious[70] weeds to spread from land after notice has been served by the Ministry of Agriculture (or the local authority acting on behalf of the Minister) to prevent the weeks from spreading. A power of entry is provided under the Act for the purpose of entering and inspecting the land in question.

Nuisance   It follows that if injurious weeks are spreading from neighbouring land, then the adjoining landowner has sufficient grounds to pursue a claim in nuisance and negligence.[71]

---

[61] *e.g. Bishop* v. *Consolidated London Properties* (1933) 102 L.J.K.B. 257 (landlord held liable for pigeon blocking gutter).

[62] See *Prosser & Sons Ltd.* v. *Levy* [1955] 1 W.L.R. 1224.

[63] *e.g. Tilley* v. *Stevenson* [1939] 4 All E.R. 207 (damage from burst pipe; defendant having good reason to believe water turned off).

[64] *e.g. Stevens* v. *Woodward* (1881) 86 Q.B.D. 318; *Hawkins* v. *Dhawan and Mishikin* (1987) 19 H.L.R. 232 (failure to check blocked overflow pipe to wash basin not negligence).

[65] s.6(1).

[66] But see *Dept. of Transport* v. *North West Water Authority* [1984] A.C. 336 for relief from liability under the Public Utilities Street Works Act 1950, s.18(2), (6) where negligence not established.

[67] *e.g. Stevens* v. *Woodward* (1881) 6 Q.B.D. 318; *Ruddiman* v. *Smith* (1889) 60 L.J. 708 (failure to turn off tap).

[68] *e.g. Blake* v. *Woolf* [1898] 2 Q.B. 426 (cistern overflowing due to plumber's negligence).

[69] s.2(1) prescribes a fine on summary conviction not exceeding £200. If no remedial steps have been taken within 14 days after the date of conviction, then a further offence will have been committed (s.2(2)).

[70] s.1(2) prescribes the following: spear thistle, creeping or field thistle, curled dock, broad-leaved dock and ragwort. At present no additional weeds have been added by any subsequent regulations.

[71] Following *Leakey* v. *National Trust* [1980] Q.B. 485. See also *Tutton* v. *A.D. Walter* [1986] Q.B. 61 (farmer can owe duty of care to neighbouring beekeepers when spraying crops) and the Control of Pesticides Regulations 1986 (S.I. 1986 No. 1510) made under s.16 of the Food and Environment Protection Act 1985. These Regulations now provide, together with the relevant Codes of Practice, comprehensive control over the sale, advertising, storage and use of all types of pesticide. They apply not only to agricultural situations (except direct

However, similar considerations to those relating to trees will apply, by analogy, to the extent that, whilst a right of abatement can be exercised, no substantive claim in damages can be pursued in the absence of actual damage. In the particular case of weeds, it is highly unlikely to be pursued in view of the practical remedies available to the injured party.

administration to livestock, including aerial spraying), but also to domestic and recreational environments (including anti-fouling paint on boats). They do not apply to pesticides used in industrial or manufacturing processes but do cover use in work places, *e.g.* herbicides and rodenticides.

6 BUILDING CONTROL

Building Regulations

Introduction

Alterations, extensions or other material changes to party structures will be subject to separate control by the local authority under the Building Regulations 1985,[1] the current enabling statute being the Building Act 1984.[2] With their predecessors, made in 1965 and 1976 (with amendments), these Regulations have collectively, since 1966, replaced the former local authority building by-laws.

Scope
    The Building Regulations are administered by the local district council through local inspectors ("the building inspector").[3] They apply to the whole of England and Wales, except for the City of London and the 12 inner London boroughs which are separately regulated under the London Building Acts.

Distinction from planning permission
    Whilst an application for Building Regulation approval will often be made at the same time as an application for planning permission, the two are separate and distinct terms of regulation. The purpose of planning permission is to regulate the use of land and buildings for which reason policy considerations (namely structure and development plans) play such an important part in the determination of such matters. The purpose of the Building Regulations, on the other hand, is to regulate the actual construction of the buildings, together with the provision of services, fittings and equipment in so far as they affect the health, safety and welfare of the occupant,[4] including facilities for disabled people.

    Accordingly, the local authority, when considering approval of plans for the purposes of Building Regulations, has no discretion to reject them if the Regulations have been complied with.[5] On the other hand, if there is any contravention, however trivial, or other defect in the plans themselves, the local authority is entitled either to reject the plans or to pass them subject to modification.[6]

[1] S.I. 1985 No. 1065.
[2] s.1. The 1984 Act has consolidated the provisions of the Public Health Acts 1936 and 1961, the Health and Safety At Work Act 1974 and the Housing and Building Control Act 1984.
[3] He may be either a local authority official or an "approved inspector" under s.49(1).
[4] Building Act 1984, Sched. 3, Pt. I; and Sched. 2 of the 1985 Regulations.
[5] Sched. 1 of the Regulations lists the following requirements: Part A (Structure); Part B (Fire); Part C (Site Preparation and Resistance to Moisture); Part D (Toxic Substances such as cavity wall insulation); Part E (Resistance to the Passage of Sound); Part F (Ventilation); Part G (Hygiene); Part H (Drainage and Waste Disposal); Part J (Heat Producing Appliances); Part K (Stairways, Ramps and Guards); Part L (Conservation of Fuel and Power).
[6] s.16(3). In the latter event, the written request or consent of the applicant will be required (s.16(4)). See also Regs. 11–13 for the requirements for the giving of a building notice and the deposit of full plans and other particulars and Reg. 14 for notice of commencement and completion of certain stages of work (such as foundations, drains and private sewers).

Application

As a general rule, all work[7] involving the erection, extension or material alteration of a building will be subject to control unless specifically exempted from the need to obtain approval under Regulation 9 of and Schedule 3 to the Building Regulations.

Exemptions   In this regard, the Regulations do not apply to the erection of the following classes of building or to the carrying out of any work to or in connection with such a building if, after the carrying out of that work it is still within one of these classes:

Class I (buildings controlled under other legislation)   *i.e.* the Explosives Acts 1875 and 1923; the Nuclear Installations Act 1965 and the Ancient Monuments and Archaeological Areas Act 1979, s.1.

Class II (buildings not frequented by people)   *i.e.* a detached building into which people cannot or do not normally go or one housing fixed plant or machinery, the only normal visits to which are intermittent visits to inspect or maintain the plant and machinery.

Class III (greenhouses and agricultural buildings)   A greenhouse will *not* be exempt if the main purpose for which it is used is for retailing, packing or exhibiting.

A building used for agriculture[8] is one which is, (a) sited at a distance not less than one and a half times its own height from any building containing sleeping accommodation, and (b) provided with an exit which may be used in case of fire which is not more than 30 metres from any point within the building, unless the main purpose for which the building is used is retailing, packing or exhibiting.

---

[7] Reg. 3 defines "building work" as:
   (a) the erection or extension of a building;
   (b) The "material alteration" of a building (*i.e.* the work, or any part of it, which carried out by itself would at any stage adversely affect the existing building in relation to compliance with the requirements contained in Part A (structure); para. B1 (means of escape in case of fire) para. B3 (internal fire-spread structure) or para. B4 (external fire-spread) of Sched. 1, or it involves the insertion of insulating material into the cavity wall of a building, or works to underpin a building);
   (c) the provision, extension or material alteration of a "controlled service or fitting" in or in connection with a building (*i.e.* a service or fitting in relation to which paras. G2 (Bathrooms), G3 (Hot water storage) or G4 (Sanitary Conveniences), Part H (Drainage and Waste Disposal) or J (Heat Producing Appliances) or para. L4 (Heating system controls) or L5 (Insulation of heating services) of Sched. 1 applies);
   (d) work required by Reg. 6 (such as requirements relating to a "material change of use") (*i.e.* where the building will now be used for the puproses of a dwelling or will contain a flat or will be used as a hotel, institution or public building, where previously it was not, or when it ceases to be an exempt building under Classes I–VI).

[8] "Agriculture" includes horticulture, fruit growing, seed growing, dairy farming, fish farming and the breeding and keeping of livestock (including any creature kept for the production of food, wool, skins or fur or for the purpose of its use in the farming of land).

Class IV (temporary buildings and mobile homes) *i.e.* a building intended to remain erected for less than 28 days or a mobile home within the meaning of the Mobile Homes Act 1983.

Class V (ancillary buildings) *i.e.* a building on an estate which is intended to be used only in connection with the disposal of buildings or building plots on that estate, (one used only by people engaged in the construction, alteration, extension or repair of a building during the course of that work or a building, other than a building containing a dwelling or used as an office or showroom, erected in connection with a mine or quarry.

Class VI (small detached buildings) *i.e.* (i) a detached building having a floor area which does not exceed 30m^2, contains no sleeping accommodation and is either (a) situated more than one metre from the boundary of its curtilage or (b) a single storey building constructed wholly of non-combustible materials; or

(ii) a detached building designed and intended to shelter people from the effects of nuclear, chemical or conventional weapons, and not used for any other purpose if (a) its floor area does not exceed 30m^2, and (b) the excavation of the building is no closer to any exposed part of another building or structure than a distance equal to the depth of the excavation plus one metre.

Class VII In addition, the Regulations do not apply to the extension of a building by the addition at ground level of—

Small domestic extensions
(a) a greenhouse, conservatory, porch, covered yard or covered way; or
(b) a carport open on at least two sides, where the floor area of that extension does not exceed 30m^2.

Breach

Any contravention may be enforced as follows:

(i) Criminal penalty Under section 35 of the 1984 Act, a fine not exceeding level 5 on the standard scale[9] may be imposed by a magistrates' court on conviction, with a further fine not exceeding £50 for each day on which the default continues after conviction. This course of action may be pursued irrespective of the local authority's rights under a section 36 notice.

Fine

(ii) Removal or alteration of offending work By section 36(1) and (2), a notice called a "section 36 notice"[10] may be served by the local authority requiring the contravening work to be pulled down, removed, or at the election of the owner, altered so as to comply with the Regulations. Failure to comply with the section 36 notice within the time allowed[11] entitles the local authority to pull down, remove or effect such alterations as they deem necessary and recover their reasonable expenses from the

Section 36 notice

---

[9] As defined by ss.126 and 75 of the Criminal Justice Act 1982—currently £1,000 under s.37 of 1982 Act. For procedure, see s.103 of 1984 Act. Appeal is to the Crown Court (s.41(1)(*a*)).

[10] See s.36(4).

[11] 28 days or such longer period as a magistrates' court may allow the owner (s.36(3)). For procedure see s.103 of 1984 Act.

owner. Section 36(4) provides a time limit of 12 months within which a section 36 notice can be served. Time runs from the date of the completion of the works. A section 36 notice cannot be issued[12] if the work has been carried out in accordance with plans passed by the local authority or notice of their rejection was not given within the relevant period[13] from their deposit.

Appeal   A right of appeal[14] lies to the magistrates' court within 28 days from the giving of the section 36 notice unless notice has been given to the local authority under section 37(1)(a) that a written report is sought from a suitably qualified person in respect of the offending work, in which event 70 days is prescribed. Pending the final determination or withdrawal of the appeal, the section 36 notice has no effect.[15]

The burden of showing non-compliance is upon the local authority who served the section 36 notice. However, if the local authority is able to show that the works did not comply with the approved document under section 6 of the 1984 Act the evidential burden will shift and it will be for the appellant to show that the requirements have been complied with.[16]

(iii) High Court injunction   Irrespective of the foregoing time limit, the local authority may apply to the High Court for an **Injunction**   injunction.[17] However, such an action can only be commenced with the consent and in the name of the Attorney-General, with the local authority acting as relator.

Relaxation

Under section 8(1), the Secretary of State for the Environment has the power to dispense with or relax a particular requirement of the Building Regulations if he is of the opinion that the operation of a regulation would be unreasonable. Except where the power is exercisable by the local authority under section 8(2), the application is made through the local authority to the Secretary of State.[18] The local authority may also apply itself.[19] Appeal is to the Secretary of State[20] where the local authority has the power to determine such matters at first instance, with a further right of appeal to the High Court.[21] The same provision applies on an application for a direction directly to the Secretary of State himself.[21a]

---

[12] s.36(5).
[13] "Relevant period" means five weeks or such extended period (not exceeding two months from the date of deposit) as may be agreed between the owner (applicant) and the local authority (s.16(12)).
[14] s.40(1).
[15] Under s.40(5) it then takes effect 28 days from the date of final determination or withdrawal.
[16] *Rickards* v. *Kerrier District Council* (1987) 15 J.P. 625.
[17] s.36(6).
[18] s.9(2).
[19] s.9(3).
[20] s.39(1).
[21] s.42(1).
[21a] s.42(1).

Other statutory controls

Building Act 1984

As well as the Building Regulations, there are other controls vested in local authorities. The Building Act 1984 covers the following matters:

(1) building over sewers (section 18);

(2) use of short-lived materials (section 19);

(3) use of materials unsuitable for permanent building (section 20);

(4) provision of satisfactory drainage (section 21);

(5) drainage of buildings in combination[21b] (section 22);

(6) provision of facilities for refuse (section 23);

(7) satisfactory exits for buildings used by the public[22] (*e.g.* theatres, halls, restaurants, shops, stores, warehouses, licensed clubs, schools,[23] churches, chapels and places of worship) (section 24)[24];

(8) provision of a wholesome water supply sufficient for domestic purposes (section 25),[25] water closets (section 26), bathrooms (section 27) and food storage (section 28)[26];

(9) sites containing offensive material (such as material impregnated with faecal or offensive animal or other offensive vegetable matter) (section 29);

(10) where a building[27] exceeds two storeys in height and the floor of the upper storey is more than 20 feet from the ground, a suitable means of escape from fire will have to be provided.

Highways Act 1980

No new building may be erected (or an existing building extended or altered) nearer to the centre of the street where an improvement line[28] or a building line[29] has been prescribed by the highway authority, without its consent.

London Building Acts

See under the separate heading below for the London Building Acts.

Remedies

The adjoining owner can benefit from the foregoing controls only indirectly. He must draw any contravention to the attention of

---

[21b] *i.e.* together into one system.

[22] A private house to which members of the public are admitted occasionally or exceptionally is specially exempted under s.24(4)(i).

[23] Includes Sunday or sabbath school (s.126) unless exempted from the Regulations.

[24] Not those before October 1, 1937 (s.24(4)(ii) and (iii)).

[25] See also s.71 in relation to fire exits.

[26] Applicable also to an occupied house under s.69, (water supply) and s.70 (food storage).

[27] By s.70(6) this includes a building let as flats or tenements or used as an inn, hotel, boarding-house, hospital, nursing home, boarding-school, children's home or similar institution and a restaurant, shop, store or warehouse where the upper floor is used as sleeping accommodation for persons employed in the premises.

[28] *i.e.* the line to which the street may be widened (s.73(1)). This includes any permanent excavations below street level other than by statutory undertakers.

[29] *i.e.* the frontage line beyond which buildings may not project (s.74(1)).

the appropriate Department[30] of the regulating authority. If the authority declines to take any action, then there may be limited grounds for seeking judicial review of the authority's determination.[31]

It should also be noted that the wording of section 36(6) of the Building Act 1984 makes express provision for the right not only of the local authority (by the Attorney-General) but also of "any other person" to apply for a High Court injunction for the removal or alteration of any work on the ground that it contravenes the Building Regulations or any provision of the 1984 Act. Arguably, therefore, the adjoining owner has sufficient *Locus standi* *locus standi* not only to bring such an application but also to seek damages, if appropriate, against the local authority for breach of its duty of care to the adjoining owner as a party affected,[32] particularly if they are aware of any consequent damage to him arising from such a breach (*e.g.* the collapse of a party structure causing damage to the adjoining property). Section 38(1) of the 1984 Act[33] will also impose liability upon any person who is in breach of the Building Regulations which results in damage.[34] Accordingly, not only the owner of the property but also the builder and the developer could be held liable.[35] The imposition of such liability is in addition rather than in substitution of any other cause of action so arising[36] but it is not retrospective in operation.[37]

London Building Acts

Introduction   Rights of adjoining owners in the City of London and the 12 inner London boroughs of Camden, Greenwich, Hackney, Hammersmith, Islington, Kensington and Chelsea, Lambeth, Lewisham, Southwark, Tower Hamlets, Wandsworth and Westminster[38] are currently governed by: the London Building Act 1930, the London Building Act (Amendments) Act 1935 and the London Building Acts (Amendment) Act 1939. These are collectively known as the London Building Acts 1930 to 1939.[39]

The Acts do not apply to property owned by the Crown, the Duchies of Lancaster and Cornwall,[40] the four Inns of Court[41] or

---

[30] Building Control will be dealt with by the Planning Department.
[31] See p. 94, above.
[32] Following *Dutton* v. *Bognor Regis U.D.C.* [1972] 1 Q.B. 373, *Ross* v. *Caunters* [1980] Ch. 297 and *Sharneyford Supplies Ltd.* v. *Edge* [1985] 3 W.L.R. 1 (duty of care established as being owed by a solicitor to a third party affected by his actions). For further consideration see also *Anns* v. *Merton London Borough Council* [1978] A.C. 728.
[33] Yet to come into force.
[34] s.38(4) defines "damage" as including the death of or injury to any person (including any disease and any impairment of a person's physical or mental condition).
[35] Following *Batty* v. *Metropolitan Property Realisations* [1978] Q.B. 554.
[36] s.38(3).
[37] s.38(2).
[38] London Government Act 1963, s.43(1).
[39] 1939 Act, s.1.
[40] *Ibid.* s.151.
[41] *Ibid.* s.152.

the Outer London Boroughs.[42] Following the abolition of the Greater London Council by section 1 of the Local Government Act 1985, all building control is now carried out by the foregoing local authorities, including the making of by-laws and the appointment and suspension of district surveyors.[43]

London Building Act 1930   The relevant provisions of the 1930 Act still in operation are as follows:

(1) Section 5—This sets out a list of statutory definitions.
(2) Sections 143 to 145 (Part XI)—These set out regulations for building near dangerous and noxious businesses.
(3) Sections 146 to 147 (Part XII)—These deal with dwellinghouses on low-lying land.
(4) Section 148—This exempts the Port of London from the provisions of the Act.

London Building Act (Amendment) Act 1935   The provisions of the 1935 Act deal with the making and administration of by-laws.[44] By section 3 they are applicable to the construction or conversion of every building or structure in inner London.

London Building Acts (Amendment) Act 1939   The layout of the 1939 Act is as follows:

(1) Pt. I (sections 1–4)—Introduction and Interpretation.
(2) Pt. II (sections 5–15)—Naming and numbering of streets, buildings, etc.
(3) Pt. III (sections 16–28)—Construction of Buildings.
(4) Pt. IV (sections 29–32)—Special and Temporary Buildings and Structures.
(5) Pt. V (sections 33–43)—Means of escape in case of fire.
(6) Pt. VI (sections 44–59)—Rights, etc. of Building and Adjoining Owners.
(7) Pt. VII (sections 60–70)—Dangerous and neglected structures.
(8) Pt. VIII (sections 71 and 72)—*Repealed*.
(9) Pt. IX (sections 73–96)—Superintending Architect, District Surveyors and Fees.
(10) Pt. X (sections 97 to 100)—By-laws.
(11) Pt. XI (sections 101–126)—Legal proceedings.
(12) Pt. XII (sections 132–157)—Miscellaneous provisions.

Those matters affecting party structures, in respect of the foregoing, have already been discussed.[45]

---

[42] s.43 of the London Government Act 1963 and para. 14(2) of Sched. 8 to the Local Government Act 1985.
[43] s.6 and para. 14(1) of Sched. 8 to the 1985 Act.
[44] See also ss.97 to 99 of the 1939 Act. Copies of the by-laws currently in force may be obtained from the Planning Department of the relevant local authority.
[45] See pp. 76–82 above.

7 PLANNING CONTROL

Introduction

The object of this chapter is to set out a summary of basic planning law as it affects, primarily, neighbouring residential properties. The mechanics of control will be a matter for the local planning authority (L.P.A.) so the adjoining occupier will be limited to making objections to the L.P.A. or to the inspector, appointed by the Secretary of State for the Environment, when he holds a local public inquiry to determine the merits of an appeal against a refusal of planning permission[1] or the making of an enforcement notice by the L.P.A. The aggrieved neighbour's remedies, in this context, are once again limited, primarily, to seeking judicial review, in cases where there is no statutory appeal procedure,[2] of these administrative decisions and, in either instance, usually, only if it can be shown that the L.P.A.[3] or the Inspector,[4] has acted in an *ultra vires* manner or in breach of the rules of natural justice.

The nature of planning control

In order to make an effective challenge against the activities, or proposed activities, of the adjoining occupier it is necessary to have an understanding of the language of planning. The primary concern of the L.P.A. is the use of the land or buildings in question in the context of their development.

Development   "Development" is defined by the Town and Country Planning Act 1971[5] as:

> "the carrying out of building[6] operations, engineering operations,[7] mining operations or other operations in, on,

---

[1] An alternative appeal procedure is by way of written representations to the Inspector (see p. 139 below).

[2] s.242 of the Town and Country Planning Act 1971 lists the orders, decisions and directions in respect of which an express right of appeal lies to the High Court.

[3] *e.g.* By the L.P.A. failing to notify the adjoining owner of the planning application or, more likely, failing to bring the objection to the attention of the planning committee via the officer's report (see also p. 94 above; p. 133 and 145 below).

[4] *e.g.* by the Inspector failing to allow the objector to present his case (adequately or at all) or, if the case is heard, failing to state any reasons (or make reference) for rejecting it; but note (a) the wide discretion given to the Inspector as to the procedure to be adopted at the inquiry under r.12 but (b) his duty to give (adequate) reasons for his decision under r.16(1) of the Town and Country Planning Appeals (Determination by Appointed Persons) (Inquiries Procedure) Rules 1974 (S.I. 1974 No. 420). See also pp. 140–142 below. The potential litigant should look further at Sweet & Maxwell's *Encyclopedia of Planning Law and Practice* for detailed comment.

[5] ss.22(1) and 290(1).

[6] "Building operations" includes rebuilding, structural alterations of or additions to buildings, and other operations normally undertaken by a person carrying on business as a builder.

[7] "Engineering operations" includes the formation or lay-out of a means of access to highways.

over or under land,[8] or the making of any material change in the use of any buildings[9] or other land."

Certain matters are expressly stated as constituting "development" including:

(1) The use of a single dwelling-house for the purpose of two or more separate dwellings (s.22(3)(a)).
(2) The display of advertisements on the external part of a building not normally used for such display (ss.22(4) and 64).

Equally, it is provided that certain matters do not constitute "development," such as:

(a) Internal or external improvements, alterations or maintenance works (not constituting the making good of war damage)[10] none of which materially affect the external appearance of the building so treated, but any works begun after December 5, 1968 for the alteration of a building by providing additional space in the building below ground level *will* constitute development (s.22(2)(a)).
(b) Maintenance or improvement works carried out by a local highway authority to, and within the boundaries of, a road (s.22(2)(b)).
(c) The breaking open of streets, etc., for the inspection, repair or renewal of sewers, mains, pipes, cables, etc., by a local authority or a statutory undertaker (s.22(2)(c)).
(d) The use of any building or other land within the curtilage of a dwelling-house for any purpose incidental to the enjoyment of the dwelling-house as a dwelling-house (s.22(2)(d)).

No requirement for planning permission

Certain matters are, however, expressly stated as not requiring planning permission. For example:

(1) The resumption, on the expiration of a planning permission to develop land granted for a limited period, of the use of the land for the purpose for which it was normally used before the limited planning permission was granted, provided that such normal use does not contravene[11] planning control (ss.23(5), (8) and (9)).

(2) The resumption, after the service of an enforcement

---

[8] "Land" means any corporeal hereditament (*i.e.* landed property) including a building.
[9] "Building" includes any structure or erection and any part of a building but does not include plant or machinery comprised in a building or any gate, wall, fence, or other means of enclosure (1977 Order, Article 2(1)).
[10] *e.g.* insertion of patio door into existing window opening. See [1987] J.P.L. 735. See also the 1977 G.D.O. Classes I.1, II.1. (Sched. 2 Pts I and II 1988 G.D.O. (*draft*)).
[11] See *Young* v. *S.S.E.* [1983] 2 A.C. 662 and *Cynon Valley B.C.* v. *S.S.W.* [1986] J.P.L. 760 (for the facts see p. 137 below).

notice in respect of any unauthorised development of land, of the lawful use of that land (s.23(6)).

No enforcement proceedings under the four-year rule

Equally, there are matters which, whilst constituting development, will not be the subject of enforcement proceedings,[12] such as the making without planning permission of a change of use of any building to use as a single dwelling-house, or the failure to comply with a condition which prohibits or has the effect of preventing such change of use, where more than four years have elapsed from the date of the breach.[13]

Requirement for planning permission

Accordingly, any building operation or change of use not falling within the following paragraphs, or amounting to "permitted development," will require planning permission. Failure to secure permission carries the sanction of enforcement control which may be exercised at the discretion of the local planning authority. This covers not only the carrying out of development without planning permission but also development which fails to comply with any condition or limitation placed upon an existing permission.

General Development Order

Under section 24 of the Town and Country Planning Act 1971 (the 1971 Act), power has been given to the Secretary of State to make regulations under which planning permission is automatically granted, or deemed to have been granted. These regulations are currently to be found in the Town and Country Planning (General Development) Order 1977 (the 1977 G.D.O.).[14] At the time of writing, however, publication of a new G.D.O. is awaited. The proposed statutory instrument, presently in draft form, will not only consolidate the 1977 G.D.O. and its six amending orders, but will make further additions (and restrictions) to the scope of permitted development. The D.o.E., in their publicity material, state that the new G.D.O. will have a simplified structure to make it more readily understandable. An explanatory manual is also expected.

1977 G.D.O.

1988 G.D.O.

In view of the forthcoming statutory instrument, references in this chapter to the 1977 G.D.O. include, where possible, references to the 1988 G.D.O. (in its present draft form) in the footnotes, and a table of comparative provisions is set out at the end of the chapter. Particular changes to be brought about by the

---

[12] ss.87, 88, 88A and 88B and see further pp. 142–147 below.

[13] s.87(4). Other developments within the "four-year rule" include the carrying out without planning permission of building, engineering, mining or other operations in, on, over or under land, or the failure to comply with any condition or limitation which relates to the carrying out of such operations and subject to which planning permission was granted for the development of that land.

[14] S.I. 1977 No. 289 (as amended).

new G.D.O. are dealt with in the relevant footnotes to this chapter and the render is directed to the Preface for the latest (known) developments immediately prior to publication.

Permitted development

Schedule 1 to the 1977 G.D.O. sets out certain classes of permitted development, of which the most relevant in this context are as follows:[14a]

Class I   Development within the curtilage of a dwelling-house.

Class II   Sundry minor operations.[15]

Class III   Development consisting of a change of use to use as a light industrial building from use either as a general industrial building or as a warehouse[16] (or vice versa) or the change of use

---

[14a] As applicable to this book, the old "Classes" set out in the text will become, under Sched. 2 of the 1988 G.D.O., "Parts" with the same numbers (*e.g.* Part 4 (Old Class IV)—Temporary Buildings and Uses) save for the Old Class V (Use by members of certain recreational organisations which now becomes Part 27).

[15] "Sundry minor operations" include gates, fences, walls and other means of enclosure not exceeding one metre in height when abutting onto a highway used by vehicles, or two metres in height elsewhere.

[16] As formerly defined by the Town and Country Planning (Use Classes) Order (S.I. 1972 No. 1385) under which ordinary shop use was Class I, office use was Class II, light industrial use was Class III, general industrial use was Class IV and warehousing was Class X. See now S.I. 1987 Nos. 764 and 765 under which ordinary shops are now Class A1 (*i.e.* excluding the following purposes):

    (a) for the retail sale of goods other than hot food (now Class A3),
    (b) as a post office,
    (c) for the sale of tickets or as a travel agency,
    (d) for the sale of sandwiches or other cold food for consumption off the premises,
    (e) for hairdressing,
    (f) for the direction of funerals,
    (g) for the display of goods for sale,
    (h) for the hiring out of domestic or personal goods or articles,
    (i) for the reception or service of goods to be washed, cleaned or repaired,

where the sale, display or service is to visiting members of the public);
light industrial use is within the new Class B1 business use (*i.e.* "Use for all or any of the following purposes)—

    (a) as an office other than a use within Class A2 (financial and professional services),
    (b) for research and development of products or processes, or
    (c) for any industrial process,

being a use which can be carried out in any residential area without detriment to the amenity of that area by reason of noise, vibration, smell, fumes, smoke, soot, ash, dust or grit");
general industrial use is now Class B2; and warehousing is now Class B8 (storage and distribution) but not retail operations. (See D.o.E. Circular 13/87).

of a shop to any use other than the sale of hot food (and drink) and motor vehicles.[17]

Class IV Temporary buildings and uses.[18]

Class V The use of land, other than buildings, not within the curtilage of a dwelling-house, for the purposes of recreation or instruction by members of an exempted organisation,[19] and the erection or placing of tents on the land for the purposes of that use.

Class VI The carrying out of building and engineering operations and the mining and working of minerals requisite for the purpose of agriculture on agricultural land of more than one acre and comprising an agricultural unit.[20]

Class VII The carrying out on land used for forestry purposes of building and other operations (other than the provision or alteration of dwellings) needed for such purposes together with the formation, alteration and maintenance of private roads on such land.

Class IX The carrying out of works required for the maintenance or improvement of an unadopted street or private way, being works carried out on land within the boundaries of the street or way.

Article 4 directions Under Article 4, the Secretary of State or the L.P.A. may direct that the provisions of the G.D.O. shall not apply to a particular locality (*e.g.* a conservation area) or to a particular development. In such circumstances, a formal application for planning permission must be made to the L.P.A.

Specific considerations for dwelling houses

"Dwelling-house" No specific statutory definition is given for the term "dwelling-house," save that it does not include a building containing one or more flats, or a flat contained within such a

---

[17] Under the 1988 G.D.O. (*draft*) the following Use Class changes will be permitted:

FROM U.C.O. CLASS	TO U.C.O. CLASS
A3 (Food & drink)	A1 (shops)
Sale etc of motor vehicles	A1 (shops)
B2 (general industrial)	B1 (business)
B8 (storage & distribution)	B1 (business)*
B1 (business)	B8 (storage & distribution)*
B2 (general industrial)	B8 (storage & distribution)*
A3 (food & drink)	A2 (financial & professional)
Premises within A2 (professional and financial) with display window at ground floor level.	A1 (shops)

    * not permitted if the floorspace in the building used for the purposes of the undertaking exceeds 235 square metres.

[18] See p. 130 below.

[19] A certificate of exemption is granted under Public Health Act 1936, s.269, *e.g.* to the Scout Association.

[20] The 1988 G.D.O. (*draft*) takes away the infamous developer's ruse of threatening a pig unit on land adjoining existing residential properties, where planning permission was being sought against strong local objections, by requiring permission for livestock units and associated structures (*e.g.* slurry tanks and lagoons) erected within 400 metres of non-agricultural buildings.

building.[21] Regard must also be paid to whether the property is used exclusively for residential purposes.[21a] The term "dwelling-house" has, accordingly, been held not to cover a Georgian house of which two ground floor rooms were used for the business of an estate agent whilst the remainder was used as his home.[22]

"Curtilage"

The term "curtilage" describes " . . . ground which is used for the comfortable enjoyment of a house or other building . . . although it has not been marked off or enclosed in any way. It is enough that it serve the purpose of the house or building in some necessary or reasonably useful way."[23]

"Incidental to the enjoyment of the dwelling-house"

The phrase "incidental to the enjoyment of the dwelling-house" can be regarded as the "litmus test" as to whether the use of that house comes within the scope of permitted development. It clearly excludes business or commercial activities[24] even for example, the parking of a commercial vehicle within the curtilage[25] or the use of part of the house for a child-minding group.[26] Certain hobbies have also been held to fall outside its scope such as the racing of stock cars (and their repair) and the assembly and repair of hang gliders.[27] On the other hand it will enable the flat roof of an extension to be used as a sitting-out area although affecting the privacy of adjoining occupiers.[28]

So far as structural alterations are concerned, enlargement, improvement or other alteration[29] of the dwelling-house is permitted under the G.D.O., provided that the external cubic content of the original house (as ascertained by external measurement) is not exceeded:

Extensions and loft conversions

(a) in the case of a "terrace house,"[30] 50 cubic metres or 10 per cent., whichever is the greater; or

(b) in any other case, 70 cubic metres or 15 per cent.,

---

[21] G.D.O. 1977 and 1988 (*draft*)), Article 2. See also *Gravesham B.C.* v. *S.S.E.* (1984) 47 P. & C.R. 142, ("dwelling-house" for planning purposes should provide all the facilities for day-to-day private domestic existence).

[21a] The building must be capable of supporting the major activities of life *i.e.* cooking, feeding and sleeping [1976] J.P.L. 326.

[22] *Scurlock* v. *Secretary of State for Wales* (1976) 33 P. & C.R. 202.

[23] *Sinclair-Lockhart's Trustees* v. *Central Land Board* (1950) 1 P. & C.R. 195.

[24] *e.g.* part-time medical business use [1973] J.P.L. 55 [1976] J.P.L. 328, but question of fact and degree [1985] J.P.L. 339.

[25] There are many decisions on this issue. Convenience is not material. See *e.g.* [1976] J.P.L. 529, [1985] J.P.L. 416.

[26] [1968] J.P.L. 536: nor use of garden and one room for nursery play-group (3 hours per day) [1966] J.P.L. 237.

[27] [1978] J.P.L. 201; [1984] J.P.L. 291 (motor sport); [1977] J.P.L. 116 (hang-gliders); [1984] J.P.L. 288 (boat-building) [1967] J.P.L. 176; [1985] J.P.L. 201 (large numbers of animals).

[28] See [1987] J.P.L. 735.

[29] This can only relate to a dwelling-house in existence when the operations are carried out. It does not cover rebuilding (see *Sainty* v. *M.H.L.G.* (1964) 15 P. & C.R. 432).

[30] "Terrace house" is defined as a dwelling-house,
    "(a) Situated in a row of three or more buildings used, or designed for use, as single dwelling-houses; and
    (b) Sharing a party wall with, or having a main wall adjoining the main wall of, the dwelling-house (or building designed for use as a dwelling-house) on either side of it;
but includes the dwelling-houses at each end of such a row of buildings" (Article 2 of the 1988 G.D.O. (*draft*)).

whichever is the greater, subject to a maximum of 115 cubic metres[31];

AND provided that:

(1) The height does not exceed the height[32] of the highest part of the roof of the original dwelling-house;

(2) No part shall project beyond the forwardmost part of any wall of the original dwelling-house which fronts the highway[33];

(3) No part which lies within a distance of two metres from any boundary of the curtilage of the dwelling-house shall have, as a result of the development, a height exceeding four metres[34];

(4) The area of ground covered by all buildings within the curtilage (other than the original dwelling-house) shall not thereby exceed 50 per cent. of the total area of the curtilage excluding the ground area of the original dwelling-house.[35]

The provisions as to volume, height and projection are of particular importance when dormer windows are proposed as

---

[31] When calculating the permissible volume any previous extensions must be included even if constructed under an express grant of planning permission ([1977] J.P.L. 113, 115). "Cubic content" is defined by Article 2 of the 1988 G.D.O. (*draft*) as meaning "the cubic content of a structure or building measured externally."

[32] "Height" is measured from "ground level" which is treated as the highest part of the land adjacent to the building (Article 2(1A)(1b) of the 1977 G.D.O. (Article 2(2) of 1988 G.D.O. (*draft*)). See *e.g.* [1986] J.P.L. 143 (pitched roof on bungalow).

[33] "Highway" includes a side road or footpath. For the statutory definition, see the G.D.O. 1977 (and 1988 (*draft*)), Article 2 and the Highways Act 1980, s.328(1).

[34] Accordingly, a balustrade taking the total height above four metres will require planning permission.

[35] Under Sched. 2 Pt. I of the 1988 G.D.O. (*draft*) the following additional restrictions will be placed upon permitted development:

"(5) it would consist of or include the installation, alteration or replacement of a satellite antenna;

(6) it would consist of or include the erection of a building within the curtilage of a listed building;

(7) it would consist of or include an alteration to any part of the roof."

For the purposes of interpretation the following considerations will apply:

"(a) the erection within the curtilage of a dwellinghouse of any building with a cubic content greater than 10 cubic metres, any part of which is within five metres of the existing dwellinghouse be treated as an enlargement of the dwellinghouse;

(b) where as a result of the development permitted above any part of the dwellinghouse would be within five metres of an existing building within the same curtilage which is used for a purpose incidental to the enjoyment of the dwellinghouse, that building will be treated as forming part of the resulting building for the purpose of calculating the cubic content of that dwellinghouse;

(c) "resulting building" means the dwellinghouse as enlarged, improved or altered, taking into account any enlargement, improvement or alteration to the original dwellinghouse whether falling within the scope of permitted development or not;

(d) the cubic content of a dwellinghouse is to be measured externally;

(e) the area of the curtilage of an original building is to be calculated excluding the area covered by the original building."

Dormer windows   part of a loft conversion. Recent appeal decisions have indicated much tighter controls by L.P.A.s on this aspect of development particularly where the majority of the roof is removed and rebuilt in mansard form or as a large box dormer window. However, if it can be shown that such work merely amounts to the insertion of a window into a wall or the roof of the original dwelling-house, or the alteration or enlargement of an existing window or "any other alteration" to any part of the roof of the original dwelling-house, no objection can be sustained.[36]

Garages and coach-houses   The construction of garages and coach-houses outbuildings will constitute "enlargement" of the original dwelling-house. In addition to the matters set out above regarding site layout, it is also a specific requirement that no part of the outbuilding shall be within a distance of five metres from any part of the dwelling-house. For these purposes, a car-port is treated as a garage. Whilst appearing to be "permitted development," construction of a driveway usually requires a separate application because it amounts to an engineering operation.

Stables or loose boxes   Stables or loose boxes are permitted under the conditions given above excepting the requirement that they be within five metres of the dwelling-house.

The erection or construction of a porch outside the house is expressly permitted provided that:

Porches
(1) the floor area does not exceed two square metres;
(2) no part of the structure is more than three metres above the ground; and
(3) no part of the structure is less than two metres from any boundary which fronts on a highway.

The installation, alteration or replacement of a satellite

---

[36] Under the 1988 G.D.O. (*draft*) this approach will be adopted for the purposes of permitted development. Henceforth the following will be permissible:
> "The insertion of a window (including a dormer window) into a wall or roof of an existing dwellinghouse, the alteration or enlargement of an existing window, or any other alteration to any part of the roof of an existing dwellinghouse."

However, development will not be permitted if—
> "(a) any part of the dwellinghouse would, as a result of the works, exceed the height of the highest part of the existing roof which is to be altered;
> (b) where the development does not include the insertion of a dormer window, the angle or position of any resulting roof, taken as a whole, would be different from that of the existing roof which is to be altered;
> (c) where the development includes the insertion of a dormer window,
>   (i) the vertical height of the resulting structure, measured at the highest part, would exceed two metres;
>   (ii) it would alter more than 50 per cent of the surface area of the existing roof-face;
>   (iii) there would be less than one metre at any point between the edge of the resulting structure and the edge of the existing roof-face in question or the boundary of the dwellinghouse."

For the purposes of interpretation,
> "(a) any area or distance to be measured in relation to a roof is to be measured in the plane of the roof;
> (b) the surface area of a roof-face is to be measured excluding the area of any part of that roof-face which is incorporated into an existing dormer window."

antenna on a dwelling-house or within its curtilage is now
permitted, provided that:

Satellite antennae

(a) the size of the antenna (excluding any projecting feed
element) does not exceed 90 centimetres in any direction;
(b) there is no other antenna already on the property;
(c) the highest part of the antenna is not higher than the
highest part of the roof of the building when it is installed
on a dwelling-house.

**Radio aerials and
masts**

Save in exceptional circumstances, radio aerials and masts
even for amateur radio use are likely to fall outside the G.D.O. so
that a formal application for planning permission will be
required.[37]

The erection, construction or placing and the maintenance,
improvement or other alteration of any building (other than a
dwelling, stable or loose-box) or enclosure[38] is permitted if it is
required for a purpose incidental to the enjoyment of the

Other buildings

dwelling-house as such. This is expressly stated to include the
keeping of poultry, bees, pet animals, birds or other livestock for
the domestic needs or personal enjoyment of the occupants of the
house. Summer-houses, greenhouses, toolsheds and dovecotes
also fall within this category. Accordingly, if the true purpose is
commercial then a specific application for planning permission
will have to be made.

**Swimming-pools,
etc.**

Swimming-pools,[39] are also treated as coming within the
term "enclosure." Ponds and underground tanks[40] are normally
regarded as being incidental to the enjoyment of a dwelling-house
subject to local policy considerations, they have all tended to be
treated as permitted development.

The erection or placing of a tank for the storage of oil for
domestic heating is permitted provided that:

Oil tanks

(1) the capacity of the tank does not exceed 3,500 litres;
(2) no part of the tank is more than three metres above the
level of the ground;
(3) no part of the tank projects beyond the forwardmost part

---

[37] See *e.g. South Staffordshire District Council* and *Smith* and various other recent
decisions all reported in (1986) 1 P.A.D. 289.
[38] Under Sched. 2, Pt. I to the 1988 G.D.O. (*draft*) the following criteria will
need to be satisfied for the building or enclosure to come within the scope of
permitted development:
"(1) the dwelling-house is *not* a listed building;
(2) the building will *not* be a dwelling or a satellite antenna;
(3) any part of the building or enclosure will *not* be nearer to any
highway which bounds the curtilage of the original
dwelling-house than the part of that original building nearest to
that highway or 20 metres, whichever is the nearer;
(4) the building erected, constructed or provided will have a cubic
content no greater than 10 cubic metres and no part of it will be
within five metres of any part of the dwelling-house;
(5) the height of it will not exceed four metres in the case of a rigid
roof and three metres in any other case;
(6) the total area of ground covered by such buildings or enclosures
within the curtilage of the original dwelling-house will not
exceed 50 per cent of the total area of the curtilage."
[39] Under the 1988 G.D.O. (*draft*), swimming pools will come within the
definition of "enclosure".
[40] *e.g.* septic tanks and ancillary works (see [1969] J.P.L. 50).

of any wall of the original dwelling-house which fronts on to a highway.

Hardstandings   Hardstandings for vehicles are permitted provided they are for a purpose incidental to the enjoyment of the dwelling-house as such, for example the parking of a dinghy or caravan. However, considerations affecting the use of the highway[41] will inevitably apply and in all probability an application for planning permission will be required.

Patios   These have been treated by most L.P.A.s as hardstanding for development control purposes.[42]

Gates, walls and fences   Under Class II the erection, construction, maintenance, improvement or alteration of gates, walls, fences and other means of enclosure is permitted provided that the structure does not exceed:

(a) one metre in height when abutting on a highway used by vehicular traffic; or

(b) two metres in height in any other case.

Road access   The formation, laying out and construction of a means of access[43] to a highway, which is not a trunk or classified road,[44] is permitted. In practice, however, most roads fall within these two categories with the result that even a small amount of work such as forming a gap in a hedge will amount to an "engineering operation" and thereby necessitate a specific application for permission.[45]

External painting   Specific provision is made under Class II[46] to permit the painting of the exterior of any building provided that it is not painted for the purposes of advertisement, announcement or direction.

Temporary buildings   Under Class IV of the G.D.O., if operations other than mining are being, or about to be, carried out, the buildings, works, plant or machinery[47] needed temporarily in connection with those operations are permitted provided that:

(1) any planning permission necessary for the main operations has been granted; and

(2) the temporary buildings, etc., are removed at the end of the operations and, if sited on adjoining land, that land is reinstated forthwith.

28-day rule   Another important exception is provided by paragraph 2 of Class IV under which land (other than a building or the curtilage of a building) may be used for any purpose or purposes, except as a caravan site, for a period of not more than 28 days in total in any one calendar year. This exception also covers the erection or

---

[41] *e.g.* sight lines (otherwise known as "visibility splays") and the lowering of the kerb edge to permit the free running of traffic over the pavement.

[42] Under the 1988 G.D.O. (*draft*), patios will be treated as "a hard surface . . . incidental to the enjoyment of the dwelling-house".

[43] This includes access for vehicles, pedestrians and animals.

[44] "Trunk road" is a national route under the responsibility of the Department of Transport. "Classified road" is defined by Article 2(1) and covers the bulk of roads maintained at the public expense.

[45] See n. 41 above.

[46] Sched. 2, Pt. 2, Class C 1988 G.D.O. (*draft*). But see specific restrictions in conservation areas, etc., p. 149 below.

[47] *e.g.* site huts, scaffolding, hoardings, cranes and the like. See Preface for (latest) position regarding "for sale" boards.

placing of moveable structures on the land in connection with its temporary use. The period is reduced to 14 days for the purpose of motor-car or motor-cycle racing or practising, or for the purpose of holding markets. Under this provision, noisy activities such as garden fêtes, pop festivals or the occasional helicopter flight may be lawfully carried out.

Material change of use

"Use" defined

As has already been indicated, "development," for the purposes of ascertaining whether planning permission is required includes the making of any material change in the use of any buildings or other land.[48] The term "use" is defined by section 290(1) not to include the use of land for the carrying out of any building or other operations thereon; but apart from two examples of what constitutes a *material* change of use given, for the avoidance of doubt, by section 22(3),[49] no further help is provided by the 1971 Act. Accordingly, this question must be determined by the given circumstances on a fact and degree basis. In essence, the new use must be substantially[50] different from the previous use to constitute a material change.[51]

Classification

What, then, is the primary use? Under the *Use Classes Order*[52] this can be categorised fairly easily into one of the relevant pigeonholes. Where it is not readily ascertainable, the use will be treated as being "*sui generis.*"[53] In the case of residential use, a material change may often occur within this category where the *character* of the use alters, for example, where a single dwelling-house is used as lodgings.[54] Indeed, in Greater

---

[48] s.22(1).

[49] See p. 122, above.

[50] "Substantial" means "considerably big or solid" (*Palser* v. *Grinling* [1948] A.C. 291).

[51] A distinction must be drawn between *primary* and *ancillary* (or *incidental*) uses *e.g.* bricks intended for building development (with planning permission) left on site over a long period of time was independent storage use [1973] J.P.L 179 but not for construction of a bungalow until fenced off for use on other buildings (*David W. Barling* v. *S.S.E.* [1980] J.P.L. 594). (See also nn. 24–27 above).

[52] See now S.I. 1987 No. 764 (operative from June 1, 1987) which revoked S.I. 1972 No. 1385 (as amended by S.I. 1983 No. 1614) and D.O.E. Circular 13/87. The functions of the U.C.O. are (i) to place into particular categories ("classes") the commonest types of land use activities and (ii) (as supplemented by the G.D.O.) the permit certain changes within a particular use class without the need for an express grant of planning permission. The courts have tended to insist that the U.C.O. should be interpreted restrictively (see *e.g.. Tessier* v. *S.S.E.* (1975) 31 P. & C.R. 161: sculptor's studio outside general industrial category). In appropriate cases a planning condition may exclude the operation of the U.C.O. (see paras. 67/68 of Circular 1/85) or restrict future changes (see *City of London Corpn.* v. *S.S.E.* (1971) 23 P. & C.R. 169).

[53] See *Tessier* v. *S.S.E.* (1975) 31 P. & C.R. 161 and *Forkhurst Ltd.* v. *S.S.E. and Brentwood D.C.* (1983) 46 P. & C.R. 89.

[54] *e.g.* Birmingham Corpn. v. *M.H.L.G. and Habib Ullah* [1964] 1 Q.B. 178 ("house let in lodgings") and *London Borough of Hammersmith* v. *S.S.E.* (1975) 73 L.G.R. 228 ("lodging house"); but see *e.g. Blackpool B.C.* v. *S.S.E.* [1980] J.P.L. 527 (house used for holiday lettings on limited basis not material change). However, the position has been relaxed to an extent by the 1987 Use Classes Order. This now provides a separate Class ("C3") for dwelling-houses, namely, use (whether or not as a sole or main residence) (a) by a single person or by people living together as a family, or (b) by not more than six residents living together as a single household (including a household where care is provided for residents).

London, statute provides that the use of any residential premises
as sleeping accommodation will involve a material change of
use.[55] Within the overall context of the primary use there may be
"incidental" or "ancillary" uses of a sufficiently different
character[56] which will not result in a material change, for
example the parking of a caravan within the curtilage of a
dwelling-house[57] or the repair of a private car in a domestic
garage.[58]

Intensification of use   If the existing use is increased or "intensified" to a
significant degree, a material change of use may then occur as, for
example, by an increase in the number of caravans on a site.[59]
The doctrine is usually only applied where it is difficult to
categorise the nature of the former use and the current use.[60]

Planning unit   In order to determine whether a material change of use has
occurred, the concept of the planning unit has been introduced in
recent years[61] as a means of identifying and classifying the
various uses to which an area of land is being put, both in terms
of physical extent and nature.

Planning permission

Procedure

Under section 53 of the Town and Country Planning Act 1971,
Section 53 determination   procedure is laid down whereby it can be determined whether
planning permission is required to make a change of use or to
carry out any operations on the land. By way of alternative

---

[55] Greater London Council (General Powers) Act 1973, s.25. It should also be
noted that the new "Class C1" provides for use as a hotel, boarding- or
guest-house or as a hostel where, in each case, no significant element of care is
provided.

[56] One of the main changes brought about by the 1987 Town and Country
Planning (Use Classes) Order is the new business use Class ("B1") namely, use
for all or any of the following purposes:
    (a) office use other than a use within Class A2 (financial and
        professional services)
    (b) research and development of products or processes, or
    (c) any industrial process,
being a use which can be carried out in any residential area without detriment
to the amenity of the area by reason of noise, vibration, smell, fumes, smoke,
soot, ash, dust or grit.

[57] See [1975] J.P.L. 104, [1976] J.P.L. 586, but a material change where the
caravan was capable of wholly independent use: [1978] J.P.L. 489.

[58] *e.g. Peake* v. *Secretary of State for Wales* (1971) 22 P. & C.R. 889.

[59] See *e.g.* [1974] J.P.L. 33 (storage of caravans from four to upwards of 24 on 3.2
acre site). For further regulation see the Caravan Sites and Control of
Development Act 1960.

[60] See *Brooks & Burton Ltd.* v. *S.S.E.* [1977] 1 W.L.R. 1294; and *Royal Borough
of Kensington & Chelsea* v. *S.S.E. and Mia Carla Ltd.* [1981] J.P.L. 50 where
Donaldson L.J. (as he then was), stated that the term "intensification" should
be used with very considerable circumspection and that intensification which
did not amount to a material change of use was merely intensification and not a
breach of planning control. Planners should therefore formulate what the use
was "before intensification" and what it was "after intensification" and judge
whether there had been a change of use accordingly.

[61] See further *Burdle* v. *S.S.E.* [1972] 3 All E.R. 240 at 244 and *Newbury D.C.* v.
S.S.E. [1981] A.C. 578.

High Court declaration

procedure,[62] an application can be made to the High Court for a declaration as to whether the proposed operations or change of use constitute development.

New Regulations

Application Regulations governing the application procedure presently form part of the 1977 G.D.O. However, re-statement by way of separate Town and Country Planning (Applications) Regulations 1988 is awaited, together with the new 1988 G.D.O. discussed above. Where possible, reference is made both to the provisions currently in force and to the draft form of the new Regulations. The reader is referred to the Preface for news of developments immediately prior to publication.

Application

Notification

With the standard form of application for planning permission issued by the L.P.A.,[63] the applicant must lodge an ownership certificate[64] to the effect that he is the sole owner of all the land to which the application relates (Certificate A) or that he has notified (Certificate B), or attempted to notify the owners (Certificate C). A separate form of notice (Certificate D) deals with the mining and working of minerals. So far as Certificate A is concerned, the applicant is not obliged to notify any third party of the application unless the land constitutes or forms part of an agricultural holding[65] or the development falls within the exceptions set out below. If Certificate A is inappropriate, then the application must be accompanied by Certificates B, C or D which deal with notice to the requisite owner, if known. In this last respect, Certificates C and D require prior notice of the application to have been published on a specified date in a local newspaper.[66] Whilst planning is concerned to ensure that in the development of land the public interest is also taken fully into account it is stated government policy[67] that "its objective" is not the safeguarding of private property rights nor, in particular, to protect the value of individual properties or the views to be had from them.[68] However, there are suggested occasions[69] when

---

[62] See *Pyx Granite Co.* v. *M.H.L.G.* [1960] A.C. 260, (s.53 does not oust jurisdiction of the court to make a declaration).

[63] See Articles 5, 6 and 7 of the 1977 G.D.O. and Development Control Policy Notes for procedure at present. See the new 1988 Applications Regulations (currently in draft form; note that these regulations only govern applications for planning permission. Application for approval of reserved matters, for approvals required by condition and for determination under s.53 of the Act are still contained within the draft 1988 G.D.O. (Articles 8, 9 and 23).

[64] s.27(1) of the 1971 Act and Article 9(1) and Sched. 4, Pt. I of the 1977 G.D.O. (Article 29 and Sched. 5 Pt. I 1988 G.D.O. (*draft*)).

[65] As defined by s.27(7) of the 1971 Act and A.H.A. 1986, s.1 in which event the current tenant must be notified (s.27(3)(*b*).

[66] See Sched. 4, Pt. II of the 1977 (and 1988 (*draft*)) G.D.O.

[67] See Circular 71/73 para. 3.

[68] Loss of light or privacy are recognised "losses of amenity" and will constitute "other material considerations" within s.29(1). See *e.g.* [1972] J.P.L. 660 (effect of extension on neighbours) and also n. 87 below.

[69] See Circular 71/73 para. 7 *e.g.*:
   (a) introducing a significant change in a homogeneous area (*e.g.* a retail warehouse);
   (b) affecting residential properties by *e.g.* smell, noise or vibration;
   (c) bringing crowds and/or noise to a generally quiet area;
   (d) causing activity and noise at late or early hours in areas where this is not usual;
   (e) otherwise having an adverse effect on the general character of

notification should be given to those affected by even a comparatively minor proposal; and it is now the practice of most L.P.A. to notify adjoining owners on either side of the application site of the proposed development at the very least or by way of a site notice.[70] Any written objections and other comments received from the neighbours must be taken into account by the L.P.A. when determining the application.[71] In addition, where the development comes within one of nine prescribed classes of development[72] which are colloquially known

"Bad neighbour" development, etc.

as "bad neighbour" development, formal notice must be advertised in the local press and on the site.[73] The site notice must be in a prescribed form[74] and be displayed for not less than seven days during the month immediately preceding the application[75] in a position which is easily visible to the public, without them needing to enter the site.[76] The prescribed classes of development are as follows:

  (1) construction of buildings for use as public conveniences;

  (2) construction of buildings or other operations, or use of land, for the disposal of refuse or waste materials,[77] as a scrap yard, a coal yard or for the winning or working of minerals[78];

  (3) construction of buildings or other operations (other than the laying of sewers, the construction of pump houses in a line of sewers, the construction of septic tanks and cesspools serving single dwelling-houses or single buildings in which not more than 10 people will normally reside, work or congregate, and works ancillary thereto) or use of land, for the purpose of the retention, treatment or disposal of sewage, trade waste or sludge;

  (4) construction of buildings to a height exceeding 20 metres;

  (5) construction of buildings, or use of land, for the purposes

---

the area *e.g.* tall buildings;

    (f) constituting a departure from the advertised development plan. The S.S.E. may also require notification of adjoining owners as part of the pre-inquiry procedure for a "called-in" application. See n. 94 below.

[70] See Circular 71/73, para. 8.

[71] s.29(3).

[72] As prescribed by s.26(1) of the 1971 Act and Article 9 of the 1977 G.D.O. (Article 11 1988 G.D.O. (*draft*)).

[73] s.26(2).

[74] s.26(3)(*a*) and Article 8 and Sched. 3, Pt. III of the 1977 G.D.O. (Article 11 and Sched. 4, Pt. III to the 1988 G.D.O. (*draft*)). This must state the name of a place in the locality where a copy of the application and of all plans and other documents will be open to public inspection at reasonable hours during a period of not less than 21 days after the posting of the notice (s.26(6)). A *pro forma* certificate must then be sent with the application stating that the requirements have been complied with or that the applicant has been unable to carry out all the requirements (s.26(9)(1)). There is a fine of £100 on summary conviction for persons supplying a false certificate. (s.26(8)).

[75] s.26(3)(*b*).

[76] s.26(4). But an applicant is excluded if, without fault or intention, a duly posted site notice is removed, obscured or defaced before the seven-day period has elapsed, provided the applicant has taken reasonable steps for protection of the notice (s.26(5)).

[77] For requirement of a specific consent for hazardous substances see ss.58B–58L (inserted by the Housing and Planning Act 1986, s.31).

[78] For specific controls over minerals see ss.51A–51F including suspension of working (inserted by the Town and Country Planning (Minerals) Act 1981— operative from May 19, 1986).

of a slaughter-house or knacker's yard; or for killing or plucking poultry.

(6) construction of buildings and use of buildings, for any of the following purposes, namely, as a casino, a funfair or a bingo hall, a theatre, a cinema, a music hall, a dance hall, a skating rink, a swimming bath or gymnasium (not forming part of a school, college or university), or a Turkish or other vapour or foam bath;

(7) construction of buildings and use of buildings or land as a zoo, or for the business of boarding or breeding cats or dogs;

(8) construction of buildings and use of land for motor-car or motor-cycle racing;

(9) use of land as a cemetery.

Provided that an objector's written representations are received by the L.P.A. before the end of 21 days from the date of the application, then the L.P.A. is obliged to consider these representations before deciding the application.[79] An objector is

Objections not normally entitled to make oral representations at the committee meeting unless called upon to do so by the chairman. Indeed, the standing orders of many committees do not even permit members of the public to attend meetings where the committee is of the opinion that a sensitive planning issue is being determined.[80] Whilst there is no procedural rule entitling an objector, other than a section 29 party, to receive a copy of the permission, it is the practice of most L.P.A.s to notify the objector of the outcome.[81]

Period for The L.P.A. is required to determine a valid planning
determination application within eight weeks of its receipt,[82] failing which the applicant will be entitled to assume there has been a "deemed refusal,"[83] thereby entitling him to appeal to the Secretary of

---

[79] s.29(2). The L.P.A. must also notify any parish or community council entitled to make representations (Local Government Act 1972, s.182 and Sched. 16) and other interested bodies, *e.g.* the Health and Safety Executive (hazardous substances) and the National Coal Board (erection of a building in an area of coal working), see Articles 15–17 of the 1977 G.D.O. (Articles 18–21 1988 G.D.O. (*draft*)).

[80] See the Public Bodies (Admission to Meetings) Act 1960, s.1.

[81] Following the implementation of the Local Government (Access to Information) Act 1985, from April 1, 1986 it is now a little easier to gain the necessary information to found an "informal objection". The relevant provisions of the Local Government Act 1972 (as amended) are as follows:
s.100A— admissions to meetings of principal councils.
s.100B— access to agenda and connected reports.
s.100C— inspection of minutes and other documents after meetings.
s.100D— inspection of background papers.
s.100E— application of ss.100A–D to committees and sub-committees.
s.100H— copying facilities.
s.100I— and Sched. 12A exempt information. (This excludes details concerning council employees, ordinary privileged documents, and any other "sensitive" material but unless planning application concerns *e.g.* the council's own scheme all material information should, normally, be supplied).

[82] Article 7(6) of the 1977 G.D.O. (Article 23 1988 G.D.O. (*draft*))—This period may be extended by the parties by agreement in writing. Under Article 7A (Article 24 1988 G.D.O. (*draft*)) a like period is prescribed for the obtaining of any consent, agreement or approval required by a condition in an existing planning permission, other than reserved matters.

[83] s.37.

State. However, the prescribed period is a directory, rather than a mandatory, provision. Accordingly, if a notice of decision is given after the expiration of the eight weeks, it will not be ineffective if accepted and acted upon by the applicant.[84] Where the application is uncontroversial, the Planning Committee of the L.P.A. is entitled to delegate its determination to the planning officer.[85]

Considerations

Under section 29 of the 1971 Act the L.P.A. must have regard to the development plan[86] for the area in question and other material considerations[87] including the protection of private interests, the planning history of the site, precedent, ulterior purposes, finance and central government policy. The L.P.A. is also directed to approach the matter on the basis that permission should be granted unless there are sound and clear-cut reasons for refusal.[88]

The L.P.A.'s decision

Planning permission can either be unconditional or subject to such conditions[89] as the L.P.A. think fit, for which reasons must be given.[90] The same requirement for giving of reasons also applies to a refusal of permission.[90] It is the written notification of the decision which constitutes the grant of the permission, rather than the resolution of the Planning Committee.[91]

"Called-in" applications

Where the Secretary of State requires that a planning application be referred to him for a decision, it is colloquially known as a "called-in" application.[92] His decision is final, subject to a right of appeal on a point of law to the High Court.[93] Such a procedure is usually adopted where the determination concerns a matter of major importance,[94] for example residential

---

[84] *James* v. *Secretary of State for Wales* [1968] A.C. 409.

[85] Local Government Act 1972, s.101.

[86] See Circular 22/84 (Memorandum on Structure & Local Plans).

[87] See *Stringer* v. *M.H.L.G.* [1970] 1 W.L.R. 1281; *Great Portland Estates plc* v. *Westminster City Council* [1985] A.C. 661 and D.O.E. Circular 22/80 (Development Policy & Practice).

[88] See D.O.E. Circular No. 22/80, paras. 3 & 4, as endorsed in Circular 14/85 para. 3 by the well-known policy statement. "There is therefore always a presumption in favour of allowing applications for development, having regard to all material considerations, unless that development would cause *demonstrable harm to interests of acknowledged importance.*" This last catchphrase has not been formally defined by D.O.E. Circular, Statutory Instrument or case law to date.

[89] See s.30; *Mixnam's Properties* v. *Chertsey UDC* [1965] A.C. 735 and Circular 1/85 (Use of Conditions in Planning Permissions). They must be necessary, relevant to planning and to the development permitted by the L.P.A., enforceable, precise and reasonable in all other respects. For relaxation procedure see s.31A.

[90] Article 7(7), Sched. 2, Pt. II of the 1977 G.D.O. (Article 25 and Sched. 3 Pt. II 1988 G.D.O. (*draft*)). "Sound and clear-cut reasons for refusal" must be given (see para. 3 of Circular 22(80)).

[91] *Co-operative Retail Services Ltd.* v. *Taff-Ely B.C.* (1978) 38 P. & C.R. 156 as confirmed by House of Lords (1980) 42 P. & C.R. 1; see also *R.* v. *West Oxfordshire D.C., ex p. Pearce Homes* [1986] J.P.L. 523.

[92] s.35 and Article 19 of the 1977 G.D.O. (Article 22 1988 G.D.O. (*draft*)). The same provisions as to notification and publication of the proposed application still apply (s.35(4)). The procedure will be a Public Inquiry conducted by an Inspector in accordance with the Town and Country Planning Appeals (Inquiries Procedure) Rules (S.I. 1974 No. 419). See also n. 14 below.

[93] Under s.242(1)(*e*), (3)(*a*) within six weeks.

[94] Government criteria are currently to be found in *Planning Appeals, Call-in and Major Public Inquiries* (Cm.43, 1986) para. 361 *e.g.*
    (a) development proposals of more than local significance;
    (b) proposals giving rise to significant public controversy (*e.g.*

development of 150 or more houses or, increasingly, where a local authority seeks deemed permission for one of its own projects.[95]

Interpretation The general rule is that regard may only be had to the permission itself (and the accompanying reasons) unless the permission incorporates the application and accompanying planning reference, in which event reference may be made to them to determine the scope of the permission[96] if the validity of the permission is challenged on the grounds that it was issued by mistake or without authority.[97] The terms of the permission should not, however, be construed narrowly or strictly or against the L.P.A..[98]

Number of permissions

Duration

Section 33(1) of the 1971 Act provides that, without prejudice to any revocation or modification,[99] a grant of planning permission will enure for the benefit of the land[1] and all persons for the time being interested therein.[2] Accordingly, more than one permission may exist in respect of the land.[3] However, under section 41(1) the duration of each permission will, unless taken up, normally be limited in time to five years beginning with the date on which the permission is granted or, as the case may be, deemed to be granted, or such other period (whether longer or

     gypsies);
  (c) retail development over 100,000 square feet;
  (d) significant development in the Green Belt;
  (e) major proposals for winning and working of minerals (*e.g.* open cast mining);
  (f) government proposals.

[95] Where the latter situation occurs (*e.g.* the siting of a gypsy encampment) the objector should write directly to the D.O.E. and call for a public inquiry. See Town and Country Planning General Regulations (S.I. 1976 no. 1419) for the procedure to be adopted by a local authority where deemed permission is sought, and in particular para. 4 (publicity) and para. 7 (lodging of application with S.S.E.). For examples of failures by local authorities to comply with requirements of the Town and Country Planning General Regulations (S.I. 1976 No. 1419) see *R.* v. *Lambeth B.C., ex p. Sharp* [1987] J.P.L. 440 and *R* v. *Doncaster M.B.C., ex p. British Railways Board* [1987] J.P.L. 444.

[96] *Wivenhoe Port Ltd.* v. *Colchester B.C.* [1985] J.P.L. 396.

[97] *Norfolk C.C.* v. *S.S.E.* [1973] 1 W.L.R. 1400, and *Co-operative Retail Services Ltd.* v. *Taff-Ely B.C.* above.

[98] *e.g. Watford B.C.* v. *S.S.E.* [1982] J.P.L. 518.

[99] ss.45 and 46 provide the procedure for the L.P.A. to revoke or modify a planning permission with the approval of the Secretary of State. The L.P.A. has no power to withdraw the permission unilaterally (*R.* v. *S.S.E., ex p. Reinisch* (1971) 22 P. & C.R. 1022 at 1025) and it may have to pay compensation under s.164. The power may be exercised only up to the time when the development is completed and will not affect operations already carried out (s.45(4)) but the L.P.A. may, where justified, serve a discontinuance order under s.51.

[1] s.33(2) also states that where planning permission is granted for the erection of the building if no purpose is specified in the permission then it will be construed as including permission to use the building for the purpose for which it was designed.

[2] See *Pioneer Agregates (U.K.) Ltd.* v. *S.S.E.* [1985] A.C. 132 (confirming that planning permission cannot be extinguished by mere conduct alone *e.g.* abandonment of land following cessation of mining operations).

[3] But see *e.g. Cynon Valley B.C.* v. *S.S.W.* [1986] J.P.L. 760: benefit of planning permission to carry on business use generally lost by subsequent change of use, requiring fresh permission before original use can be resumed; but on the facts reversion from temporary use as an antique shop back to a fish and chip shop permitted as permission granted under s.23(8), "subject to limitations." (See also *Young* v. *S.S.E.* [1983] 2 A.C. 662).

shorter) as the L.P.A. may direct. This time limit does not apply, though, to planning permission granted by a development order, or for a limited period under the terms of a conditional grant of planning permission,[4] or for permission to retain buildings or works, or continue the use of land,[5] or to any outline planning permission. In this last respect, under section 42(1) outline

Outline permission planning permission is defined as permission (with the reservation for subsequent approval by the L.P.A. or the Secretary of State of matters (known as "reserved matters") not particularised in the application, for example the form of construction of the proposed building. In such circumstances, the time limits will be as follows:

(1) in the case of any reserved matter, application for approval must be made not later than the expiration of three years from the date of the grant; and

(2) the development must be commenced[6] either within five years from the date of grant or two years from the final approval of reserved matters, or the last such matter if approval is given on different dates.

If the development has been commenced but not completed by the expiration of the time limit contained in the permission, and it appears unlikely to the L.P.A. that it will be completed

Completion notice within a reasonable period, then a completion notice may be served under section 44(2) stating that the planning permission will cease to have effect at the expiration of a further period specified in the notice, being a period of not less than 12 months after the notice takes effect.[7] The confirmation of the Secretary of State is required before the notice takes effect, for which purpose oral representations may be made to an Inspector, provided notice is given within 28 days from the service of the completion notice.[8]

Appeal Under section 36(1) of the 1971 Act, there is a right of appeal to the Secretary of State against a decision of the L.P.A.

---

[4] s.30(1). Article 5(3) of the 1977 G.D.O. (Article 7 1988 G.D.O. (*draft*); see also the proposed Town and Country Planning (Application) Regulations which provides a special procedure for the renewal of a time-limited permission which, as a general rule, will be renewed unless there has been some material change of planning circumstances since the permission was granted, or continued failure to begin the development.

[5] s.32.

[6] Under s.43(1) development is commenced on the earliest date on which a "specified operation" is begun. "Specified operation" means:

(a) any work of construction in the course of the erection of a building;

(b) the digging of a trench which is to contain the foundations, or part of the foundations of a building;

(c) the laying of any underground main or pipe to the foundations or part of the foundations of a building, or to any such trench as is mentioned in the preceding paragraph;

(d) any operation in the course of laying out or constructing a road or part of a road;

(e) any change in the use of any land, where that change constitutes material development as defined by s.43(3).

[7] The notice authorises development carried out up to and including that date (s.44(5)).

[8] s.44(4).

Procedure refusing the application,[9] or imposing excessive or unreasonable conditions. A like procedure exists under section 37 where there has been a deemed refusal. Notice of appeal must be given within six months of receipt of the notice of the decision[10] in a prescribed form except where the appeal is in respect of an application for any consent, agreement or approval, required by a condition imposed on a grant of planning permission, (other than an application for approval of a reserved matter), or a section 53 determination, in which event notice in writing will be sufficient.[11] With the appeal notice, the applicant must supply all relevant documentation, including all plans and drawings in support of the proposed development.[12]

Under section 36(8) and Schedule 9, certain prescribed appeals are to be heard and determined by an Inspector appointed by the Secretary of State. These are known as **Transferred** "transferred appeals" and include the following:
appeals

(1) an appeal relating to a planning decision (s.36(8));
(2) an appeal against an enforcement notice (s.88(9));
(3) an appeal relating to the certification of an established use (s.95(7));
(4) an appeal against a listed building enforcement notice (s.97(7));
(5) an appeal against an enforcement notice relating to the duty to replace trees (s.103(4)); and
(6) an appeal against the refusal of listed building consent or the grant thereof subject to conditions (Sched. 11, para. 8(6)).

The decision of the Inspector then becomes that of the Secretary of State (Schedule 9, para. 2(3)).

The powers of the Secretary of State through his Inspector **Disposal of appeal** are wide ranging. Before determining the appeal, the Inspector can, if so requested by either the applicant or the L.P.A., call for written representations[13] or an informal hearing.[13a] Otherwise,

---

[9] Under s.36(1) the applications to which a right of appeal lies are as follows:
    (a) for planning permission to develop land;
    (b) for any consent, agreement or approval of that authority required by a condition imposed on a grant of planning permission; or
    (c) for any approval of that authority required under a development order.

[10] s.36 and Article 20(1) of the 1977 G.D.O. (Article 26 1988 G.D.O. (*draft*))—"month" means calendar month (see Article 2(2)).

[11] Article 20(1A) of the 1977 G.D.O. (Article 26 1988 G.D.O. (*draft*)).

[12] As set out under Article 20(2). (Article 26 1988 G.D.O. (*draft*)).

[13] This procedure arises if the parties waive their rights to a hearing and is now used in over 85 per cent. of planning appeals. The format is set out in the Appendix I to Circular 18/86 (Planning Appeals Decided By Written Representations). See also Circular 11/87 and Town and County Planning (Appeals) (Written Representations Procedure) Regulations 1987 (S.I. 1987 No. 701). These Regulations require S.S.E. to notify parties of the "starting date" for the procedural timetable. Under Reg. 9(1) the S.S.E. has power to proceed to a decision on appeal upon the basis of such written representations and supporting documents that have been submitted within the time limits.

[13a] In appropriate cases the S.S.E. may offer, or the parties may agree, to an informal hearing (*e.g.* where only real dispute is on a point of law). Time scales for exchange of documents are shortened and the right to cross-examine witnesses is waived by the parties.

the Inspector will hear the appeal at a public local inquiry.[14]
However, it should always be borne in mind that the Secretary of
State is entitled to decline to determine an appeal if satisfied that
planning permission could not have been granted at all, or could
only have been granted subject to the conditions of which
complaint is now made.[15] Procedure at the inquiry is at the
discretion of the Inspector.[16] The appellant, the L.P.A., other
relevant planning authorities[17] and section 29 parties may appear
as of right. Although it is now acknowledged practice to allow
other persons to appear, in law, such right lies entirely within the
discretion of the Inspector.[18] Until it has been exercised in favour
of that person he is not entitled to participate. Thereafter, that
person can have his representations considered in accordance
with the procedural Rules.[19] An aggrieved neighbour should bear
this consideration in mind when making his appearance at the
inquiry and obviously not upset the Inspector by his behaviour.[20]
As the whole of the application will be considered as if it were at
first instance, the Secretary of State, by his Inspector, is not only
entitled to confirm or reverse the decision of the L.P.A. but may

[14] See s.36(4) and also Sched. 9. The procedure at the public inquiry is currently
governed by the Town and Country Planning Appeals (Inquiry Procedure)
Rules 1974 (S.I. 1974 No. 419) and the Town and Country Planning Appeals
(Determination by Appointed Persons) (Inquiries Procedure) Rules 1974 (S.I.
1974 No. 420) for certain transferred appeals (such as planning appeals) and
tree preservation, listed building consent and advertisement consent appeals.
Under Rule 5(2) provision is made for notification in the local press and to
parties affected (usually neighbours, objectors at first instance and other
interested parties) who, under Rule 9, have a right to be heard together with
any other person at the discretion of the Inspector. At least 28 days before the
enquiry, the L.P.A. must serve a statement (known colloquially as a "Rule 6
Statement") of its submissions on the applicant, and all section 29 parties (such
as owners of the land concerned and any agricultural tenant thereof). Where
the appeal concerns issues of complexity or environmental sensitivity it is now
the practice of the D.o.E. to ask the appellant to prepare his own statement
under Rule 7(5) of the Appointed Persons Rules 1974, which must be served
on all other parties in like manner to the Rule 6 statement. At the time of
writing the D.o.E. are proposing to extend the requirement that both the
L.P.A. and the Appellant should serve pre-inquiry statements. See the Preface
for further developments in respect of the 1988 (Inquiries Procedure) Rules.
[15] s.36(7).
[16] S.I. 1974 No. 419, r. 10(1); S.I. 1974 No. 420, r. 12(1). Unless otherwise
directed, the appellant will open his case at the beginning of the inquiry and
will have the final right of reply. The order of other witnesses is at the
discretion of the Inspector but usually will be the L.P.A. plus other objectors.
Evidence is normally given in the form of written proofs which are read out to
the inquiry followed by cross-examination. Oral representations are
permissible. Documentary and hearsay evidence can be admitted and taken
into account provided it can be fairly regarded as reliable (see *Knights Motors* v.
S.S.E. [1984] J.P.L. 584. The rules of natural justice may be satisfied by
allowing parties to comment and contradict such evidence (*Miller (T.A.) Ltd.*
v. *M.H.L.G.* [1968] 1 W.L.R. 992).
[17] *e.g.* parish or community councils if they have made representations in the
prescribed manner.
[18] S.I. 1974 No. 419, r. 7(2); S.I. 1974 No. 420, r. 9(2).
[19] See *Turner* v. *S.S.E.* (1973) 23 P. & C.R. 123 at 134–139.
[20] See *e.g. Lovelock* v. *S.S.T.* (1979) 39 P. & C.R. 468 where a road inquiry
proceeded in the absence of a party ejected for disruptive behaviour. See also
e.g. Nicholson v. *S.S. for Energy* (1977) 76 L.G.R. 693 (failure to permit cross-
examination held to be breach of rules of natural justice).

add more onerous conditions if he considers it appropriate.[21] The Inspector is required to give reasons for his decision[22] save where the matter is determined by written representations.[23]

Notification of the decision will then be sent by the Department of the Environment to the appellant.[24] If requested, all objectors, not only section 29 parties, will be able to receive a copy of the decision.

High Court appeal   A further right of appeal lies to the High Court under section 245(1) of the 1971 Act on a point of law. Such a right extends to "any person aggrieved" and not just to the major participants, so that any third party who has participated at the public inquiry can, in principle, pursue an appeal.[25] The statutory grounds of challenge are limited to establishing either that the order is not within the powers of the 1971 Act,[26] or that any of the relevant requirements have not been complied with[27] (*i.e.* there has been a breach of natural justice or a failure to give reasons).[28] Accordingly, it is doubtful whether a third party is likely to succeed to any significant degree at this stage in view of the restricted method of review procedure by the High Court (and the costs involved).[29] Moreover, in practical terms, if the

---

[21] s.36(3). The Inspector's role is to consider the contentions of the parties and to advise the S.S.E. whether there are any "sound and clear cut reasons" for refusing planning permission. He is not obliged to investigate though he may call for information if necessary (*Federated Estates Ltd.* v. *S.S.E.* [1983] J.P.L. 812). Equally there is no burden of proof on the L.P.A. to justify its reasons for refusal although the very nature of the procedure will lead to such reasons being challenged both in evidence and cross-examination (see *Pye (Oxford) Estates Ltd.* v. *S.S.E.* [1982] J.P.L. 575). The inspector will require the parties to agreee such conditions. These should comply with the model forms set out in Circular 1/85 to be acceptable to the S.S.E. Only if it can be shown that the L.P.A. has acted unreasonably can an application for costs at the inquiry be properly made or be successful (see Circular 2/87).

[22] S.I. 1974 No. 419, r. 13(1); S.I. 1974 No. 420, r. 16(1). The lack of sufficient reasons may form a useful ground for appeal under s.245(1).

[23] But see *Grenfell-Baines* v. *S.S.E.* [1986] J.P.L. 256 where the duty may be inferred now from the broader requirement to have regard to all material considerations.

[24] The S.S.E. may either uphold or reject the Inspector's recommendation. A copy of the Inspector's report will be attached to the decision letter.

[25] For decisions on *locus standi* see *Turner* v. *S.S.E.* (1973) 23 P. & C.R. 123 (Objector heard at public inquiry); *Bizony* v. *S.S.E.* [1976] J.P.L. 306 and *Hollis* v. *S.S.E.* [1983] J.P.L. 164 (parties whose amenities are likely to be affected by the appeal proposals).

[26] *i.e.* that the Inspector has erred in law on the same principles as a judge at first instance (see *Ashbridge Investments Ltd.* v. *M.H.L.G.* [1965] 1 W.L.R. 1320 but the weighing of evidence and decisions of fact and degree are for the S.S.E. and his Inspector not the court (*Catton* v. *S.S.E.* [1976] J.P.L. 663). Errors of fact if material, are errors of law (*Elmbridge B.C.* v. *S.S.E.* [1980] J.P.L. 463). If this is established, the High Court has power to suspend the order or action pending final determination of the proceedings (s.245(4)(*a*)).

[27] Substantial prejudice must be established before the order will be quashed (s.245(4)(*b*)). See *e.g. Peak Park Joint Planning Board* v. *S.S.E.* (1979) 39 P. & C.R. 361 at 385 and *G.L.C.* v. *S.S.E.* [1983] J.P.L. 793.

[28] It should always be remembered that the court can only interfere if it thought that the Inspector came to a decision which no reasonable Inspector could have come to (*Behrman* v. *S.S.E.* [1979] J.P.L. 622).

[29] Even though the S.S.E.'s decision is quashed the appeal is regarded as still standing. The S.S.E. is therefore entitled to come to a fresh decision in accordance with the ruling of the court, to which end he may re-open the inquiry but only to allow the parties to deal with matters upon which the court has made a particular finding e.g. evidence on a point overlooked or prerepresentational on a point wrongly determined (see e.g. *H. Sabey Ltd* v.

aggrieved neighbour is against the proposed development then the L.P.A. is likely to have supported his objections, in which event, if the objection is sufficiently meritorious, they are likely to continue to pursue the matter on appeal.[30] If an appeal is to be pursued the originating motion must be entered within six weeks of the date of the decision letter.[31]

Issue of notice

Enforcement   The L.P.A. has a discretion to issue an enforcement notice[32] where it appears to the authority that a breach of planning control[33] has occurred after the end of 1963.[34] Such a resolution will be determined by matters of expediency having regard to the provisions of the development plan and to any other material considerations.[35] However, an enforcement notice can be issued in respect of the following breaches within

The four-year rule   the period of four years[36] from the date of the breach:

(1) the carrying out without planning permission of building, engineering, mining or other operations in, on, over or under land; or

(2) the failure to comply with any condition or limitation which related to the carrying out of such operations and subject to which planning permission was granted for the development of that land; or

(3) the making without planning permission of a change of use of any building to use as a single dwelling-house; or

(4) the failure to comply with a condition which prohibits, or has the effect of preventing, a change of use of a building to use as a single dwelling-house.

Accordingly, apart from exceptions (3) and (4), any material change of use will be subject to enforcement proceedings, as will a development which results in both a change of use and building or other operations.[37]

The fifth exception from enforcement proceedings is where the use in contravention of planning control began:

S.S.E. [1978] 1 All E.R. 586). If the decision letter has been quashed for inadequate or unintelligble reasons the S.S.E. need do no more than issue a fresh decision letter making those reasons clear (see *Price Bros. (Rode Heath) Ltd.* v. *S.S.E.* (1978) 38 P. & C.R. 579 and *Rogelen Building Group Ltd.* v. *S.S.E.* [1981] J.P.L. 506).

[30] See p. 121 above and pp. 145–146 (esp. n. 55) below.

[31] s.245(1). The court has no discretion to extend this period. Time runs from the date on the decision letter rather than its receipt by the applicant (see *Griffiths* v. *S.S.E.* [1983] 1 All E.R. 439).

[32] s.87(1).

[33] s.87(3) defines "breach of planning control." This is development (*a*) carried out, whether before or after the 1971 Act, without planning permission or (*b*) which fails to comply with any conditions or limitations subject to which the planning permission has been granted. The L.P.A. will not have to show that there has been a breach of planning control but simply that there appeared to be such a breach in order to justify the service of an enforcement notice (*Ferris* v. *S.S.E.*, *The Times*, January 21, 1988). However, issue estoppel can apply to both s.36 and s.88 appeals (*Thrasyvoulon* v. *S.S.E.*, *The Times*, February 3, 1988, C.A.).

[34] This relates to established use; see further p. 143 below.

[35] See p. 136 above. A right of withdrawal *before* the enforcement notice takes effect exists under s.87(10).

[36] s.87(4).

[37] *Burn* v. *S.S.E.* (1971) 219 E.G. 586.

(a) before the beginning of 1964 without planning permission and has continued ever since the end of 1963; or

(b) before the beginning of 1964 under a planning permission granted subject to conditions or limitations which have either never been complied with at all, or have not been complied with since the end of 1963; or

(c) after the end of 1963 as a result of a change of use which did not require planning permission and since the end of 1963 there has been no change of use which did require planning permission.[38]

Established use certificates

In such circumstances, an application may be made for a certificate from the L.P.A. known as an "established use certificate."[39] This certificate will then be conclusive proof in any subsequent enforcement proceedings that the continuing use is no longer illegal.[40]

Service of enforcement notice

Under section 87(5) the enforcement notice must be served not later than 28 days after the date of its issue, and not later than 28 days *before* the date specified in the notice as the date on which it is to take effect on the owner and occupier of the land to which it relates, and on any other person having an interest in the land who will be materially affected by the notice.

Contents

The enforcement notice must specify[41]:

(1) the matters alleged to constitute the breach of planning control (s.87(6));

(2) the steps, if any required by the L.P.A. to be taken to remedy the breach by either restoring the land to its condition before the development took place or securing compliance with the conditions or limitations subject to which planning permission was granted, including the demolition or alteration of any building or works, the discontinuance of any use or the carrying out of any necessary building or other operations (s.87(7), (9));

(3) the period within which the steps are to be taken (s.87(8)).[42]

There is no prescribed form for an enforcement notice.[43] However, because of its draconian effect, careful consideration should be given to the whole document, and in particular, to the

---

[38] s.94(1).

[39] See Article 22 of the 1977 G.D.O. (Article 29 1988 G.D.O. (*draft*)). The procedure basically follows that for the obtaining of planning permission. A power of "calling in" can be exercised by the Secretary of State under s.95(1).

[40] s.94(7).

[41] See generally D.o.E. Circular 38/81. The reasons for the issue of the enforcement notice and a location plan must also be given (see Town and Country Planning (Enforcement Notices and Appeals) Regulations (S.I. 1981 No. 1742) Regs. 3, 4).

[42] This must be at least 28 clear days following completion of service before the date upon which the enforcement notice can be said to take effect (s.87(5)). Time can be extended provided an application is made to the L.P.A. *before* the initial period prescribed has expired (s.89(6)). If the appropriate steps are taken, planning permission is deemed to be granted for the retention of the buildings or works as they stand as a result of the compliance (s.87(16)).

[43] The L.P.A. will, however, have its own *pro forma* notice. (See generally D.o.E. Circular No. 38/81). The reasons for the issue of the enforcement notice and a location plan must be provided as part of the notice.

wording describing the alleged breach. This must be correctly identified[44]; otherwise, the enforcement notice may be a nullity. If the notice is defective by reason of one of the grounds of appeal **Appeal** set out below, then the only remedy will be by way of appeal.

Under section 88(2) these grounds of appeal are as follows:

(a) that planning permission ought to be granted for the development to which the notice relates or, as the case may be, that a condition or limitation alleged in the enforcement notice not to have been complied with ought to be discharged[45];

(b) that the matters alleged in the notice do not constitute a breach of planning control;

(c) that the breach of planning control alleged in the notice has not taken place;

Grounds
(d) in the case of a notice which, by virtue of section 87(4) of the 1971 Act, may be issued only within the period of four years from the date of the breach of planning control to which the notice relates, that the period had elapsed at the date when the notice was issued;

(e) in the case of a notice not falling within paragraph (d) above, that the breach of planning control alleged by the notice occurred before the beginning of 1964;

(f) that copies of the enforcement notice were not served as required by section 87(5) of the 1971 Act;

(g) that the steps required by the notice to be taken exceed what is necessary to remedy any breach of planning control, or to achieve a purpose specified in section 87(10) of the 1971 Act;

(h) that the period specified in the notice as the period within which any step is to be taken falls short of what should reasonably be allowed.

Procedure   Notice of appeal in writing[46] must be sent to the Secretary of State before the expiration of the date stated on the enforcement notice from which the notice is to take effect.[47]

---

[44] See *Miller-Mead* v. *M.H.L.G.* [1963] 2 Q.B. 196. Minor errors will not invalidate the notice and can be corrected on appeal under s.88A(2), *e.g.* to alter the steps to be taken; but the L.P.A. cannot correct a defect which "goes to the substance of the matter" (*Miller-Mead*) which would cause "injustice" to the appellant (see *Wealdon D.C.* v. *S.S.E.* [1983] J.P.L. 234) *e.g.* where the body of the notice makes an allegation of material change of use whilst the schedule alleges breach of conditions (*Epping Forest D.C.* v. *Matthews* [1987] J.P.L. 132) or where the plan fails to identify the correct planning unit (*De Mulder* v. *S.S.E* [1974] Q.B. 792).

[45] Appeal on this ground will amount to a deemed application for planning permission.

[46] The use of a standard form of appeal issued by the D.O.E. is not mandatory. In addition a written statement of the grounds of appeal should be lodged at the same time or within 28 days of a request from the S.S.E. and any other prescribed information (see Reg. 5(1), 1981 Regs.) If the appellant fails to provide such information the Secretary of State may dismiss the appeal (s.88(6)(a)). The L.P.A. must in turn provide a statement setting out their case, also colloquially known as a "Rule 6" Statement, at least 28 days before the inquiry (see further Town and Country Planning (Enforcement) (Inquiries Procedure) Rules (S.I. 1981 No. 1743)—Failure to comply may result in the notice being quashed (s.88(6)(b)).

[47] s.88(1).

As with a planning appeal, the Secretary of State is given the discretion to determine the appeal. Unless the matter is determined summarily by reason of procedural irregularities under section 88(6) a public inquiry presided over by an Inspector appointed by the Secretary of State will normally take place.[48] The onus of proof will be on the appellant to establish that no breach of planning control has occurred.[49] Under sections 88A and 88B the Secretary of State has the power to quash, correct or vary the enforcement notice. He may also grant planning permission in respect of the unauthorised development, or discharge the condition or limitation which has not been complied with. If the enforcement notice is upheld on appeal under section 88, the notice will take effect on the date of the Secretary of State's decision letter[50] unless a further appeal is pursued to the High Court under section 246(1).[51] This right of appeal exists only on point of law. It can only be exercised by the appellant, the L.P.A. or any other person having an interest in the affected land, and within 28 days of the date of the decision letter.[52] Accordingly, the aggrieved neighbour has no *locus standi*. Such rights of objection that he does have are limited in the first instance to making representations to the L.P.A., and in the second instance to making representations at the public inquiry in respect of the section 88 appeal.[53] Unless there are overwhelming grounds for contending that the L.P.A. has wrongly exercised its discretion in not pursuing enforcement proceedings in the first instance, following *Wednesbury*[54] principles, no grounds are likely to be made out for an application for judicial review to compel the L.P.A. to act. It should also be borne in mind that under R.S.C., Ord. 53, r. 3, the leave of the court must first be obtained. Accordingly, unless

High Court appeal

Aggrieved neighbour

---

[48] The written representations procedure can be used but not where factual evidence is likely to be in dispute or where the subject matter of the enforcement notice is of special local interest or concern. For the overriding powers of S.S.E. to hold a public inquiry see s.282(1). In practice, therefore, written representations are unlikely to be appropriate where the grounds of appeal include (b) (c) (d) (e) or (f).

[49] *Nelsovil* v. *M.H.L.G.* [1962] 1 W.L.R. 404.

[50] See *Dover District Council* v. *McKeen* (1985) 50 P. & C.R. 250. Thereafter, under s.87(10) the landowner must comply with the terms of the enforcement notice. e.g. a requirement to cease a use should be read as a permanent cessation (ss.93(1), 93(2)). Thereafter, the requirements of the notice automatically revive if the unauthorised development (to which it relates) recommences, unless permitted by a subsequent planning permission (see s.92(1)).

[51] The decision of the Divisional Court in the *Dover* case is clear where no s.246 appeal is lodged. In the subsequent case of *London Parachuting Ltd.* v. *S.S.E.* [1987] J.P.L. 279 the Court of Appeal also expressed the view that s.246 created a separate right of appeal. The Court of Appeal has now concluded, on the wording of s.88(10) that the "final determination" of a s.88 appeal by the S.S.E., cannot be known until after that appeal has either been withdrawn or it has been determined under s.246 by the High Court, Court of Appeal, or House of Lords (see *R.* v. *Kuxhaus, The Times*, February 22, 1988).

[52] R.S.C. Ord. 55, rr. 2, 4.

[53] If permission is granted under s.88(2)(*a*) an appeal could be pursued under s.245(1) (see also p. 140 above).

[54] *i.e.* that no reasonable local authority would have reached the decision in question (see *Associated Provincial Picture Houses Ltd.* v. *Wednesbury Corporation* [1948] 1 K.B. 223).

the applicant can show that he has a sufficient interest in the matter to which his application relates[55] he will fall at this first hurdle.

Suspension of enforcement notice

Upon the making of the appeal to the Secretary of State, the enforcement notice will be suspended until such time as the appeal is finally determined or withdrawn.[56] However, where a section 246 appeal then takes place, it will be advisable to apply to the High Court for a stay pending the determination of that further appeal, in view of current judicial uncertainty as to when the suspension ends.[57]

Penalties for non-compliance   If the enforcement notice takes effect, under section 89(1) criminal proceedings which can result on summary conviction, in a fine not exceeding £2,000, and, on

Fine

indictment, in a fine without limit, will be taken by the L.P.A.[58] If the enforcement notice relates to the use of land, the defendant can be fined on a daily basis at a rate on summary conviction, of up to £100 for each day the use continues, and on indictment, at a rate without limit.

Once the enforcement notice has been served and irrespective of whether an appeal has been lodged, the L.P.A.

Stop notice

may, under section 90(1), serve a stop notice if they consider it expedient to prevent before the expiry of the period allowed for compliance with the notice, the carrying out of any activity which is, or is included in, a matter alleged by the notice to constitute a breach. Such a resolution is usually only taken where it is apparent that continuing harm is likely to be caused to the neighbourhood pending the determination of the appeal, or where use of the appeal procedure appears to be an abuse of this process of redress. The decision is also likely to be affected by the liability of the L.P.A. under section 177 to pay compensation for any loss or damage directly attributable to the prohibition contained in the stop notice if the enforcement notice is subsequently withdrawn, varied or quashed other than under ground (a), namely, that planning permission should be granted for the unauthorised activity. A stop notice cannot, however, prohibit the use of any building as a dwelling-house, or land as the site for a caravan occupied by any person as his only or main residence, or the taking of any steps specified in the enforcement notice. Penalties for non-compliance are the same as for breach of the enforcement notice.

In addition to criminal sanctions, the L.P.A. may also apply, under its general powers to prosecute and defend legal proceedings under section 222(1) of the Local Government Act

Injunction

1972, for an injunction to enforce the provisions of the stop

---

[55] R.S.C. Ord. 53, r. 3(7) *e.g.* where the development would be detrimental to a neighbour's privacy (see *R.* v. *North Hertfordshire D.C., ex p. Sullivan* [1981] J.P.L. 752), or where a group of residents is likely to be affected (see *Covent Garden Community Assocn. Ltd.* v. *G.L.C.* [1981] J.P.L. 183).

[56] s.88(10). See also n. 51 above.

[57] This course of action was proved, successfully, by the appellant in the *London Parachuting* case under R.S.C. Ord. 55, r. 3(3). Until this area of law is finally clarified by the House of Lords it would be prudent to take this step.

[58] The offences created by ss.89(1)–(5) are single and not continuing offences (see *Hodgetts* v. *Chiltern D.C.* [1983] A.C. 120).

notice if there has been a clear breach and a deliberate and flagrant flouting of the law and a plain breach of the law.[59]

Planning register

Under section 34,[60] every L.P.A. is required to keep a register. Part I contains a copy of every pending application for planning permission, for approval of reserved matters and for section 53 determinations together with copies of all plans and drawings submitted with them. Part II contains a permanent record of all applications and decisions, including any decision of the Secretary of State or a deemed application arising out of an enforcement appeal. A separate register is also kept of all enforcement and stop notices.[61] Public access extends to the taking of notes of all the aforementioned documents and the receiving of copies of applications and permissions but not accompanying documents. Despite this restriction, the register does provide an important source of information.

Local land charges

Notice of the existence of all enforcement and stop notices, listed buildings, conservation areas and tree preservation orders is also to be found in the register of local land charges kept by the local authority.

Listed building consent

Principles Under section 54(1) of the 1971 Act, the Secretary of State is required to compile a list of buildings of special architectural or historic interest.[62] They are classified as either of exceptional interest, (Grade I), or of special interest, (Grade II). Once a building is on the approved list, any work which will affect the special character of that building, whether constituting development in planning terms or not, will require "listed building consent."[63] This procedure is concurrent with but separate from an application for planning permission. The L.P.A. will grant the application, subject to such conditions as may be deemed necessary to preserve the character of the building.[64] Such consent will last for five years beginning with the date of the grant or such other period (whether longer or shorter) as the L.P.A. considers appropriate.[65] Furthermore, where consent is granted for the demolition of the listed building, the L.P.A. are entitled to grant a condition that the building is

[59] See *Westminster City Council* v. *Jones* [1981] J.P.L. 750, (*per* Whitford J.) and *Stoke-on-Trent City Council* v. *B & Q (Retail) Ltd.* [1984] A.C. 754.
[60] See also Article 20 of the 1977 G.D.O. (Article 27 1988 G.D.O. (*draft*)).
[61] s.92A and Article 21A. (Article 28 1988 G.D.O. (*draft*)).
[62] See further Circular 8/87.
[63] See Sched. 11.
[64] ss.56(4), (4A) and (4B).
[65] s.56A(1).

not to be demolished before a contract for the carrying out of the works of redevelopment has been made and planning permission granted for such development.[66]

Compensation   Minimum compensation is payable by the Secretary of State under section 117 where, on appeal, listed building consent is refused or made subject to conditions and the building is deliberately left derelict. In such circumstances, the owner may choose to serve a purchase notice on the L.P.A. if he can show that the building is not capable of beneficial use either without listed building consent or subject to the conditions which have been imposed, and there are no works which could reasonably be carried out to make the land capable of beneficial use.[67]

Repairs notice   Where the owner allows the building to fall into a state of disrepair, the L.P.A. may serve a "repairs notice" setting out the works necessary to put the building back into a reasonable state of preservation.[68] Such a notice is a preliminary step[69] to the compulsory acquisition of the property under section 114 if the Secretary of State determines that reasonable steps are not being taken for properly preserving it. A right of appeal lies to the magistrates' court within 28 days of the service of the notice.[70] Express provision is made preventing a higher level of compensation being obtained under section 117 in the event that this course is pursued, so as to prevent the unscrupulous owner[71] from benefiting from his acts of omission.

Where works are carried out without listed building consent,[72] the L.P.A. may serve a listed building enforcement **Listed building** notice under section 96(1). This must specify the alleged **enforcement** contravention and the steps required within such period as may **notice** be there stated for the purpose of:

(1) restoring the building to its former state; or
(2) if such restoration is not reasonably practicable or is undesirable, for alleviating the effect of the unauthorised works; or
(3) bringing the building to the state in which it would have been if the terms and conditions of any listed building consent had been complied with.

The same provisions as to service and enforcement apply as with an ordinary enforcement notice. A right of appeal lies to the Secretary of State under section 97.

Conservation areas

Creation   Under section 277 the L.P.A. is obliged to determine and designate any area within their control or which they consider is of special architectural or historic interest as a conservation area,

---

[66] s.56(3). If the building is not listed a "building preservation notice" can be served under s.58(1) where it is of special architectural or historic interest and is in danger of demolition or alteration in such a way as to affect its character.
[67] s.190(1).
[68] s.115(1). See also s.56(c) for dangerous structure orders.
[69] It must be served at least two months before compulsory purchase is initiated.
[70] s.114(6).
[71] ss.116 and 180(4).
[72] e.g. repainting the exterior of the building had to be an alteration requiring consent (*Windsor and Maidenhead B.C.* v. *S.S.E.*, *The Times*, January 6, 1988).

and where they deem it desirable, to preserve or enhance the character and appearance of such an area. These areas will vary in size from a group of buildings to the whole of a town centre or a village. Notice of the designation of a conservation area must be publicised in the London Gazette and in a local newspaper

Effect circulating in the locality in question.[73] Designation will constitute a local land charge. Within the conservation area, the grant of all forms of planning permission, including permitted development under the General Development Order, will be strictly regulated. Details of all applications for planning permission must be publicised in the local press and at the site. This form of regulation, whilst at times taken to extremes (for example, a restriction on the colour of front doors), is a useful adjunct to the powers of an L.P.A. in its attempts to preserve and maintain the architectural and visual amenities of a particular area by, for example, curbing the less attractive features of "modernisation" (such as certain types of replacement windows and stone cladding). In such circumstances, the L.P.A. is obliged to consider all representations made not only by interested parties but also by members of the public.[74] Where a building is to be demolished within the area, listed building consent must be obtained.[75] Special provision is also made for trees in conservation areas,[76] by which all trees are automatically protected even though no tree preservation order has been made,[77] unless protection would be contrary to the interests of good forestry.[78]

Tree preservation orders

Section 60(1) makes provision for the preservation "in the interest of amenity"[79] of trees, groups of trees or woodlands by prohibiting felling, topping, lopping, uprooting, wilful damage or wilful destruction without the consent of the L.P.A., and by securing the replanting of trees. Such powers are in addition to the duty of the L.P.A. under section 59 to ensure by the imposition of conditions that adequate provision is made for the preservation and planting of trees.

Procedure In fulfilment of this duty, the L.P.A. are required[80] to identify the location of the trees, groups of trees or woodlands in question and once a preservation order is made, to supply the Conservator of Forests and the District Valuer with copies of the

---

[73] s.277(7).
[74] s.28. See also Circular 8/87.
[75] s.277A.
[76] s.61A.
[77] See s.61(A)(2).
[78] See Town and Country Planning (Tree Preservation) (Amendment) and (Trees in Conservation Areas) (Exempted Cases) Regulations (S.I. 1975 No. 148), Reg. 3.
[79] See *Re Ellis and Ruislip-Northwood U.D.C.* [1920] 1 K.B. 343. See also D.O.E. Circular 36/78.
[80] For procedure, see Town and Country Planning (Tree Preservation Orders) Regulations (S.I. 1969 No. 7 as amended by S.I. 1975 No. 148 and S.I. 1981 No. 14).

order, a map and a list of the persons affected.[81] The L.P.A. must also serve the order upon such people, together with a notice setting out the grounds for the making of the order, the place where it can be inspected by the public, and stating that objections and representations may be made within 28 days from the date of service of the notice. Every objection must be made in writing,[82] within the aforementioned period, identifying the trees and setting out the grounds for objection. These grounds must then be taken into account before the order is confirmed. Provision is also made for a local inquiry. Once again, the aggrieved neighbour has an opportunity to make representations. The foregoing provisions as to notification apply equally to the notice of confirmation of the preservation order.

Definition of "tree"

Unfortunately, the 1971 Act contains no definition of the term "tree."[83] A distinction is now drawn between mature trees and saplings, and as a rough rule of thumb the L.P.A. tends to make an order only where the diameter of the trunk is greater than seven or eight inches.[84]

High Court appeal

Any "person aggrieved" or an "Authority directly concerned" with the making of the order is also entitled to challenge the validity of the order on the same basis as with a planning appeal by appealing to the High Court on a point of law.[85]

Contravention

Under section 102(1), any contravention of a tree preservation order is a strict liability.[86] On summary conviction, the defendant is liable to a fine not exceeding level 4 on the Standard Scale[86a] or twice the value of the tree (whichever is the greater) for cutting down, uprooting or wilfully destroying[87] a tree or treating it in such manner as is likely to destroy it. On indictment, the court is also directed to have regard to any financial benefit which has accrued or appears likely to accrue to him in consequence of the offence. Another contravention will lead to a further fine on summary conviction. Continuing offences incur a further fine not exceeding £5 per day.

Injunction

In addition to these matters, the L.P.A. is entitled to seek the civil remedy of an injunction in order to prevent a possible contravention.[88]

However, where a tree is dying or dead or has become dangerous or an obligation is imposed by Act of Parliament, it

---

[81] Reg. 5(*b*). "The persons affected are the owners and occupiers of the land and any other person known to the L.P.A. as being entitled to work by surface working any minerals in the land or to fell any of the trees affected by the order" (Reg. 5(*c*)).

[82] Reg. 7.

[83] For an attempt at a definition see [1979] J.P.L. 483—"a woody perennial plant which can attain a stature of six metres or more on a single stem. The stem may divide low, but must do so above ground level. Hawthorn qualifies under this rule, elderberry and dogwood do not, whilst hazel is usually given the benefit of the doubt".

[84] See *Kent County Council* v. *Batchelor* (1976) 33 P. & C.R. 185 at 189 (*per* Lord Denning M.R.).

[85] ss.242(1)(*d*), (2)(*c*) and 245(1). See also p. 141 above.

[86] See *Maidstone B.C.* v. *Mortimer* [1980] 3 All E.R. 552. Accordingly, ignorance of the tree preservation order is no defence.

[86a] Criminal Justice Act 1982, s.46. Currently a maximum of £2,000.

[87] For the definition of wilful destruction, see *Barnet L.B.C.* v. *Eastern Electricity Board* [1973] 1 W.L.R. 430.

[88] *Kent C.C.* v. *Batchelor* (*No. 2*) [1978] 3 All E.R. 980 at 986.

Exceptions may be cut down, uprooted, topped or lopped. Indeed, as the ultimate statutory preservation of the neighbour's first and foremost right of self-help, the foregoing activities may be lawfully carried out for the purposes of preventing or abating a nuisance caused by a tree.[89]

General Development Orders—Table of Comparative Provisions

ARTICLE			
	1977	1988 (*draft*)	
Application, citation and commencement	1	1	Application, citation and commencement
Interpretation	2	2	Interpretation
Permitted development	3	3	Permitted development
Directions restricting permitted development	4	4	Directions restricting permitted development
	—	5	Approval of Secretary of State for article 4 directions
	—	6	Directions restricting permitted development under Pt. 22 Class B and Pt. 23 Class B
Applications for planning permission	5	—	**New 1988 Town and Country Planning (Applications) Regulations**
		7	Outline applications
Other forms of application	6	8	Application for approval of reserved matters
		9	Application for determination under s.53
General provisions relating to applications (including time periods)	7	10	General provisions relating to applications
		(23)	(*Time periods*)
Applications made under planning condition	7A	(24)	(*Applications made under planning condition*)
Notice under s.26	8	11	Notice under s.26
Certificates & notices under s.27	9	—	*See Sched. 5 for certificates & notices under s.27*
	—	12	Notification of applications to owners & agricultural tenants
	—	13	**New notification of mineral applications**
Directions restricting the grant of permission	10	14	Directions by the Secretary of State restricting the grant of permission
Special provisions as to permission for development affecting certain existing and proposed highways	11	15	Special provisions as to permission for development affecting certain existing and proposed highways
Power of local highway authority to issue directions restricting the grant of planning permission	12	—	**Highway authorities' powers of direction deleted to be removed and replaced by requirement for consultation**

[89] s.60(6). See also *e.g.* [1985] J.P.L. (permission to fell where the amenity value of the tree was not great and it cast a dense shadow, but made subject to a re-planting condition. See s.62 for statutory powers of replacement.

ARTICLE			
	1977	1988 (*draft*)	
Application of bye-laws in relation to construction of new streets	13	16	Application of bye-laws in relation to construction of new streets
Development not in accordance with the development plan	14	17	Development not in accordance with development plan
Consultation before the grant of permission	15	18	Consultation before the grant of permission
	—	19	Consultation with county planning authority
Applications relating to county matters	16	20	Applications relating to county matters
Notice to parish and community councils	17	21	Notice to parish and community councils
Provisions for applications affecting listed buildings Revoked by S.I. 1980 No. 1946, art. 2	18	—	
Notice of reference of applications to the Secretary of State	19	22	Notice of reference of applications to the Secretary of State
	—	23	Time periods
(*Applications made under planning condition*)	(7A)	24	Applications made under planning condition
	—	25	Written notice of decision or determination relating to an application
Appeals	20	26	Appeals
Register of Applications	21	27	Register of Applications
Register of Enforcement and Stop Notices	21A	28	Register of Enforcement and Stop Notices
Established Use Certificates	22	29	Established Use Certificates
Directions and notices	23	30	Directions and notices
Revocations and savings	24	31	Revocations and savings

SCHEDULE			
	1977	1988 (*draft*)	
	—	1	**New Sched. 1 —Land in National Parks, areas of outstanding natural beauty, conservation areas, etc. —Land in and adjoining National Parks**
Permitted development	1	2	Permitted development
Notification to be sent to applicant on receipt of his application, refusal of planning permission or on grant of permission subject to conditions	2	3	Notification to be sent to applicant on receipt of his application, refusal of planning permission or on grant of permission subject to conditions
Prescribed forms of notices and certificate under s.26	3	4	Prescribed forms of notices and certificate under s.26

SCHEDULE			
1977		1988 (*draft*)	
Prescribed forms of notices and certificate under s.27, and notice under ss.27 and 36 of appeal	4	5	Prescribed forms of certificate under s.27 and article 29, notices under s.27 and notice under ss.27 and 36 of appeal
Prescribed forms of certificate and notices under article 22, and notices under article 22 of appeal	5	6	Prescribed forms of notices under article 29, and notices under article 29 of appeal
Notification to be sent to applicant on receipt of his application for an established use certificate Prescribed form of established use certificate	6	7	Notification to be sent to applicant on receipt of his application for an established use certificate Prescribed form of established use certificate
Statutory Instruments revoked	7	8	Statutory Instruments revoked

8 LITIGATION

Introduction

The object of this chapter is twofold. First, to provide a reference guide to those points of practice and procedure requiring a quick answer; secondly, to highlight certain procedural matters pertinent to the type of litigation contemplated by this book. For further detail the reader is referred to the standard texts and references.

Jurisdiction

County court

Rateable value

Recovery of land and declarations as to title   The net annual value for rating[1] of the hereditament[2] in question should not be in excess of £1,000[3] at the time when proceedings are commenced.

Easements and licences   The same rateable value limit applies in respect of the hereditament on, through, over or under which the easement or licence is claimed by the prospective plaintiff.[4]

No limit

Consent   The court does, of course, have jurisdiction to hear an action with the parties' consent whatever the net annual value may be,[5] but not, somewhat surprisingly, if the action would have been adjourned to the Chancery Division or to the Family Division had proceedings been commenced in the High Court.[6] The County Courts Act 1984[7] expressly provides that such consent must be given in the form of a memorandum. This is known as a "jurisdiction agreement."[8] It must be signed either by the parties or by their respective solicitors, and it must state

Jurisdiction agreement

---

[1] s.147(2) of the County Courts Act 1984 states that this is to be determined by reference to the valuation list in force at the time in question. When part of the property is unrated that part will be deemed to have a net annual value for rating not exceeding that of the whole (s.147(3)(a)), but for all other purposes it will be taken to have a net annual value equal to its value by the year (s.147(3)(b)).

[2] "Hereditament" includes both corporeal (e.g. land and houses) and incorporeal (e.g. easements and rentcharges) hereditaments (s.147(1)).

[3] Administration of Justice Act 1973, Sched. 2.

[4] s.21(2)(a) of the 1984 Act. Dealing with slightly different wording, in R. v. Judge Drucquer [1939] 2 K.B. 588 it was held that under s.51(a) of the County Courts Act 1934 the court's jurisdiction was ousted if the value of the dominant or the servient tenement exceeded the limit. Similarly, in Wong v. Beaumont Property Trust Ltd. [1965] 1 Q.B. 173, Lord Denning M.R. was of the view that the court had jurisdiction so long as neither property exceeded the limit, then fixed at £400 under s.51(4) of the County Courts Act 1959 (as amended).

[5] R. v. Judge Willes, ex p. Abbey National Building Society [1954] 1 W.L.R. 136.

[6] s.18 of the 1984 Act.

[7] s.18 and also s.24 (certain equity proceedings).

[8] As defined by s.34(3).

that the county court in question shall have jurisdiction in the action.

Equity jurisdiction The current limit is fixed at £30,000.[9]

Contract or tort **Money claims** The limit is currently fixed at £5,000[10] in respect of any action founded in contract or tort where the debt, demand or damage claimed does not exceed this amount.[11] A plaintiff is entitled to abandon any excess part of his claim to enable the county court to have jurisdiction,[12] but he cannot divide his claim for the purpose of enabling two or more actions to be brought in one or more county courts.[13]

Exceeding the limit **Counterclaims** The value of a counterclaim, or a set-off and counterclaim, can exceed the county court limit provided that an application has been made for an order under section 42(1)(c) of the County Courts Act 1984 to transfer the action to the High Court, or that such an application has been made and refused.[14]

Transfer of proceedings Section 42(1) of the 1984 Act provides that at any stage in proceedings the county court may, either of its own motion or on the application of any party to the proceedings, order the transfer of the whole or any part of the proceedings to the High Court[15] if

(1) the court considers that some important question of law or fact is likely to arise; or
(2) the court considers that one or other of the parties is likely to be entitled, in respect of a claim or counterclaim, to an amount exceeding the amount recoverable in the county court; or
(3) any counterclaim, or set-off and counterclaim, of a defendant involves matters beyond the jurisdiction of the county court.[16]

High Court A similar power exists under section 40 for the High Court,

---

[9] Currently fixed by the County Courts Jurisdiction Order 1981 (S.I. 1981 No. 1123), operational from October 1, 1981. See, *e.g.* s.23(*d*) which gives the county court all the jurisdiction of the High Court to hear and determine proceedings for the specific performance or for the rectification, delivery up or cancellation of any agreement for the sale, purchase or lease of any property where, in the case of a sale or purchase the purchase money, or in the case of a lease the value of the property, does not exceed the limit. See also s.38 for the county court's general ancillary jurisdiction, *e.g.* to grant damages in lieu of specific performance (see s.50 of the Supreme Court Act 1981) or to enforce an undertaking to re-erect a fence (see *Bourne* v. *McDonald* [1950] 2 K.B. 422).
[10] See the County Courts Jurisdiction Order 1981.
[11] 1984 Act, s.15(1).
[12] *Ibid.* s.17(1).
[13] *Ibid.* s.35(1).
[14] s.43.
[15] s.41(1) also enables the High Court at any stage to transfer or retransfer proceedings to itself.
[16] s.42(2) provides that execution of the judgment of any part of the proceedings determined by the county court shall be stayed until that part transferred to the High Court has been concluded.

either of its own motion,[16a] or on the application of any party to the proceedings, to transfer the whole or any part of the proceedings to a county court if the parties consent, or the amount (or balance) of the claim is within the county court limits, or if the proceedings are suitable for determination in the county court.

In either instance the costs of the whole proceedings both before and after transfer will be in the discretion of the court to which the proceedings are then transferred, subject to any order of the court making the transfer.[17]

Normally, proceedings commenced in a county court in which that court has no jurisdiction will be transferred to the High Court.[18] Nevertheless, section 34(2) provides that where, on the application of any defendant, it appears to the court that the plaintiff, or one of the plaintiffs, knew or ought to have known that the court had no jurisdiction in the proceedings the

Striking out   court may, if it thinks fit, instead of ordering that the proceedings be transferred, order that they be struck out.

At the other end of the scale, under C.C.R. Ord. 19, r. 2, if any proceedings in which the sum claimed or amount involved does not exceed £500, the action will stand referred for

Arbitration   arbitration by the registrar upon receipt by the court of a defence to the claim.[19] The object of this procedure is to save time and costs[20] by the use of less formality.[21] Accordingly, under sub-rule 3(4), the reference may be rescinded on the application of any party, provided that the registrar can be satisfied that:

(1) a difficult question of law or a question of fact of exceptional complexity is involved; or
(2) a charge of fraud is in issue; or
(3) the parties are agreed that the dispute should be tried in court; or
(4) it could be unreasonable for the claim to proceed to arbitration having regard to its subject matter, the circumstances of the parties or the interests of any other person likely to be affected by the award.

[16a] See further *Practice Statement (Listings), The Times,* January 13, 1988: In order to reduce the backlog of cases in the Q.B.D. non-jury list, all cases will be reviewed by the judge in charge and all proceedings which do not seem likely to raise any important questions of law or fact will be transferred to the county court under s.40(1)(*d*) of the 1984 Act. Illustrative categories of retained cases include: actions where the amount in dispute exceeds £20,000, professional negligence claims, actions involving the police, or allegations of fraud or undue influence, fatal accidents, or matters of public interest and lengthy cases.

[17] See s.45(1). It should also be noted that s.45(2) expressly provides for the part heard by the High Court to be taxed on the High Court scale subject to the provisions of s.19 (limitation on recoverable costs of actions in contract or tort commenced in High Court which could have been commenced in county court (see below)).

[18] See also s.34(1).

[19] See C.C.R. Ord. 19, r. 2(3)—an amendment to increase the amount of the claim will rescind the reference (see *Linton* v. *Thermabreak* [1984] C.L.Y. 467).

[20] Under sub-rule 6 no solicitors' charges are allowed except for the cost of the summons, the costs of enforcing the award and such costs as are certified by the arbitrator to have been incurred due to unreasonable conduct of the other party.

[21] See sub-rule 9. See also *Chilton* v. *Saga Holidays* [1986] 1 All E.R. 841 (legally represented party not prevented from cross-examining unrepresented party).

Invariably this means that any action involving neighbours is heard by a judge[22] for one of the foregoing reasons.

High Court

General jurisdiction

Section 19 of the Supreme Court Act 1981 now formally governs the general jurisdiction, for all practical purposes unlimited, of the High Court. Apart from matters which have been brought by statute within the exclusive jurisdiction of the county court (*e.g.* proceedings under the Rent Act 1977) the only governing factor will be the question of costs. In this regard, sections 19(1) and 20(2) of the County Courts Act 1984 provide that where an action founded on contract or in tort which could have been commenced in the county court is commenced in the High Court, and the plaintiff fails to recover in respect of his claim an amount[23]

The costs penalty

exceeding the county court "higher" limit of £3,000, his costs will be taxed on the county court scale. If he recovers *less* than the county court "lower" limit[24] of £600, the plaintiff will be allowed no costs at all in the High Court. However, if it appears to the High Court that there was reasonable ground for supposing the amount recoverable in respect of the plaintiff's claim to be in excess of the amount recoverable in an action in the county court, then the question of costs will not be affected, for example, where

Avoiding the penalty

the plaintiff's claim is brought below the limit by a counterclaim, or where a smaller sum of money is paid into court and accepted in full and final satisfaction of the action.[25] Similarly if the High Court is satisfied that:

(1) there was sufficient reason[26] for bringing the action in the High Court; or
(2) the defendant, or one of the defendants, objected to the transfer of the action to a county court;

then it can make an order allowing the costs, or any part of the costs, on the High Court scale, or such one of the county court scales[27] as it may deem appropriate.

However, certain case law authorities[28] indicate that if the monetary claim of the plaintiff is not his substantial claim, or if he makes a claim for other substantial relief of a non-monetary nature, then the court's discretion in this respect cannot be

---

[22] Under sub-rule 2(3) the arbitration may be heard by the judge (or by an outside arbitrator) but the same provisions as to costs under sub-rule 6 still apply. As to distribution of business between judge and registrar see generally C.C.R. Ord. 50, r. 3.

[23] This includes a payment into court (*Parkes* v. *Knowles* [1957] 1 W.L.R. 1040).

[24] These "higher" and "lower" limits are currently fixed by the 1981 Order and s.20(9) of the 1984 Act. By s.19(4) these provisions do not apply to proceedings by the Crown.

[25] See, *e.g. Utal* v. *May* (1899) 15 T.L.R. 307. In this context money paid under a compromise is also treated as money "recovered" (*Colton* v. *McCaughey* [1970] 1 W.L.R. 63).

[26] *e.g.* it is not a "sufficient reason" that the plaintiff erroneously believed that a personal injury was much more serious than ultimately transpired (*Finch* v. *Telegraph Construction and Maintenance Co. Ltd.* [1949] 1 All E.R. 452).

[27] Currently these are as follows: exceeding £25 and not exceeding £100 (Lower Scale); £100 to £500 (Scale 1); £500 to £3,000 (Scale 2); exceeding £3,000 (Scale 3).

[28] *Keates* v. *Woodward* [1902] 1 K.B. 532; *Deverell* v. *Milne* [1920] 2 Ch. 52.

Injunction and damages invoked. Accordingly, where in addition to damages an injunction is obtained, High Court costs can be recovered even if only a modest sum, within foregoing county court limits, is ultimately awarded in damages.[29]

Choice of division Section 64(1) of the 1981 Act states that without prejudice to the power of transfer under section 65, the person by whom any cause or matter is commenced in the High Court shall in the **Allocation** prescribed manner allocate[30] it to whichever division he thinks fit. This right is, however, subject to the power of the court under section 65(1) to direct the transfer of those proceedings to the appropriate division. In this regard, Schedule 1, paragraph 1 provides that all causes and matters relating to, *inter alia*:

(1) the sale,[31] exchange or partition of land, or the raising of charges on land; and
(2) the rectification, setting aside or cancellation of deeds or other instruments in writing;

are assigned to the Chancery Division.

In essence, therefore, any action relating to the title of, or any rights over, land should be commenced in the Chancery Division. On the other hand, actions in nuisance or trespass are **Nuisance or trespass** usually pursued in the Queens Bench Division[32] although, if the action is likely to raise declaratory issues rather than a claim for monetary compensation, it is preferable for it to proceed in the Chancery Division. It should also be borne in mind that all **District Registries** District Registries now have equal jurisdiction in both Chancery and Queens Bench actions.[32a]

Pleadings

County court By C.C.R. Ord. 3, r. 1, all proceedings where the object is to obtain relief against any person, or to compel any **Commencement** person to do or abstain from doing any act, must be commenced by issue of a summons together with particulars of claim.[33] Sub-rule 2(2) requires every claim, whether liquidated or unliquidated, to be brought by *default* summons except where the plaintiff claims some relief other than money, in which case it should be brought by a *fixed date* summons. Both types of summons should be accompanied by particulars of claim.

Any other proceedings may be commenced by originating

---

[29] *Doherty* v. *Thompson* (1906) 94 L.T. 626; but see the opposite view in *Cooper* v. *Straker* (1888) 40 Ch.D. 21 where the court was of the view that proceedings could have been brought in the county court.
[30] It should be noted that s.64(2) expressly states that once allocated to a Division all subsequent interlocutory or other steps or proceedings in the High Court in that cause or matter should be taken in that division.
[31] See also R.S.C. Ord. 31, rr. 1–4 (sale of land by order of the court).
[32] It is to be noted that under s.1, para. 2(*b*) all applications for judicial review are assigned to Q.B.D., as are other administrative law proceedings, *e.g.* appeals under ss.243–246 of the Town & Country Planning Act 1971.
[32a] See R.S.C., Ord. 32, r. 24, Practice Note 32/23–24/3 and *Practice Direction (Trial Out of London)* [1987] 1 W.L.R. 1322 (Practice Note 34/4/6).
[33] For service of an admission, defence or counterclaim within 14 days of the summons: see C.C.R. Ord. 9, r. 1. See Appendix for Precedents of Particulars of Claim (CC1) and Reply and Defence to Counterclaim (CC9).

application[34] but in the context of this book it is highly unlikely that proceedings other than by summons will be warranted unless **Construction of** the relief sought amounts, in essence, to the construction of a **deeds** deed. A declaration relating to land may be sought in the county court, as in the High Court, without the necessity of claiming other relief, such as damages.

High Court   By R.S.C. Ord. 5, r. 2, proceedings must be **Writ** begun by writ if the plaintiff's claim is for any relief or remedy arising out of a tort other than trespass to land,[35] if the claim is based upon an allegation of fraud, if a claim is made for damages for breach of duty (whether the duty exists by virtue of a contract or of a provision made by or under an Act or independently of any such contract or provision), or if the damages consist of, or include, damages in respect of the death of or personal injuries to any person, or in respect of damage to any property.[36]

In the context of this book the use of an originating **Originating** summons[37] is only likely to be required in the following **summons** circumstances:

(1) where the sole or principal question in issue is, or is likely to be, one of the construction of an Act or of any instrument made under an Act or of any deed, will, contract or other document or some other question of law; or

(2) where there is unlikely to be any substantial dispute of fact.

Accordingly, if the plaintiff intends in those proceedings to apply for summary judgment under either R.S.C. Ord. 14 or Ord. 86 or for any other reason he considers that it would be

---

[34] C.C.R. Ord. 3, r. 4(1). For the Answer: see C.C.R. Ord. 9, r. 18. Not every originating application requires an Answer. If there is any doubt an affidavit should be filed so that the court is aware of the respondent's case.

[35] Practice Note 5/2/1 suggests that these words do not mean that an action for trespass should not be begun by writ, but that where the main question concerns the title to the land or an easement it may conveniently be tried by originating summons rather than by writ. See Appendix for Precedent of General Indorsement on Writ (HC1) and Statement of Claim (HC2).

[36] The Acknowledgment of Service must be filed within 14 days of service of the writ (R.S.C. Ord. 12, r. 5). The Defence should be served within 14 days after the Acknowledgment of Service has been returned where the Statement of Claim is indorsed upon or accompanies the writ (R.S.C. Ord. 18, r. 2(1)), otherwise 14 days after service of the Statement of Claim (sub-rule 2(2)). It should be noted that since the Statement of Claim must be served within 14 days of the Acknowledgment of Service a defendant has effectively 27 days within which to prepare the Defence if time limits are strictly adhered to.

[37] As with a writ, an Acknowledgment of Service must accompany the originating summons (unless it is made *ex parte* or for summary possession of land under R.S.C. Ord. 113). It must also be filed within 14 days of service of the originating process (R.S.C. Ord. 12, r. 9). In addition, under R.S.C. Ord. 28, r. 1A(1) the plaintiff must, before the expiration of 14 days after the defendant has acknowledged service, file the affidavit evidence upon which he intends to rely. A defendant has 28 days in which to file any affidavit evidence in reply (sub-rule 1A(4)) and the plaintiff has a further 14 days in which to file further affidavit evidence (sub-rule 1A(5)). Under R.S.C. Ord. 28, r. 7(1) the defendant may make a counterclaim in the action without having to bring separate proceedings.

more appropriate for the proceedings to be begun by writ,[38] he should so begin them.

In practice, therefore, essentially declaratory proceedings alone should be brought by originating summons, in respect of which the High Court has an unfettered jurisdiction under R.S.C. Ord. 15, r. 16.

Documents Since documents are often referred to in the pleadings of a "neighbours action" it should be borne in mind that such reference makes them *part of* the pleadings. As a result they can be looked at by the court without the need for them to be exhibited by affidavit or put formally in evidence.[39] Their disclosure may also be sought by the other side prior to discovery under C.C.R. Ord. 14, r. 4,[40] or R.S.C. Ord. 24, r. 10.[40a] This can be a useful tactical weapon by which the other side's case may be probed and tested prior to discovery, *.e.g* where the full contents of a material letter or the other party's title deeds need to be studied.[41]

Reference to documents

Tactics

Content of pleadings Particular regard should always be paid to the matters which must be pleaded specifically. R.S.C. Ord. 18, r. 8 reads in full as follows:

High Court

"(1) A party must in any pleading subsequent to a statement of claim plead specifically any matter, for example, performance, release, any relevant statute of limitation, fraud or any fact showing illegality.
   (a) which he alleges makes any claim or defence of the opposite party not maintainable; or
   (b) which, if not specifically pleaded, might take the opposite party by surprise; or
   (c) which raises issues of fact not arising out of the preceding pleading.
(2) Without prejudice to paragraph (1) a defendant to an action for the recovery of land must plead specifically every ground of defence on which he relies, and a plea that he is in

---

[38] R.S.C. Ord. 28, r. 8 also enables proceedings to be continued as if begun by writ.

[39] See *Day* v. *William Hill (Park Lane) Ltd.* [1949] 1 K.B. 632.

[40] The scope of this rule covers both pleadings and affidavits. Notice under sub-rule 10(2) is often given in the course of a Request for Further and Better Particulars but should usually be made by separate notice. This requires the respondent to respond within four days of the service of the applicant's notice stating a time within seven days of which he will produce those documents which he does not object to producing. Failure to produce the stated document can be followed up by an order of the court under R.S.C., Ord. 24, r. 11(1) of necessary documents (see also Ord. 24, r. 13(1)). In *Rafidain Bank* v. *Agom Universal Sugar Trading Co. Ltd.* [1987] 1 W.L.R. 1606 the Court of Appeal held that discovery would be ordered under Ord. 24, r. 11(1) notwithstanding that the documents were not within the possession, custody or power of the person against whom the order was sought but that factor could be taken into account when considering whether to exercise the courts discretion in favour of the applicant.

[40a] Under R.S.C. Ord. 24, r. 11A(1) any party who is entitled to inspect any documents under Ord. 24 may, at or before the time fixed for inspection, give notice requiring a true copy of any such document capable of being copied by photographic or similar process.

[41] In the case of title deeds, the rule preventing production by any person other than a party to the proceedings was abolished by Civil Evidence Act 1968, s.16(1)(*b*).

possession of the land by himself or his tenant is not sufficient.

(3) A claim for exemplary damages must be specifically pleaded together with the facts on which the party pleading relies.

(4) A party must plead specifically any claim for interest under section 35A of the Act or otherwise."

County court   Whilst the application of the County Court Rules is, generally, less strict[42] it should still be borne in mind, if only as a matter of good practice, that under section 76 of the County Court Act 1984 the general principles of practice in the High Court may be adopted and applied to proceedings in a county court.

Defence   It is often tempting when drafting a defence either to put the plaintiff strictly to proof of his case or to preserve the defendant's position as much as possible by advancing a general
Difficulties at trial   denial of liability. However, this approach can lead to difficulties at trial if an affirmative case is then advanced. As Lord Evershed M.R. pointed out in the case of *Regina Fur Co. Ltd.* v. *Bossom*[43]:

> "I think a defendant—whether he is an underwriter or any other kind of defendant—is entitled to say, by way of defence, 'I require this case to be strictly proved, and admit nothing.' Where such is the defence, the onus remains throughout upon the plaintiffs to establish the case they are alleging. Where such is the form of pleading, it is not only obligatory upon the defendants but it is not even permissible for them to proceed to put forward some affirmative case which they had not pleaded or alleged; and it is not therefore right that they should, by cross-examination of the plaintiffs
> **Regina Fur Co.**   or otherwise, suggest such an affirmative case. The
> **Ltd. v. Bossom**   defendants are acting correctly if they follow the course adopted in this case—that is, so to challenge at each point, and by proper evidence, where it is admissible, and by cross-examination, the case which the plaintiffs seek to make good.
>
> The result, where such is the form of defence and of the issues raised, is no doubt such that the Judges will watch

---

[42] But see C.C.R. Ord. 6, r. 1A requiring a claim for interest under s.69 of the 1984 Act to be pleaded specifically. Sub-rules 3 and 4 require, in the case of actions for the recovery of land and for injunctions or declarations relating to land, that the particulars of claim should contain the following:
> (a) the land sought to be recovered;
> (b) the net annual value of the land for rating or, if the land does not consist of one or more hereditaments having at the time when the action is commenced a separate net annual value for rating—
> > (i) the net annual value of that hereditament where the land forms part of a hereditament having a net value for rating not exceeding the county court limit under s.21 of the Act, or
> > (ii) in any other case, the value of the land by the year.
> (c) the rent, if any, of the land;
> (d) the ground on which possession is claimed, and
> (e) in a case to which s.138 of the Act applies, the daily rate at which the rent in arrear is to be calculated.

[43] [1958] 2 Lloyd's Rep. 428.

carefully that defendants, first, do not attempt, by evidence or cross-examination, to establish some affirmative case of which no proper notice has been given by way of pleading to the other side; and second, do not attempt to lead evidence solely directed to the credit of witnesses."

Such an approach is often taken because of the rule that a defendant cannot be ordered to give particulars of a mere denial.[44] However, R.S.C. Ord. 18, r. 12(3)[45] provides that "the court may order a party to serve on any other party particulars of any claim, defence or other matter stated in his pleadings, or in any affidavit of his ordered to stand as a pleading, or a statement of the nature of the case on which he relies." Accordingly, such **"Opening up"** denials are capable of being "opened up" to ensure that the trial is conducted fairly, openly and without surprises, and to reduce costs.[46] The extent of such "opening up" will depend upon the form of the traverse. Certainly it is now well recognised that if the denial relates to a negative statement in the claim or is, in itself, a denial "pregnant with affirmation" so that it really sets up an affirmative case, further particulars can be ordered.[47]

Further and better particulars   In addition, under R.S.C. Ord. 18, r. 12(2),[48] one party is, of course, entitled to particulars of any averment in the other party's pleading. However, the **Scope** scope of this procedure is often misunderstood; for the court can only order particulars to be given of material facts relied upon[49] and not where a party, in effect, seeks advance disclosure of evidence.[50] The dividing line between what amounts to fact as opposed to evidence is not always easy to define. If any doubt exists, then as a matter of procedure it is better to decline to answer with the simple averment "not entitled," rather than divulge too much of the client's case.[50a] If the applicant still seeks such particulars, the matter can then be dealt with at the summons for directions. Such a review will not delay the general prosecution of the action; for under R.S.C. Ord. 18, r. 20(1)[51] pleadings in an action are deemed to be closed at the expiration of 14 days after service of the reply, or if there is no reply but only a defence to counterclaim, at the expiration of 14 days after service of the defence, notwithstanding that any request or order for

---

[44] This rests on the common sense basis that there is nothing which the defendant can particularise (see *Pinson* v. *Lloyds and National Provincial Foreign Bank Ltd.* [1941] 2 K.B. 72 at 85, *per* Stable J.).

[45] See C.C.R. Ord. 9, r. 1(2) for comparable county court procedure.

[46] See further Practice Note 18/12/2.

[47] *Pinson* v. *Lloyds* (above) at 80, *per* Goddard L.C.J.

[48] See C.C.R. Ord. 6, r. 7 for county court procedure.

[49] See further Practice Notes 18/7/3 and 18/7/4.

[50] See *Philipps* v. *Philipps* (1878) 4 Q.B.D. 127; *Re Dependable Upholstery Ltd.* [1936] 3 All E.R. 741.

[50a] See Appendix for Precedent of Further And Better Particulars (CC8).

[51] Under the County Court Rules no provision is made for the service of a reply or defence to counterclaim. If these pleadings are required they are dealt with at the pre-trial review under C.C.R. Ord. 17, r. 1. Pleadings are therefore deemed to be closed after the service of the defence. See Appendix for Precedent of Reply and Defence to Counterclaim (CC9).

further and better particulars has been made but has not been complied with at that time.[52]

Application to strike out   Continuing failure to serve further and better particulars will invariably lead to an application to strike out the other side's pleading in default of service.[53]

Interlocutory proceedings

Affidavits   Due to increasing judicial complaint in recent years about both the content and, more particularly the layout[54] and making, of affidavits, the following matters should be borne in mind.

R.S.C. Ord. 41, r. 1 states as follows[54a]:

"(1) Subject to paragraphs (2) and (3) every affidavit sworn in a cause or matter must be entitled in that cause or matter.

(2) When a cause or matter is entitled in more than one matter, it shall be sufficient to state the first matter followed by the words 'and other matters,' and where a cause or matter is entitled in a matter or matters and between parties, that part of the title which consists of the matter or matters may be omitted.

Form   (3) Where there are more plaintiffs than one, it shall be sufficient to state the full name of the first followed by the words 'and others,' and similarly with respect to defendants.

(4) Every affidavit must be expressed in the first person and, unless the court otherwise directs, must state the place of residence of the deponent and his occupation or, if he has none, his description, and if he is, or is employed by, a party to the cause or matter in which the affidavit is sworn, the affidavit must state that fact.

In the case of a deponent who is giving evidence in a professional, business or other occupational capacity the affidavit may, instead of stating the deponent's place of residence, state the address at which he works, the position he holds and the name of his firm or employer, if any.

(5) Every affidavit must be in book form, following continuously from page to page, both sides of the paper being used.

---

[52] See R.S.C. Ord. 18, r. 20(2).

[53] See generally R.S.C. Ord. 18, r. 19 and C.C.R. Ord. 13, r. 5.

[54] See Appendix for layout (CC3).

[54a] The comparable provision in the county court, C.C.R. Ord. 20, r. 10(1) reads: "Subject to the following paragraphs of this rule, the provision of the R.S.C. with respect to:—

  (a)   the forms and contents of an affidavit;

  (b)   the making of an affidavit by two or more deponents or by a blind or illiterate deponent;

  (c)   the use of any affidavit which contains an interlineation, erasure or other alteration or is otherwise defective;

  (d)   the striking out of any matter which is scandalous, irrelevant or otherwise oppressive;

  (e)   the insufficiency of an affidavit sworn before any agent, partner or clerk of a party's solicitor; and

  (f)   the making and marking of exhibits to an affidavit,

        shall apply in relation to an affidavit for use in a county court as they apply in relation to an affidavit for use in the High Court."

(6) Every affidavit must be divided into paragraphs numbered consecutively, each paragraph being as far as possible confined to a distinct portion of the subject.

(7) Dates, sums and other numbers must be expressed in an affidavit in figures and not in words.

(8) Every affidavit must be signed by the deponent and the jurat must be completed and signed by the person before whom it is sworn.''

R.S.C. Ord. 66, r. 1 requires the affidavit to be on A4 ISO[55] paper of durable quality, having a margin not less than one and a half inches wide, to be left blank on the left side of the face of the paper and on the right side of the reverse. The contents must be in black ink, though they may be printed, written or typed otherwise than by means of a carbon.[56]

Contents
R.S.C. Ord. 41, r. 5(1) states that an affidavit may contain only such facts as the deponent is able of his own knowledge to prove, but sub-rule 5(2) does enable an affidavit sworn for the purpose of being used in interlocutory proceedings to contain statements of information or belief, provided that the sources and grounds thereof are also given. In practice such sources are frequently not stated, but this does not preclude the other side from objecting, and if the objection is one of substance, the court is bound to pay regard to it.[57]

Any affidavit, exhibit or bundle of documents which does not comply with R.S.C. Ord. 41 and the Lord Chief Justice's Practice Direction dated July 21, 1983[58] as to markings and **Rejection of** exhibits may now be rejected by the court, or made the subject of **affidavits** an order for costs. The full terms of the Practice Direction are set out below.

"Affidavits

Marking
1. At the top right hand corner of the first page of every affidavit, and also on the backsheet, there must be written in clear permanent dark blue or black marking:
    (i) the party on whose behalf it is filed;
    (ii) the initials and surname of the deponent;
    (iii) the number of the affidavit in relation to the deponent; and
    (iv) the date when sworn. *For example*: 2nd Dft: E.W. Jones: 3rd: 24.7.82.

Binding
2. Affidavits must not be bound with thick plastic strips or anything else which would hamper filing.

---

[55] The term "A4 ISO" refers to the size of paper specified by the International Standards Organisation.

[56] See R.S.C. Ord. 66, r. 2(1).

[57] See *Re Birrell (Anthony) & Co.* [1899] 2 Ch. 50. In the county court the rule is generally more relaxed. Under C.C.R. Ord. 20, r. 10(4), unless the court otherwise orders, *any* affidavit may be used notwithstanding that it contains statements of information or belief. See Appendix for specimen affidavit supporting application for interlocutory injunction (CC3).

[58] [1983] 1 W.L.R. 922.

Exhibits

Markings generally

3. Where space allows, the directions under para. 1 above to the first page of every exhibit.

Documents other than letters

4. (i) Clearly legible photographic copies of original documents may be exhibited instead of the originals provided the originals are made available for inspection by the other parties before the hearing and by the judge at the hearing.

(ii) Any document which the court is being asked to construe or enforce, or the trusts of which it is being asked to vary, should be separately exhibited, and should not be included in a bundle with other documents. Any such document should bear the exhibit mark directly, and not on a flysheet attached to it.

(iii) Court documents, such as Probates, Letters of Administration, Orders, Affidavits or Pleadings, should never be exhibited. Office copies of such documents prove themselves.

(iv) Where a number of documents are contained in one exhibit, a front page must be attached, setting out a list of the documents, with dates, which the exhibit contains, and the bundle must be securely fastened. The traditional method of securing is by tape, with the knot sealed (under the modern practice) by means of wafers; but any means of securing the bundle (except by staples) is acceptable, provided that it does not interfere with the perusal of the documents and it cannot readily be undone.

(v) This direction does not affect the current practice in relation to scripts in Probate matters, or to an affidavit of due execution of a will.

Letters

5. (i) Copies of individual letters should not be made separate exhibits, but they should be collected together and exhibited in a bundle or bundles. The letters must be arranged in correct sequence with the earliest at the top, and properly paged in accordance with para. 6 below. They must be firmly secured together in the manner indicated in para. 4 above.

(ii) When original letters, or original letters and copies of replies, are exhibited as one bundle, the exhibit must have a front page attached, stating that the bundle consists of so many original letters and so many copies. As before, the letters and copies must be arranged in correct sequence and properly paged.

Paging of documentary exhibits

6. Any exhibit containing several pages must be paged consecutively at centre bottom.

Copies of documents generally

7. It is the responsibility of the solicitor by whom any affidvait is filed to ensure that every page of every exhibit is fully and easily legible. In many cases photocopies of documents, particularly of telex messages, are not. In all cases of difficulty, typed copies of the illegible document (paged with 'a' numbers) should be included.

Exhibits bound up with affidavit

8. Exhibits must not be bound up with or otherwise attached to the affidavit itself.

Exhibits other than documents

9. The principles are as follows.

(i) The exhibit must be clearly marked with the exhibit mark in such a manner that there is no likelihood of the contents being separated; and

(ii) Where the exhibit itself consists of more than one item (*e.g.* a cassette in a plastic box), each and every separate part of the exhibit must similarly be separately marked with at least enough of the usual exhibit mark to ensure precise identification.

This is particularly important in cases where there are a number of similar exhibits which fall to be compared. According:

(*a*) The formal exhibit should, so far as practicable, be written on the article itself in an appropriate manner (*e.g.* many fabrics can be directly marked with an indelible pen), or, if this is not possible, on a separate slip which is securely attached to the article in such a manner that it is not easily removable. (N.B. Items attached by Sellotape or similar means are readily removable.) If the article is then enclosed in a container, the number of the exhibit should readily appear on the outside of the container unless it is transparent and the number is readily visible.

Alternatively, the formal exhibit marking may be written on the container, or, if this is not possible, on a separate slip securely attached to the container. If this is done, then either:

(i) the number of the exhibit and, if there is room, the short name and number of the case, the name of the deponent and the date of affidavit must be written on the exhibit itself and on each separate part thereof; or

(ii) all these particulars must appear on a slip securely attached to the article itself and to each separate part thereof.

(*b*) If the article, or part of the article, is too small to be marked in accordance with the foregoing provisions, it must be enclosed in a sealed transparent container of such a nature that it could not be reconstituted once opened and the relevant slip containing the exhibit mark must be inserted in such container so as to be plainly visible. An enlarged photograph or photographs showing the relevant characteristics of each such exhibit will usually be required to be separately exhibited.

Numbering

10. Where a deponent deposes to more than one affidavit to which there are exhibits in any one matter, the numbering of such exhibits should run consecutively throughout, and not begin again with each affidavit.

Reference to documents already forming part of an exhibit

11. Where a deponent wishes to refer to a document already exhibited to some other deponent's affidavit, he should not also exhibit it to his own affidavit.

Multiplicity of documents

12. Where, by the time of the hearing, exhibits or affidavits have become numerous, they should be put in a consolidated bundle, or file or files, and be paged consecutively throughout in the top right hand corner, affidavits and exhibits being in separate bundles of files.

Bundles of documents generally

13. The directions under 5, 6 and 7 above apply to all bundles of documents. Accordingly they must be:

(i) firmly secured together;

(ii) arranged in chronological order, beginning with the earliest;

(iii) paged consecutively at centre bottom; and

(iv) fully and easily legible.

14. Transcripts of judgments and evidence must not be bound up with any other documents, but must be kept separate.

15. In cases for trial where the parties will seek to place before the trial

judge bundles of documents (apart from pleadings) comprising more than 100 pages, it is the responsibility of the solicitors for all parties to prepare and agree one single additional bundle containing the principal documents to which the parties will refer (including in particular the documents referred to in the pleadings) and to lodge such bundle with the court at least two working days before the date fixed for the hearing."

Injunctions   These are considered later in this chapter, at page 171.

Inspection   Normally the other side will allow facilities to a surveyor or other nominated representative to inspect and take photographs of the land in question on the giving of reasonable notice.[59] Sometimes, however, steps will need to be taken to accelerate the arrangement of such an inspection where, for example, there is likely to be an alteration in the relevant ground conditions or where the opposing party is being obdurate by

Proposition   refusing permission to inspect. It is suggested that in such circumstances the court can order that party to allow facilities for inspection in the exercise of its powers under R.S.C. Ord. 29, r. 3(1).[60] This states that:

> "where it considers it necessary or expedient for the purpose of obtaining full information or evidence in any cause or matter, the court may, on the application of a party to the cause or matter, and on such terms, if any, as it thinks just, by order authorise or require any sample to be taken of any property which is the subject-matter of the cause or matter or as to which any question may arise therein, any observation to be made on such property or any experiment to be tried on or with such property."

Authority   In *Colls* v. *Home & Colonial Stores*,[61] the only authority on this point, Lord Macnaghten referred in passing to the benefits of calling in an expert surveyor to report, in that case, on the degree of diminution which the plaintiff's ancient rights had undergone so that the court had such a report for its own guidance.[62] Since most expert evidence will, to some extent, assist the court, there cannot be anything untoward in the making of such an order. Indeed, by analogy, if it is permissible to allow a party to take photographs of documents in the possession of the other party,[63] then it is equally appropriate for such powers to be exercised in relation to inspecting or photographing land.

Interrogatories   These are a means by which to elicit the other side's evidence in advance of the trial. Unlike a request for

---

[59] Failing an exchange of solicitors' letters, matters can usually be dealt with at the Summons for Directions.

[60] See C.C.R. Ord. 13, r. 7(1)(*e*) for the equivalent power in the county court.

[61] [1904] A.C. 179 at 192.

[62] See also *Abbott* v. *Holloway* [1904] W.N. 124 where, after personal inspection by the judge, a consent order was made referring the matter to an independent surveyor to report.

[63] See *Lewis* v. *Earl of Londesborough* [1893] 2 Q.B. 191 dealing with the equivalent provision under the former Rules of the Supreme Court.

further and better particulars,[64] which is meant to identify the
issues in the case, interrogatories are designed to secure
admissions so as to ease the burden of proving the case.[65] Under
Procedure R.S.C. Ord. 26, r. 1, the necessary application is made to the
master by summons, or by notice under the summons for
directions. A copy of the proposed interrogatories must be
attached to the summons. The respondent is required to answer
on affidavit.

Scope The right to interrogate is not limited to the facts directly in
issue but may extend to any facts, the existence or non-existence
of which is relevant to the existence or non-existence of the facts
directly in issue.[66] It has also been said that answers to
interrogatories need not be conclusive as to the question in issue.
It is enough if they have some bearing upon it and may form a
step in establishing liability.[67] In essence, therefore,
interrogatories will be admissible if it can be established that they
either go to support the applicant's case, or to impeach or destroy
the opponent's case.[68]

Limitations On the other hand, "fishing interrogatories" will not be
allowed, for example, interrogatories to establish a cause of action
against a third party,[69] to obtain evidence for use in subsequent
proceedings[70] or to prove a cause of action or a defence not yet
pleaded.[71] Equally, they will not be allowed if they are thought to
be oppressive, for example, if they seek to obtain admissions of
all the statements in the applicant's pleadings,[72] if they do not
precisely formulate the question asked[73] or if they seek the names
of witnesses.[74] In this last respect, Practice Note 26/1/6 suggests
that questions as to the names of persons in whose presence an
event took place will not generally be allowed[75]; but questions
asking to whom a consent was given are proper, as are questions
asking with whom an oral contract was made or to whom goods
were resold, and even questions about the addresses of such
persons will be permissible[76] because in such cases the answers
identify the parties to an alleged act or transaction.

Disallowance Interrogatories will be disallowed if their object is to seek the
admission of a fact solely within the knowledge of the party
applying,[77] of a fact which can be proved by a witness who will in

---

[64] It shall be noted that the court will not sanction an attempt to serve
interrogatories under the guise of a Request for Particulars (see *G & W Young
& Co. Ltd.* v. *Swedish Union & National Insurance Co., Same* v. *North Bristol &
Mercantile Insurance Co.* (1907) 24 T.L.R. 73).
[65] *Att–Gen.* v. *Gaskill* (1882) 22 Ch.D. 537.
[66] *Marriott* v. *Chamberlain* (1886) 17 Q.B.D. 154 at 163; *Nash* v. *Layton* [1911] 2
Ch. 71.
[67] *Blair* v. *Haydock Cable Co.* (1917) 34 T.L.R. 39.
[68] *Plymouth Mutual Co-Op Society* v. *Traders Publishing Association* [1906] 1 K.B.
403 at 416–417.
[69] *e.g. Sebright* v. *Hanbury* (1916) 2 Ch.D. 245 (whether the defendant was acting
as an agent for an undisclosed principal).
[70] *Lovell* v. *Lovell* [1970] 1 W.L.R. 1451.
[71] *Hennessy* v. *Wright (No. 2)* (1890) 24 Q.B.D. 445 at 448.
[72] *Heaton* v. *Goldney* [1910] 1 K.B. 754 at 759.
[73] *Oppenheim* v. *Sheffield* [1893] 1 Q.B. 5.
[74] *Knapp* v. *Harvey* [1911] 2 K.B. 725 at 732.
[75] Citing *Eade* v. *Jacobs* (1877) 3 Ex.D. 335.
[76] Citing *Marriott* v. *Chamberlain* (1886) 17 Q.B.D. 154; *Nash* v. *Layton* [1911] 2
Ch. 71; *Osram Lamp Works* v. *Gabriel Lamp Co.* [1914] 2 Ch. 129.
[77] *Maskell* v. *Metropolitan Railway Co.* (1890) 7 T.L.R. 49.

any case be called at trial,[78] if it is plain that no admission can be obtained, or if they relate to a matter of opinion.[79]

In the context of this work, the following interrogatories[79a] would be admissible:

Examples

(1) As to the substance, but not the details and words, of conversations during which agreements are made or consents given.[80]

(2) As to questions which might have been asked by way of a request for particulars.[81]

(3) As to the system of keeping noise to claimed levels in a nuisance action.[82]

(4) As to the covenants in a lost document.[83]

(5) As to whether a party wrote a particular document.[84]

Corporate bodies

Where the interrogated party is, for example, a company, the court will decide which member or officer is most likely to be able to answer the interrogatories satisfactorily.[85] In cases of doubt, the order will be in terms that the answers will be by "the Secretary or other proper officer of the company."[86]

Insufficient answer

R.S.C. Ord. 26, r. 5 enables the applicant to apply for an order requiring the interrogated party to make a further answer, either by affidavit or on oral examination as the court may direct.

Non-compliance

Failure to comply with an order under rules 1 or 5 may lead to the action being dismissed or the defence struck out and judgment entered.[87]

R.S.C. Ord. 26, r. 7 states as follows:

"A party may put in evidence at the trial of a cause or matter, or of any issue therein, some only of the answers to interrogatories, or part only of such an answer, without putting in evidence the other answers or, as the case may be, the whole of that answer, but the court may look at the whole of the answers and if opinion that any other answer or other part of an answer is so connected with an answer or part thereof used in evidence that the one ought not to be so

---

[78] See Practice Note 26/1/4; but it will not apply if the admission shifts the onus of proof or to avoid calling unnecessary witnesses (see *Lyell* v. *Kennedy* (1883) 8 App.Cas. 217 at 228).

[79] *e.g.* if he has to consult an expert (see *Rofe* v. *Kevorokian* [1936] 2 All E.R. 1334).

[79a] See also Appendix for Precedents of Request for and Answer to Interrogatories (HC14, HC15 and HC16).

[80] *Eade* v. *Jacobs* (1877) 3 Ex.D. 335 at 337; *Att.–Gen.* v. *Gaskill* (1882) 20 Ch.D. 519 at 527, 529.

[81] *e.g. Bidder* v. *Bridges* (1885) 29 Ch.D. 29 (whether a beerhouse and cottages had any land appurtenant thereto as the plaintiff had failed to plead that they had, and the defendant applicant had pleaded that they had not).

[82] See the First Pearson Commission Report, para. 363.

[83] See Practice Note 26/1/12 and *Herschfeld* v. *Clarke* (1856) 11 Exch. 712.

[84] *e.g. Dalrymple* v. *Leslie* (1881) 8 Q.B.D. 5: the interrogated party is entitled to see the relevant document before answering.

[85] See R.S.C. Ord. 26, r. 2 and *Berkeley* v. *Standard Discount Co.* (1879) 13 Ch.D. 97.

[86] *Chaddock* v. *British South Africa Co.* [1896] 2 Q.B. 153; *Att.–Gen.* v. *North Metropolitan Tramways Co.* [1892] 3 Ch. 70.

[87] By R.S.C. Ord. 6, r. 3 service on a party's solicitor of an order to answer interrogatories will be sufficient service to found an application for committal of the party disobeying the order, but the party may show in answer to the application that he had no notice or knowledge of that order.

used without the other, the court may direct that that other answer or part shall be put in evidence."

Those answers to the interrogatories which are put in will form part of the general body of evidence in the case. However, the party who puts them in is not bound to accept their truthfulness, and may call other evidence to contradict them.[88]

County Court   The comparable county court provision is under C.C.R. Ord. 14, r. 11, which follows, almost exactly, procedure in the High Court.

Notices to admit and produce   Under R.S.C. Ord. 27, r. 2(1), any party, no later than 21 days after the action has been set

Procedure   down for trial, may serve a notice calling on any other party to admit any specific fact or facts, or such part of the case as is specified in the notice. If the party upon whom such a notice has been served refuses or neglects to admit the specific fact or facts within seven days after service of the notice, or such further time as may be allowed by the court, then the costs of proving the fact or facts or part of the case in question must be paid by the party so neglecting or refusing unless the court orders otherwise.[89] A party may withdraw or amend any admission of fact with leave on such terms as may be just.[90] It has been suggested[91] that there is no reason why a statement of claim so framed (*i.e.* particularised in accordance with the rules) should not be accompanied by, or typed upon, a form incorporating a notice to admit facts.

Apart from the cost factor, it is, of course, open to any party to apply[92] under R.S.C. Ord. 27, r. 3 for leave to enter judgment

Judgment on   on those admissions without waiting for the remainder of the
admissions   action to be determined. Provided they are clear, such admissions need not be expressly[93] made, and can be relied upon whether they are made in a pleading, or in a letter, or even orally if they can be proved.[94] Subject to the foregoing, such a procedure can be used as an alternative to R.S.C. Ord. 14 where, for example, the defendant admits the claim but pleads a counterclaim.[95] The service of a notice to admit facts will not, however, preclude the delivery of interrogatories for the same purpose.[96]

In the county court, C.C.R. Ord. 20, r. 2(1) requires the notice to be served no later than 14 days before trial or hearing, and the counter-notice to be served within seven days after service of the notice.

Under R.S.C. Ord. 27, r. 5(1), and again after the action has been set down for trial, any party may call upon any other

---

[88] *Endeavour Wines Ltd.* v. *Martin & Martin* (1948) 92 S.J. 574.
[89] R.S.C. Ord. 62, r. 3(5).
[90] R.S.C. Ord. 27, r. 2(2).
[91] See Pearson Committee Report, para. 256.
[92] In the Ch.D. the application will be made on motion for judgment unless the defendant consents to the application being made by summons. In the Q.B.D. the application may be made by summons (*e.g.* on the directions hearing).
[93] See *Ellis* v. *Allen* [1914] 1 Ch. 904; *Ash* v. *Hutchinson & Co. (Publishers)* [1936] Ch. 489 at 503 and *Technistudy* v. *Kelland* [1976] 1 W.L.R. 1042.
[94] See Practice Note 27/3/2 and *Re Beeney* [1894] 1 Ch. 499.
[95] In such circumstances there will be a stay of execution pending trial (see *Showell* v. *Bouron* (1883) 52 L.J.Q.B. 284; *The Mersey Steamship.* v. *Shuttleworth* (1883) 11 Q.B.D. 531.
[96] See *Hellier* v. *Ellis* [1884] 9 W.N. 9.

Admission of documents party to admit any document specified in the notice. If the other party wishes to challenge the authenticity of the document he must, within 21 days after service of the notice, give notice himself that he does not admit the document and requires it to be proved at trial. If no such notice is given under sub-rule 5(2) he will be deemed, under sub-rule 5(3), to have admitted the document unless the court orders otherwise.

County court In the county court the comparable provision is C.C.R. Ord. 20, r. 3. Such a notice must be served no later than 14 days before the trial or hearing. Under sub-rule 3(2), counter-notice must be served within seven days after service of the notice. No form of admission is prescribed by the Rules.

Benefit The benefit of such an admission is that the authenticity of the document in question need not be proved by the calling of its maker. The strictures of the rules of evidence governing such **Presumption of** matters are, in any event, mitigated by the presumption in the **genuineness** High Court that documents disclosed on discovery are genuine.[97] Equally, documents produced from proper custody can be admitted in evidence and, if ancient documents, will prove themselves.[98]

The effect of a notice to produce under C.C.R. Ord. 20, r. 4(4), or of a notice disputing authenticity under R.S.C. Ord. 27, r. 4(2), is that the original document must be shown to the applicant named in it.[99] This may be material where evidence **Forgery or** of forgery or alteration is raised, although the matter will usually **alteration** have been considered in advance under the court's powers of inspection, already discussed above.

Specific discovery Allied to the issue of producing documents specified in the other party's list is the question of how documents not so listed can be brought to light. If one party suspects non-disclosure, he should certainly insist upon discovery **Discovery on** being made on affidavit, rather than by list.[1] In addition, an **affidavit** application can, of course, be made for specific discovery under R.S.C. Ord. 24, r. 7.[2] Such an application will be of particular benefit where, for example, the other side has failed to produce all the documents relevant or necessary to establish their claim in damages. Insisting on an affidavit, once again, can assist on the issue of credibility at trial.

Interlocutory injunctions

High Court Practice Note 29/1/2 explains the general principles as follows:

General principles "The basic purpose of the grant of an interlocutory

---

[97] See R.S.C. Ord. 27, r. 4(1) as applied to the county court under s.76 of the 1984 Act.
[98] See C.C.R. Ord. 20, r. 11; Evidence Act 1938, s.4 and pp. 11–12 above.
[99] See also R.S.C. Ord. 24, rr. 9 and 11; C.C.R. Ord. 14, rr.3 and 5 for inspection and production of documents upon discovery.
[1] See R.S.C. Ord. 24, r. 3(1) and C.C.R. Ord. 14, r. 1(1)—the affidavit verifies the list.
[2] See also C.C.R. Ord. 14, r. 8.

injunction is to preserve the status quo until the rights of the parties have been determined in the action."

The grant of an interlocutory injunction is a remedy that is both temporary and discretionary, and in exercising its discretion whether or not to grant such an injunction, the court is not justified in embarking upon anything resembling a trial of the action upon conflicting affidavits in order to evaluate the strength of either party's case. It is sufficient to show that there is a serious question to be tried. Unless the material available to the court shows that the plaintiff has no real prospect of succeeding in his claim at the trial, or the court is satisfied that the claim is "frivolous or vexatious," the court must go on to consider whether the balance of convenience lies in favour of granting or refusing the interlocutory relief sought. The governing principle is that if the recoverable damages would be an adequate remedy, no interlocutory injunction should normally be granted however strong the plaintiff's claim appears to be at the interlocutory stage. Equally if the recoverable damages under the plaintiff's undertaking as to damages would be an adequate remedy for the defendant, and the plaintiff is in a financial position to pay them, then there is no reason to refuse the plaintiff an interlocutory injunction. Where other factors appear to be evenly balanced, the prudent course for the Court is to preserve the status quo.[2a] The phrase "frivolous or vexatious" case should be read in a different sense from its meaning in relation to striking out under R.S.C. Ord. 18, r. 19, and as resembling the phrases "a serious question to be tried" and "a real prospect of succeeding."[3]

Landowners   In the particular case of a plaintiff landowner unless the defendant can show that he has an arguable claim to a right of entry then the plaintiff will be entitled to an interlocutory injunction to restrain a trespass on his land even if he suffers no harm.[3a]

Application   An application for the grant of an injunction can, of course, be made before or after the trial of any cause or matter, whether or not a claim for an injunction was included in that party's writ, originating summons, counterclaim or this third-party notice.[4]

Undertaking as to damages   It is a prerequisite to the granting of an interlocutory injunction that the plaintiff give an undertaking as to damages. This is usually done through his counsel.[5] The rationale for this practice is that if it is established at trial that the defendant has been unjustly restrained, he is then entitled to damages for the loss he has sustained during the currency of the injunction.

In exceptional cases the undertaking may be dispensed with,

[2a] See *American Cyanamid Co.* v. *Ethicon Ltd.* [1975] A.C. 396.
[3] See *Mothercare Ltd.* v. *Robson Books Ltd.* [1979] F.S.R. 466; [1979] C.L.Y. 2698.
[3a] See *Patel* v. *Smith (W.H.) (Eziot)* [1987] 1 W.L.R. 853, C.A..
[4] See R.S.C. Ord. 29, r. 1(1). See Appendix for following Precedents: HC3—Intended Affidavit for *Ex Parte* Injunction Before Issue of Writ; HC4—Draft Minute of Order (*Ex Parte*); HC5—Summons To Continue *Ex Parte* Order; HC6—Summons for Interlocutory Injunction; CC3—General Layout for Affidavit.
[5] See *Manchester & Liverpool. Banking Co.* v. *Parkinson* (1889) 60 L.T. 47 (such a procedure necessary on behalf of a limited company), but a local authority may give the undertaking itself (*East Molesey Local Board* v. *Lambeth Waterworks Co.* [1892] 3 Ch. 389).

for example, where the applicant is the Crown.[6] Whilst the court has no jurisdiction to compel a plaintiff to give such an undertaking, his application is likely to fail unless he does give

Condition of grant one. As a condition of granting the injunction the court may also require a sum of money to be paid into court to "fortify the undertaking"[7] if there is any doubt concerning, for example, the plaintiff's solvency,[8] or if he is outside the jurisdiction.[9] In general, however, questions of financial stability (*e.g.* where one party is legally aided) should not affect the value of an undertaking or cross-undertaking in the context of when the court considers whether it is in the essential justice of the case that an injunction should be granted.[10]

Provision is made under R.S.C. Ord. 29, r. 1 for *ex parte* applications in the following terms:

Ex parte applications
"(1) Where the applicant is the plaintiff and the case is one of urgency such application may be made *ex parte* on affidavit but, except as aforesaid, such application must be made by motion or summons.

(2) The plaintiff may not make such an application before the issue of the writ or originating summons by which the cause or matter is to be begun except where the case is one of urgency, and in that case the injunction applied for may be granted on terms providing for the use of the writ or summons and such other terms, if any, as the court thinks fit."

It follows that the application should be made promptly and **Real urgency** only in cases of "real urgency where there has been a true impossibility of giving notice."[11] Frequently, all that the plaintiff will be able to produce to the court is a sworn affidavit and draft order since at this stage speed is likely to be of the essence.[12] Since procedure at the hearing is in the discretion of the judge,

---

[6] See *Att.–Gen. Albany Hotel Co.* [1896] 2 Ch. 696; *Hoffman-La Roche AG* v. *Secretary of State for Trade & Industry* [1975] A.C. 295. Since *Practice Direction* (1974) 2 All E.R. 400 the undertaking has been abolished in matrimonial proceedings in both the High Court and the county court unless it is specifically required in property matters, *e.g.* under s.17 of the Married Womens Property Act 1882.

[7] *Baxter* v. *Claydon* [1952] W.N. 376 (sum paid in to account in the joint names of the parties' solicitors).

[8] This power is separate from a claim for security for costs under R.S.C. Ord. 23, r. 1. However, it should also be borne in mind that insolvency or poverty is equally no ground in itself for giving security for costs, even though the plaintiff may be an undischarged bankrupt, but not if he is a nominal plaintiff, *i.e.* a person who does not have a good cause of action but allows his name to be used by someone else as opposed to someone suing in a representative capacity (sub-rule 1(*b*)).

[9] *Harman Pictures NV* v. *Osborne* [1967] 1 W.L.R. 723.

[10] See *Allen* v. *Jambo Holdings Ltd.* [1980] 1 W.L.R. 1252.

[11] See *Bates* v. *Lord Hailsham of St. Marylebone* [1972] 3 All E.R. 1019 at 1025, *per* Megarry J. and Practice Note 29/1/13.

[12] Where an undertaking is given to the court to issue the writ "forthwith" or "as soon as practicable" this must be done properly and expeditiously by the plaintiff's solicitor; otherwise it will, prima facie, be a grave breach of his duty to the Court (see *Refson (P.S.) & Co. Ltd.* v. *Saggers* [1984] 1 W.L.R. 1025). See Appendix for Precedents HC3, HC4 and HC5.

evidence can, if required, be given on oath. During normal court hours, application for a hearing will need to be made through the listing officer. Outside these hours, a duty judge system is operated in the High Court and by some county courts.[13] Where no judge[14] is available locally, it will be necessary to apply to the duty judge in London. Upon the giving of appropriate undertakings[15] an *ex parte* order can, if necessary, be made by the duty judge over the telephone. The defendant is entitled to attend the hearing if he learns of the application. He can either take no part, or he can take another role, albeit without the benefit of any, or any adequate, supporting affidavit evidence.[16]

Duty judge

Due to the potentially draconian effects of an injunction, an early return date will normally be fixed at the *ex parte* hearing. Usually this *inter partes* hearing will be no later than seven days after the initial order has been made. In cases of delay, or where the terms of the injunction are particularly severe, provision will be made in the order for the terms to be varied or discharged before the return date on the giving of a prescribed period of notice[17] by the defendant to the plaintiff. However, the absence of such notice does not prevent the court from discharging the injunction in the rare case when this is found to be appropriate.[18]

Provision for delay

An injunction is binding upon the defendant from the moment upon which he is notified of its contents, whether by telephone, telegram or otherwise.[19] The order must, of course, be endorsed with a penal notice.[20]

Effect

The question of costs is always reserved to the *inter partes* hearing, discussed below.

Inter partes hearing   Prior to any hearing *inter partes*, the defendant must have been served with a copy of the motion or summons and supporting affidavit or affidavits at least two clear days before the return date.[21] In addition the writ, if only generally endorsed, should have been issued if not actually served on the defendant. Usually all these documents will have been served together. The defendant should, of course, have prepared and sworn affidavits answering the plaintiff's case.

Where the hearing *inter partes* is on the return date of an *ex*

---

[13] Jurisdiction is neither confirmed nor excluded by locality; and the hearing may be conducted at the judge's private residence (see, generally, *St Edmundsbury and Ipswich Diocesan Board of Finance* v. *Clarke* [1973] Ch. 323).

[14] A master or district registrar may only grant an injunction by consent of the parties (R.S.C. Ord. 32, r. 11(2)).

[15] Namely, as to the issue of proceedings and the drawing, service and filing of the material order, affidavits, etc.

[16] See *Pickwick International Inc. (GB) Ltd.* v. *Multiple Sound Distributors* [1972] 1 W.L.R. 1213.

[17] Usually either 24 hours or 48 hours notice.

[18] See *London City Agency (JCD) Ltd.* v. *Lee* [1970] Ch. 597 and *W.E.A. Records Ltd.* v. *Visions Channel 4 Ltd.* [1983] 1 W.L.R. 721.

[19] See R.S.C. Ord. 45, r. 7(6).

[20] See Practice Note 45/7/6.

[21] See in High Court R.S.C. Ord. 8, r. 2(2) (Motions) and R.S.C. Ord. 32, r. 3 (Summons) and in county court C.C.R. Ord. 13, r. 2. See Appendix for following Precedents: HC5, HC6, and CC2—Draft Summonses; HC7, CC4, and CC5—Draft Orders; HC9, HC10—Penal Notices.

Discharge of *ex parte* order *parte* order, the court has an inherent jurisdiction to discharge the earlier order even though the parties concerned have not entered an appearance and have not themselves applied for the injunction to be discharged.[22]

Where there is a direct conflict of fact which makes it inappropriate for a decision to be made on affidavit alone, the plaintiff can apply in the Chancery Division for the motion or **Standing over** summons to be "stood over for trial" on terms.[23] This practice has become a matter of some controversy since it may allow the plaintiff to go on a "fishing expedition" without having to abandon his application.[24] The alternative course is for the court to adjourn the matter for further affidavit evidence to be filed.

Speedy trial Equally, the nature of the case may warrant an early trial. Where the court makes such an order under R.S.C. Ord. 29, r. 5 it is required to direct the plan and mode of trial at the same time.[25]

Directions The other major benefit resulting from an interlocutory injunction is the opportunity to obtain immediate directions under R.S.C. Ord. 29, r. 7 for the further conduct of the action.

Undertakings While an undertaking is technically voluntary, amounting to a concession that the plaintiff is likely to obtain his injunction, in reality it has the same effect as an injunction[26] to **Penal notice** the extent that the order should have a penal notice endorsed upon it to be enforceable by committal.[27] The plaintiff is not obliged to accept the offer of an undertaking and can insist on an injunction.[28] However, it is not good practice for the order to declare that the plaintiff is entitled to an injunction in the terms of the undertaking.[29] The plaintiff must ensure that such terms have been carefully and properly worded,[30] since he cannot reopen his application for an interlocutory injunction, save where

[22] See *Harbottle Mercantile Ltd.* v. *National Westminster Bank Ltd.* [1978] Q.B. 146.

[23] See, *e.g. Société Française* v. *Electronic Concepts Ltd.* [1976] 1 W.L.R. 51.

[24] *e.g. Pictograph Ltd.* v. *Lee-Smith Photomechanics* [1964] 1 W.L.R. 402.

[25] In Q.B.D. see Practice Direction [1958] 3 All E.R. 678. In Ch.D. see Practice Directions [1974] 1 All E.R. 1039 and [1979] 1 All E.R. 364. For Specimen Order see Appendix (HC8).

[26] See *Biba Ltd.* v. *Stratford Investments Ltd.* [1973] Ch. 281 (a director who has neither aided nor abetted a contempt can be liable under Ord. 45, r. 5 for breach by his company of its undertaking to abstain, given to the court and embodied in a written order—equivalent to an injunction).

[27] In *Hussain* v. *Hussain* [1986] Fam. 134 the Court of Appeal took the view that R.S.C. Ord. 29 does not apply to undertakings and it is the undertaking and not the order which requires the giver to act in accordance with its terms. However, as a matter of general practice a penal notice should be endorsed on the order; and its absence may provide good mitigating grounds. See Appendix for Specimen Penal Notices (HC9, HC10 and CC4).

[28] *Oliver* v. *Dickin* [1936] 2 All E.R. 1004.

[29] *S.* v. *S.* (1980) 10 Fam. Law 153 (such a declaration would be "meaningless").

[30] To ensure enforcement the following steps should be taken: (1) the undertaking should be included as a recital or preamble to an order of the court; (2) the order incorporating the undertaking should be issued and served on the person who gave it; (3) the order should be indorsed with a suitably worded notice explaining the consequences of a breach of the undertaking, *per* Neill L.J. in *Hussain* v. *Hussain* above. See Appendix, Precedent CC5 for Draft Order incorporating undertaking (but *no* Penal Notice).

a breach occurs, simply because the defendant's undertaking does not give adequate protection before trial.[31]

Mandatory injunctions Although the court has jurisdiction to grant a mandatory injunction upon an interlocutory application,[32] including a mandatory *quia timet* injunction, it will

Requirements for grant

do so only if it can be shown that: (a) there is a proven probability of damage, and (b) there is an immediate means by which remedial steps can be effected to restore the plaintiff's property.[33] It must also be established that there is every likelihood that a similar injunction will be granted at trial.[34] The terms of the order must be expressed in such a form that the person against

Terms of order

whom it is made knows exactly what he has to do,[35] for example, the execution of specific works to prevent further deterioration of the plaintiff's property, the restoration of a staircase,[36] or the demolition of part of a building put up after the defendant learned that a writ had been issued.[37] If the defendant fails to carry out the works within the necessary time, the plaintiff, without prejudice to the court's powers of committal,[38] can seek leave of the court under R.S.C. Ord. 45, r. 8 to have the works carried out at the expense of the defendant.[39]

Costs At the hearing *inter partes* the following orders for costs[40] may be sought by or against the plaintiff:

(1) plaintiff's costs in any event;
(2) defendant's costs in any event;
(3) plaintiff's costs in the cause;
(4) defendant's costs in the cause;
(5) costs in the cause;
(6) costs reserved;
(7) no order as to costs.

Suspending the injunction Where the plaintiff has proved his right to the injunction but there may be difficulties in removing the injury immediately, for example, the reinstatement of land[41]

Purpose

is involved, the court may suspend the operation of the

---

[31] *e.g. GCT (Management) Ltd.* v. *Laurie Marsh Group Ltd.* [1972] F.S.R. 519; [1973] C.L.Y. 3325.

[32] See *Bonner* v. *G.W. Railway* (1883) 24 Ch.D. 1 and *Canadian Pacific Railway* v. *Gaud* [1949] 2 K.B. 239 ("a very exceptional form of relief").

[33] *Hooper* v. *Rogers* [1975] Ch. 43 (damages in lieu awarded).

[34] See *Shepherd Homes Ltd.* v. *Sandham* [1971] Ch. 340.

[35] See *Redland Bricks Ltd.* v. *Morris* [1970] A.C. 652. For specimen wording, see first recital in Appendix, Precedent HC8.

[36] *Allport* v. *The Securities Corporation* (1895) 64 L.J. Ch. 491.

[37] *Daniel* v. *Ferguson* [1891] 2 Ch. 27; *Von Joel* v. *Hornsey* [1895] 2 Ch. 774.

[38] Namely, under R.S.C., Ord. 45, r. 5.

[39] See *Mortimer* v. *Wilson* (1885) 33 W.R. 927 (failure to carry out an undertaking).

[40] And see generally new R.S.C. Ord. 62, r. 3.

[41] See *Charrington* v. *Simons & Co.* [1971] 1 W.L.R. 598 where the suspension of a mandatory injunction for three years to enable the defendants to carry out ameliorative works was reversed on appeal as such works amounted to acts of trespass and interfered with the plaintiff's farming operations; but if the plaintiff's consent was not forthcoming then the injunctions would be discharged. For example, in dispute over a right of way see *Jameson* v. *Manley*, September 4, 1986 (C.A.T. No. 779); [1987] 10 C.L. 256.

injunction for a period.[42] Equally, a short period of suspension may be required to give the defendant the opportunity to cease his activities,[43] or to allow certain works to be completed.[44] As an alternative, the court may make no order but grant the plaintiff liberty to apply for an injunction after a certain period if it is thought that the problem will disappear, but the plaintiff may well have to establish that fresh circumstances have arisen to justify the subsequent imposition of an injunction after the trial has been concluded.

Even after an order has been made, the defendant is at liberty to apply for an injunction, but not an undertaking,[45] to be suspended. Such a situation may arise if there has been a change in the defendant's circumstances, in which event his application should be made to the trial judge.[46]

Discharge An interlocutory injunction may be discharged at any time prior to trial on the application of the defendant. It is for this reason that the expression "until trial or further order" is **Grounds for** used. Possible grounds for discharge are:
discharge

(1) if the injunction has become oppressive[47];
(2) where the terms of any order have not been fulfilled by the plaintiff[48];
(3) where the law has been changed or clarified by an appeal in a court since the injunction was granted,[49] but not if it was made by consent[50];
(4) if the plaintiff fails to proceed expeditiously with the substance of the action[51]; and
(5) where there has been a change of circumstances since the interim order was made.[52]

Whilst the court will not vary an undertaking once given, it

---

[42] *Att.-Gen.* v. *Colney Hatch Lunatic Asylum* (1868) 4 Ch.App. 146; *Stollmeyer* v. *Petroleum Development Co. Ltd.* [1918] A.C. 498n.

[43] *Lotus Ltd.* v. *British Soda Co. Ltd.* [1972] Ch. 123.

[44] *e.g. Woollerton Hinton Ltd.* v. *Richard Costain Ltd.* [1970] 1 All E.R. 483 (injunction granted to restrain trespass by crane but suspended for 12 months to allow for completion of the building works); but contrary approach taken in *Trenberth* v. *National Westminster Bank Ltd.* (1979) 39 P. & C.R. 104 where suspension was refused although the defendants were obliged to carry out works on the plaintiff's land, for which purpose they had erected scaffolding on it.

[45] See *Chanel Ltd.* v. *F.W. Woolworth* [1981] 1 W.L.R. 485.

[46] See *Shelfer* v. *City of London Electric Lighting Co.* (1895) 2 Ch. 388.

[47] This ground will usually arise when a *Mareva* injunction has been sought freezing assets; but in the context of this work it could arise where, *e.g.* excessive time restrictions are placed on building operations or the use of a way.

[48] *Spanish General Agency Corporation* v. *Spanish Corporation Ltd.* (1890) 63 L.T. 161.

[49] *Regent Oil Co.* v. *J.T. Leavesley Ltd.* [1966] 1 W.L.R. 1210.

[50] See *Chanel Ltd.* v. *F.W. Woolworth* above.

[51] *e.g.* by failing to serve the statement of claim (see R.S.C. Ord. 19, r. 1); default in discovery (R.S.C. Ord. 24, r. 16(1)); default in taking out summons for directions (R.S.C. Ord. 25, r. 4); default in setting down (R.S.C. Ord. 34, r. 2). For questions concerning "want of prosecution" generally, see Practice Note 25/1/5.

[52] *Ushers Brewery Ltd.* v. *P.S. King & Co. Ltd.* [1972] Ch. 148.

Release from undertaking may release the party giving it if sufficient reason[53] is shown but not simply as a result of a change in the law.[54] To be effective, the application for release must be supported by evidence.[55]

Inquiry as to damages Where an interlocutory injunction is discharged the defendant is entitled to enforce the plaintiff's **Defendant's losses** undertaking. The assessment of his losses is known as an "inquiry as to damages." It cannot be ordered until either the plaintiff's case has failed on its merits at trial or it has been established, before trial, that the injunction should not have been granted in the first place,[56] for example, where the plaintiff discontinues the action,[57] or it is established that an *ex parte* order was improperly obtained leading to its discharge at the hearing *inter partes*,[58] or where the injunction is discharged on appeal,[59] but not if a change in circumstances leads to its discharge.[60]

An inquiry will be refused if the damage allegedly suffered by the defendant appears to be trivial, or if there has been excessive delay in the making of the application.[61]

County court Within the general ancillary jurisdiction of the county court under section 38 of the County Courts Act 1984, the **Power** power is given to grant interlocutory injunctions on the same basis as in the High Court.

C.C.R. Ord. 13, r. 6 provides as follows:

"(1) An application for the grant of an injunction may be made by any party to an action or matter before or after the trial or hearing, whether or not a claim for the injunction was included in that party's particulars of claim, originating application, petition, counterclaim or third party notice, as the case may be.

(2) Rule 1(6) shall not apply and, unless the registrar has power under any other provision of these rules to grant the injunction, the application shall be made to the judge.

(3) Where the applicant is the plaintiff and the case is one of urgency, the application may be made *ex parte* on affidavit but, except as aforesaid, the application must be made on notice, and in any case the affidavit or notice must state the terms of the injunction applied for.

(4) The plaintiff may not make an application before the issue of the summons, originating application or petition by which the action or matter is to be commenced except where the case is one of urgency and in that case.

[53] See *Cutler* v. *Wandsworth Stadium Ltd.* (1945) 172 L.T. 207 (application to vary terms of undertaking as being too wide refused).
[54] See *Chanel Ltd.* v. *F.W. Woolworth* above. Where a motion or summons seeking an interlocutory injunction is adjourned generally upon the defendant giving undertakings, there is no restriction on his right to seek their discharge but this will only be the case where the motion is adjourned *generally* rather than stood over until trial of the action. (See *Butt* v. *Butt* [1987] 1 W.L.R. 1351, explaining and distinguishing *Chanel* v. *Woolworth*.
[55] See *Cutler* above.
[56] See *Ushers Brewery Ltd.* v. *P.S. King & Co. Ltd.* above.
[57] *Newcomen* v. *Coulsen* (1878) 7 Ch.D. 764.
[58] *Ross* v. *Buxton* [1888] W.N. 55.
[59] *Hubbard* v. *Vosper* [1972] 2 Q.B. 84.
[60] *Ushers Brewery Ltd.* v. *P.S. King & Co. Ltd.* above.
[61] *Smith* v. *Day* (1882) 21 Ch.D. 421.

(a) the affidavit on which the application is made shall show that the action or matter is one which the court to which the application is made has jurisdiction to hear and determine, and

(b) the injunction applied for shall, if granted, be on terms providing for the issue of the summons, originating application or petition in the court granting the application and on such other terms, if any, as the court thinks fit.

(5) Unless otherwise directed, every application not made *ex parte* shall be heard in open court.

(6) Except where the case is one of urgency, a draft of the injunction shall be prepared beforehand by the party making an application to the judge under paragraph (1) and, if the application is granted, the draft shall be submitted to the judge by whom the application was heard and shall be settled by him.

(7) The injunction, when settled, shall be forwarded to the proper office for filing."

Except in matrimonial matters, interlocutory applications are normally heard in open court rather than in chambers.[62]

Permanent injunctions

Procedure   A plaintiff is entitled to seek a permanent injunction under R.S.C. Ord. 14, but not under C.C.R. Ord. 9, r. 14. However, he must have an exceptionally strong case[63] since the application is for final judgment, albeit on a summary basis. In view of the Master's inability to grant an injunction save by consent,[64] the summons must be issued directly to, and heard by, the judge in chambers.[65] In the Chancery Division the summons will also be made returnable to the judge,[66] but unless there is a need for speed the plaintiff should apply by way of motion.[67]

Summary judgment

A plaintiff is not permitted to obtain an injunction by way of an application for judgment in default of appearance[68] unless he abandons his claim for the injunction. In such circumstances the plaintiff should file an affidavit proving due service of the writ and then proceed with the action as if the defendant had acknowledged service as set out by R.S.C. Ord. 13, r. 6(1).

Default of appearance

Where no defence is served the plaintiff should apply to the judge[69] for judgment in default of defence. This order is discretionary,[70] and the judge will determine the application

Default of defence

---

[62] Practice Direction (Interlocutory Applications: Chambers) [1974] 2 All E.R. 1119 and C.C.R. Ord. 47, r. 8(4). See Appendix for Precedents CC2 to CC5.
[63] See *Shell Mex & B.P. Ltd.* v. *Manchester Garages Ltd.* [1971] 1 W.L.R. 612.
[64] See R.S.C. Ord. 32, r. 11(1)(*d*).
[65] See *Shell Mex* above.
[66] See *Practice Direction (Chancery: Applications and Change of Name)* [1984] 1 All E.R. 720.
[67] *Sony Corporation* v. *Anand (No. 2)* [1982] F.S.R. 200; [1982] C.L.Y. 447.
[68] See generally Practice Note 13/6/1.
[69] In Q.B.D. by summons. In Ch.D. on motion.
[70] See *Wallersteiner* v. *Moir* [1974] 1 W.L.R. 991.

solely on the pleadings[71] in the action. Accordingly, as a matter of good practice it is prudent to ensure that the statement of claim errs on the side of maximum detail when a permanent injunction is sought in the prayer for relief, since neither oral nor affidavit evidence[72] will be admissible.

Damages in lieu

Final judgment The court has a general power to award damages in lieu of an injunction even when no separate claim has been made, although in practice damages will usually be pleaded as part of the prayer for relief following the presumption in law that damages should normally be an adequate permanent remedy.[73] Consequently, where the wrongdoing has ceased and there is no likelihood of any continuing recurrence, a permanent injunction will generally be refused.[74] Whilst the public interest, if relevant, must be considered, the plaintiff's rights will prevail if substantial damage is likely to continue in the absence of such a restraint.[75] Questions of convenience do not, however, arise where the defendant is in breach of covenant upon the basis that the court is merely sanctioning the parties' contractual rights and duties[76] and, arguably, the enforcement of restrictive covenants on a permanent basis[77] (but only where adequate compensation cannot be found in damages).

General damages

In the absence of proof of any special damages, a plaintiff will not normally recover general damages beyond a nominal amount in addition to an injunction where that relief is the real remedy in the action, for example, where the action concerns nuisance by noise or vibration.[78]

Liberty to apply

Alternative additional remedies It is sometimes the case that a permanent mandatory injunction may be required in addition to certain declarations and damages. Certain matters, such as the use of a right of way to maintain a right of access, can be dealt with effectively by the making of a declaration,[79] coupled with liberty to apply for an injunction if this should prove necessary.[80] In the case of breach of a declaratory order (without the express sanction of an injunction) the plaintiff will have to seek such an injunction to enforce the order since the defendant's refusal to comply does not, of itself, amount to contempt of court.[81]

---

[71] See *Smith* v. *Buchan* (1888) 58 L.T. 710; *Young* v. *Thomas* [1892] 2 Ch. 134.
[72] This includes any affidavit evidence filed in connection with interlocutory applications. The cost of any affidavits in support of the default application will be disallowed (see *Jones* v. *Harris* (1887) 55 L.T. 884).
[73] See p. 172 above.
[74] *Proctor* v. *Bayley* (1889) 42 Ch.D. 390; *Pride of Derby and Derbyshire Angling Association Ltd.* v. *British Celanese Ltd.* [1953] Ch. 149.
[75] See *Kennaway* v. *Thompson* [1981] Q.B. 88 (restriction of use of lake by speedboats).
[76] See *Doherty* v. *Allman* (1878) 3 App.Cas. 709, though in fact the breach of covenant could not be sanctioned by injunction as it was ameliorating waste.
[77] See *Hampstead & Suburban Properties Ltd.* v. *Diomedous* [1969] 1 Ch. 248.
[78] See *Lipman* v. *George Pullman & Sons Ltd.* (1904) 91 L.T. 132; *Gilling* v. *Grey* (1910) 27 T.L.R. 39.
[79] *e.g.* that a party should not use the right of way in such a manner as to cause substantial interference with its use by the other party.
[80] See *Jelbert* v. *Davis* [1968] 1 W.L.R. 589.
[81] *Webster* v. *Southwark LBC* [1983] Q.B. 698.

Committal for contempt

High Court　Although the power to commit is rarely invoked in the type of litigation considered in this book the following aspects of procedure may be helpful.

Power　R.S.C. Ord. 45, r. 5(1) states:

"Where—
(a) a person required by a judgment or order to do an act within a time specified in the judgment or order refuses or neglects to do it within that time or, as the case may be, within that time as expanded or abridged under Order 3, rule 5, or
(b) a person disobeys a judgment or order requiring him to abstain from doing an act,

then subject to the provisions of these rules, the judgment or order may be enforced by one or more of the following means, that is to say—
(i) with the leave of the court, a writ of sequestration against the property of that person;
(ii) when that person is a body corporate, with the leave of the court, a writ of sequestration against the property of any director or other officer of the body;
(iii) subject to the provisions of the Debtors Acts 1869, and 1878, an order of committal against that person or, where that person is a body corporate, against any such officer."

It is a prerequisite for enforcement by way of committal that the terms of the order have been brought to the attention of the **Procedure**　defendant by one of the following means, specified by R.S.C. Ord. 45, r. 7:

(1) by personal service[82] with a copy of the judgment or order containing the injunction endorsed with a penal notice,[83] together with any order extending or abridging the time for the required act to be done under Ord. 3, r. 5[84]; failing which, in the case of prohibitory orders only
(2) by the court being satisfied that the person against whom, or against whose property, it is sought to enforce the order has had notice thereof, either
(a) by being present when the order was made, or
(b) by being notified of the terms of the order whether by telephone, telegram or otherwise,

pending personal service of the order.

Procedure　All applications for committal in the High Court must be made by notice of motion[85] stating the date and place of

---

[82] This is obligatory in the case of mandatory injunctions. For the court's powers to order substituted service see R.S.C. Ord. 65, r. 4. Under R.S.C. Ord. 45, r. 7(7), and without prejudice to such powers, the court may dispense with service if it thinks it is just to do so.

[83] For the position with regard to undertakings see *Hussain* v. *Hussain* [1986] Fam. 134 and p. 175 above.

[84] See R.S.C. Ord. 45, r. 7(5).

[85] See R.S.C. Ord. 52, r. 4(1). For Draft Notice of Motion see Appendix Precedent HC11.

Personal service the hearing, the grounds of the application and accompanied by affidavit.[86] These documents must also be personally served on the person sought to be committed; the attendance at the hearing of the contemnor will not, of itself, waive the necessity of service.[87] If the initial hearing is adjourned, notice of the date of any new hearing must also be personally served on the contemnor.[88] The grounds of the application must be clearly set out in the notice of motion, in order that the contemnor is fully aware of the breaches alleged and can meet them at the hearing, either orally or on affidavit. As with most High Court

Notice applications, at least two clear working days' notice must be given between the date of service and the date of the hearing.[89]

Since committal for contempt forms part of the High Court's quasi-criminal jurisdiction, the hearing must take place in open court unless the exceptions set out in R.S.C. Ord. 52, r. 6(1) apply.[90] The criminal standard of proof will apply.[90a] Except with leave of the court, the applicant may not rely upon any grounds other than those set out in the notice of motion,[91] and the evidence given must be sufficient to prove the breach.[92] It is advisable that all deponents of the affidavits in support of the application should attend court for the purpose of

Oral evidence cross-examination.[93] The contemnor is also entitled to give oral evidence on his own behalf should be wish so to do.[94] If time permits, an affidavit in reply will usually be prepared on his behalf.

Should the contemnor fail to attend the hearing, a new date will have to be fixed.[95] The court will only make an order for

Ex parte orders committal _ex parte_[96] in exceptional circumstances, for example, when a flagrant breach has occurred and a further breach is threatened.[97]

Scope of the power As a general rule of policy, the court will not immediately commit the contemnor to prison unless the breach is so deliberate that no alternative course can be taken.[98]

First hearing Certainly at a first hearing the court is likely to suspend the

---

[86] R.S.C. Ord. 52, r. 4(2). For comparable powers to dispense with personal service see sub-rule 4(4), _e.g._ where the contemnor can be proved to be evading service.

[87] _Mander_ v. _Falcke_ [1891] 3 Ch. 488.

[88] See _Chiltern District Council_ v. _Keene_ [1985] 1 W.L.R. 619 and also _Phonographic Performance Ltd._ v. _Tsang_ (1985) L.S.Gaz. 2331.

[89] See _Chiltern D.C._ v. _Keene_ above and also _Williams_ v. _Fawcett_ [1986] Q.B. 604.

[90] _e.g._ cases involving children, secret processes, national security, mental disorder or in the interests of the administration of justice.

[90a] See _Dean_ v. _Dean_ [1987] 1 F.L.R. 517.

[91] R.S.C. Ord. 52, r. 6(3).

[92] See _Churchman_ v. _Joint Shop Stewards' Committee of the Port of London_ [1972] 3 All E.R. 603 at 608.

[93] See Practice Note 38/2/3 and _Comet Products U.K. Ltd._ v. _Hawkex Plastics Ltd._ [1971] 2 Q.B. 67. See also _Aslam_ v. _Singh, The Times,_ June 12, 1986, where defendant denied opportunity to cross-examine plaintiff's witnesses.

[94] R.S.C. Ord. 52, r. 4.

[95] For requirements of personal service of this order see n. 82 above at p. 181.

[96] See R.S.C. Ord. 90, r. 30(4).

[97] See _Warwick Corporation_ v. _Russell_ [1964] 1 W.L.R. 613 where a circus owner had broken into and entered the Corporation's land and set up tents, intending to give performances on the following two days.

[98] _e.g._ in _Warwick Corporation_ v. _Russell_ above; see also _O'Donovan_ v. _O'Donovan_ [1955] 1 W.L.R. 1086 (threat to remove child from jurisdiction).

execution of the committal order for a period of time or on specified terms.[99] The court will continue to retain its discretion to do whatever is just in the circumstances even when the order becomes operative as a result of the contemnor's failure to comply with a condition of that order.[1]

Since the court's powers arise from its inherent jurisdiction to enforce its own orders, the court will not be fettered by any concurrent criminal proceedings arising from the same set of facts, and the Court of Appeal have now stated that since contempt proceedings should be dealt with swiftly and decisively, the court should not adjourn them until any pending criminal proceedings have been concluded.[2]

Imprisonment

Sentencing By section 14 of the Contempt of Court Act 1981, the court can commit a contemnor to prison for a fixed period not exceeding two years. It can only pass sentence on one occasion and cannot impose a more severe sentence at a later date unless evidence of further breaches is adduced.[3] However, it has the power not only to suspend the initial term but also to impose consecutive sentences in respect of separate contempts.[4]

Particulars of the contempt

Terms of order The order must conform with the oral judgment of the court.[5] It should recite with sufficient particularity what has been proved against the contemnor[6] in terms of the evidence that has been adduced of the breach. In this regard the particulars of the contempt must not contain references to matters not comprised in the supporting affidavits, since the contemnor will have had no notice of such matters.[7] If the defect is more than an "insignificant" or "quite trivial" one, the order will not be upheld.[8] Moreover, a second valid order cannot be substituted for one that is initially defective,[9] nor by the warrant of committal. However, where the application is not in the proper form, the court has jurisdiction to entertain a further application in order that matters may be put right.[10]

Execution of the order

The committal order is usually executed by the tipstaff, failing which, by the usher or some other official to whom the order of the court is addressed. Their authority arises from a

[99] See R.S.C. Ord. 52, r. 7(U). Where execution is suspended the applicant must, unless the court otherwise directs, serve on the contemnor a notice informing him of the making and terms of the order under sub-note 7(1) (see sub-note 7(2)). In the case of a breach of declaratory order it is not a contempt if the party affected refuses to comply so the applicant must seek an injunction to enforce the order (see *Webster* v. *Southwark L.B.C.* [1983] Q.B. 698).
[1] *Re W (B) (An Infant)* [1969] 2 Ch. 50.
[2] *Szczepanski* v. *Szczepanski* [1985] F.L.R. 468; *Caprice* v. *Boswell* (1986) 16 Fam.Law 52.
[3] *Lamb* v. *Lamb* (1984) 14 Fam.Law 60.
[4] *e.g. Lee* v. *Walker* [1985] Q.B. 1191.
[5] *Re C (A Minor) (Wardship: Contempt)* [1986] 1 F.L.R. 578.
[6] *McIlraith* v. *Grady* [1968] 1 Q.B. 468; *Chiltern D.C.* v. *Keene* above; *Williams* v. *Fawcett* above; and *Nguyen* v. *Phung* (1985) 15 Fam.Law 54. For Draft Order see Appendix, Precedent HC12.
[7] *Tabone* v. *Seguna* [1986] 1 F.L.R. 591; see also *Nguyen* v. *Phung* above.
[8] See *Burrows* v. *Iqbal* (1985) 15 Fam.Law 188 (failure to specify the precise dates of the breaches and the contemnor present in court for hearing).
[9] See *Smith* v. *Smith* (1983) 133 New L.J. 234; *Hegarty* v. *O'Sullivan* (1985) 135 New L.J. 557.
[10] See *Jelson (Estates) Ltd.* v. *Harvey* [1984] 1 All E.R. 12 where alleged breaches had not been set out in sufficient detail.

warrant signed by the judge or one of the other judges at the court where the order was made. If the contemnor is present in court, the tipstaff will take him to prison immediately.[11] If he is absent, the tipstaff will arrest him either at his known address or through the local police, who will hold him in the cells at the police station until the tipstaff arrives to convey him to the prison specified in the warrant.[11a]

Remission   Where a contemnor is detained in prison for a stated term of more than five days he is eligible for up to one-third remission of the term of imprisonment, provided that the actual period served is not reduced below five days.[12]

Discharge   The court may, on the application of any person committed to prison for any contempt of court, discharge him. Such an application is made on motion and should, where practicable, be made to the judge who made the committal order. The contemnor will usually be released from prison if the court is **Purging the** satisfied that he has sufficiently "purged his contempt," in other **contempt** words, if his disobedience has been sufficiently punished and it is clear that further imprisonment will not secure any greater compliance.[13]

Appeal   The Court of Appeal has the power to reverse or vary the committal order or to make any other order, including releasing the contemnor on bail, as may be just.[13a] The appeal can be made without leave of the court. The normal practice is to hear appeals as expeditiously as possible, usually within one or two days of setting down.

Sequestration   Because of its recent topicality, readers should **Nature of remedy** be aware that a writ of sequestration is a means by which a judgment or order requiring an act to be done, for example, payment of money or costs or delivery of goods or documents, can be enforced against real property. Under R.S.C. Ord. 46, r. 5, leave to issue the writ must be obtained from the court on motion supported by affidavit evidence. Personal service of these documents should be effected.[14]

Effect   The writ will bind both real[15] and personal[16] property in the possession of the contemnor from the time that it is issued.[17] Until registered, it will not create a charge on land.[18] The property sequestered may be applied to meet the applicant's demand. However, an order for sale will be required from the court, and all money recovered will have either to be paid into court[19] or otherwise accounted for fully. The applicant will be entitled to his costs out of the fund.[20]

---

[11] See Practice Note 52/7/2.
[11a] In London, Brixton or Holloway according to sex (see Practice Note 52/7/2).
[12] Prison Rules 1964, rr. 5(1) and 63(3) (as amended 1981).
[13] *Re Barrell Enterprises* [1972] 3 All E.R. 631.
[13a] See R.S.C. Ord. 59, r. 20 and Practice Note 59/20/1.
[14] R.S.C. Ord. 46, r. 5(3).
[15] *Re Lush* (1870) L.R. 10, *e.g.* 442; and the rents and profits thereof.
[16] *e.g.* pensions and bank balances (see, *e.g. Guerrine* v. *Guerrine* [1959] 1 W.L.R. 760; *Eckman* v. *Midland Bank Ltd.* [1973] Q.B. 519).
[17] *Dixon* v. *Rowe* (1876) 35 L.T. 548.
[18] Land Charges Act 1972, s.6.
[19] *e.g. Miller* v. *Huddlestone* (1882) 22 Ch.D. 233.
[20] *Etherington* v. *Big Blow Gold Mines* [1897] W.N. 21.

Discharge A discharge may be obtained on motion or summons. The order will direct the sequestrators ("commissioners") to withdraw from possession. Any balance after all costs have been met will be paid to the contemnor.

This procedure is rarely used against an individual defendant nowadays, and will normally be utilised when, for example, an overseas company has assets within the jurisdiction,[21] or when, as recently, a recalcitrant trade union has repeatedly broken court orders.[22]

Fine R.S.C. Ord. 52, r. 9 preserves the inherent power of the court[23] to impose a fine, or to seek security for good behaviour as a result of a contempt of court. Today such a remedy tends to be adopted as an alternative to sequestration,[24] or when a person has misbehaved in court or refused to attend to give evidence,[25] rather than as a means of enforcing an injunction. Payment of the fine may be enforced, upon order of the court, in like manner to either a judgment for the payment of money in the High Court, or a fine imposed by the Crown Court.

Alternative remedy

County court The provisions of C.C.R. Ord. 29, r. 1 are as follows:

"1. (1) Where a person required by a judgment or order to do an act refuses or neglects to do it within the time fixed by the judgment or order or any subsequent order, or where a person disobeys a judgment or order requiring him to abstain from doing an act, then, subject to the Debtors Acts 1869 and 1878 and to the provisions of these rules, the judgment or order may be enforced, by order of the judge, by a committal order against that person or, if that person is a body corporate, against any director or other officer of the body.

(2) Subject to paragraphs (6) and (7) a judgment or order shall not be enforced under paragraph (1) unless—

(a) a copy of the judgment or order has been served personally on the person required to do or abstain from doing the act in question and also, where that person is a body corporate, on the director or other officer of the body against whom a committal order is sought, and

(b) in the case of a judgment or order requiring a person to do an act, the copy has been so served before the expiration of the time within which he was required to do the act and was accompanied by a copy of any order, made between the date of the judgment or order and the date of service, fixing that time.

---

[21] *e.g. Hospital for Sick Children* v. *Walt Disney Productions Inc.* [1968] Ch. 52.

[22] *e.g. Reed (Richard) Transport* v. *National Union of Mineworkers (South Wales Area), The Times,* March 1985 (application to end sequestration after end of strike).

[23] See *Phonographic Performance Ltd.* v. *Amusement Caterers (Peckham) Ltd.* [1963] 3 All E.R. 493 at 497, *per* Cross J. For Draft Order for Payment of a Fine see Appendix, Precedent HC13.

[24] See, *e.g. Steiner Products Ltd.* v. *Willy Steiner Ltd.* [1966] 1 W.L.R. 986 where sequestration would adversely affect the livelihood of innocent parties.

[25] See also R.S.C. Ord. 39, r. 5 for additional remedy in costs.

(3) Where a judgment or order enforceable by committal order under paragraph (1) has been given or made, the proper officer shall, if the judgment or order is in the nature of an injunction, at the time when the judgment or order is drawn up, and in any other case on the request of the judgment creditor, issue a copy of the judgment or order, indorsed with or incorporating a notice as to the consequences of disobedience, for service in accordance with paragraph (2).

(4) If the person served with the judgment or order fails to obey it, the proper officer shall, at the request of the judgment creditor, issue a notice calling on that person to show cause why a committal order should not be made against him, and subject to paragraph (7) the notice shall be served on him personally.

(5) If a committal order is made, the order shall be for the issue of a warrant of committal and a copy of the order shall be served on the person to be committed either before or at the time of the execution of the warrant unless the judge otherwise orders.

(6) A judgment or order requiring a person to abstain from doing an act may be enforced under paragraph (1) notwithstanding that service of a copy of the judgment or order has not been effected in accordance with paragraph (2) if the judge is satisfied that, pending such service, the person against whom it is sought to enforce the judgment or order has had notice thereof either—

    (a) by being present when the judgment or order was given or made, or

    (b) by being notified of the terms of the judgment or order whether by telephone, telegram or otherwise.

(7) Without prejudice to its powers under Order 7, rule 8, the court may dispense with service of a copy of a judgment or order under paragraph (2) or a notice to show cause under paragraph (4) if the court thinks it just to do so."

Notice to show cause

Draft notice

The principal difference from procedure in the High Court is the requirement to issue the "notice to show cause" under C.C.R. Ord. 29, r. 4.[26] This is dealt with by the court officer at the written request[26a] of the applicant. The notice itself[27] must set out the grounds of the application with the same degree of particularity[28] as is expected in the High Court. Because of a succession of appeal decisions in recent years highlighting bureaucratic errors,[29] it is advisable to submit a draft notice which need only be sealed by the court office before service is effected. While C.C.R. Ord. 29 makes no specific reference to the need to serve supporting affidavit evidence it is now the invariable practice, as well as a matter of prudence, to ensure that

[26] See Appendix, Precedent CC6.
[26a] No prescribed form is given for this request. See Appendix Precedent CC7.
[27] County Court Form N. 78 and Precedent CC6.
[28] See, *e.g. Williams* v. *Fawcett* [1986] Q.B. 604 (detailing the requirements for a valid Form N. 78).
[29] In *Williams* v. *Fawcett* above the Court of Appeal held that it was undesirable for the notice (a) to be addressed to the registrar or proper officer (in addition to the contemnor) and (b) to be signed by the applicant's solicitors.

any affidavits upon which reliance will be placed at the hearing are served at this stage, if only to save the costs of further service.[30] The court can dispense with the formalities of service of the judgment or order and the notice to show cause if it thinks it just to do so.[31] The hearing must be in open court and the applicant should attend with his witnesses.

Sentencing

Scope of the power   Under section 14 of the Contempt of Court Act 1981[32] the county court is treated as a "superior court." The judge's powers of sentencing are limited to a fixed period of imprisonment not exceeding two years. In addition, his powers under section 14 allow him to impose a fine on the same occasion.[33] A county court judge's jurisdiction to commit for contempt is restricted to cases of contempt in the face of the court or disobedience to an order of the court.[34] Accordingly, where a judge found the defendant in contempt for supplying to two newspapers information prejudicial both to the plaintiff and to the judge, it was held that the judge had no jurisdiction to order the defendant to pay the plaintiff's costs in the absence of any intervention by the Attorney-General or of an application of the plaintiff to the divisional court pursuant to R.S.C. Ord. 82, r. 2.[34a]

Discharge

Under C.C.R. Ord. 29, r. 3(1),[35] where the committal arises out of an act of disobedience, an application for discharge[36] should be made to the court in writing attested by the governor of the prison (or any other officer of the prison not below the rank of principal officer). This should be served not less than one day before the hearing on the other party at whose instance the warrant or order was issued. The hearing will take place before a judge.[37]

Trial

Documents

Setting down bundles   In the High Court it is an express requirement of the setting down procedure[37a] that two bundles of documentation are lodged, containing the writ, the pleadings (including any affidavits ordered to stand as pleadings), any request or order for particulars and the particulars given, any orders made on the summons for directions and any requisite

---

[30] See C.C.R. Ord. 20, rr. 5–7 for use of affidavit evidence.
[31] See C.C.R. Ord. 29, r. 1(7).
[32] As amended by the County Court (Penalties for Contempt) Act 1983.
[33] *i.e.* on the same basis as in the High Court (see p. 185 above).
[34] See *Bush* v. *Green* [1985] 1 W.L.R. 1143.
[34a] *Ibid.*
[35] An exception is made in the case of committals under C.C.R. Ord. 27, r. 8 (failure to obey an order to attend an adjournal hearing. An application for an attachment of earnings order and a judgment summons) and Ord. 28, r. 4 (committal under s.5 of the Debtors Act 1869).
[36] Sub-rule 3(3) as that this application does not preclude any application for discharge by the Official Solicitor.
[37] With leave of the judge it can take place before the Registrar (sub-rule 3(2)).
[37a] R.S.C. Ord. 34, r. 3(1).

"Working bundle" legal aid documents. At least one bundle will be put before the judge. However, it has become a growing practice for a "working bundle"[38] of the essential pleadings to be lodged with the court before trial. This will usually assist the plaintiff's counsel when opening the case and during trial of the action.

In the county court no setting down bundle is required, presumably because all the material pleadings or orders are to be found in the court file. Nonetheless, where there have been **Lengthy pleadings** lengthy pleadings, adoption of the foregoing practice may well assist with the orderly management of the action.

Expert reports If copies have not been filed with the court at the time of disclosure it is, once again, helpful to lodge a bundle of both parties' reports, whether their contents are agreed or not.[38a] Clearly, where there is a dispute as to the contents of a report (*e.g.* where one party has been late in effecting disclosure and has not sought leave to extend the time for service) this practice should be avoided. In ordinary circumstances, the trial judge will obviously welcome the opportunity to read these reports prior to the trial which, in turn, is bound to save court time and costs.

Evidential bundles It is a matter for the parties how many bundles should be put before the court, and in what form they are prepared and laid out. As a rule of thumb, a minimum of four sets will be required, including photographs, *i.e.* one each for the judge and the witness box and two for the parties' counsel, or one each for each side's "team" of counsel and instructing solicitor. Whilst a degree of latitude still remains in practice (*e.g.* as to the use of ring-bound loose-leaf files) the spirit of the Lord Chief Justice's Practice Direction of July 21, 1983[39] should always be borne in mind as to legibility, pagination and chronology. Where bundles comprising more than 100 pages occur,[39a] it is the responsibility of the solicitors for all parties to prepare and agree one additional bundle containing the principal documents to which the parties will refer (including, in particular, the documents referred to in the pleadings). This bundle should be lodged with the court at least two days before the date fixed for hearing. As a matter of good practice, particularly concerning the average county court action, prior lodgement should always take place in order to save time and costs.

Content of bundles Three misconceptions often arise as to the content of the bundles. In the first instance, a bundle should only contain those documents upon which the respective parties wish to rely at trial to prove their case. Secondly, copies of documents can and should where possible be agreed "as documents" to save time even if their contents are disputed. Clearly, if the authenticity of

---

[38] This should be suitably bound and paginated. This is now the practice in the Official Referees Court (see generally Practice Note 36/1–9/12 *et seq.*).

[38a] See R.S.C. Ord. 38, r. 37 (direction as to disclosure) and Ord. 38, r. 38 (direction as to "without prejudice" meeting of experts and joint statement as to matters of agreement.

[39] [1983] 1 W.L.R. 922 and see p. 164 above; whilst it is the duty of the plaintiff to prepare the court bundles usually the parties' solicitors will work in consultation to ensure common pagination. From the foregoing it follows that the plaintiff has the ultimate say as to presentation.

[39a] See Practice Direction of 1983 para. 15.

a document is disputed, or where surprise is required as a necessary part of cross-examination, this practice cannot be adhered to. Where no agreement can be reached, it is better, for the purposes of presentation and accessibility, that a separate paginated bundle is prepared.[40] The same practice should be adopted with regard to material inter-solicitor correspondence concerning some point of procedure or the issue of costs.[41]

Thirdly, a bundle may sometimes contain "without prejudice" correspondence. As a matter of law, a "without prejudice" qualification does not, of itself, conclusively or automatically make the particular document privileged.[42] It will, however, extend to all documents so marked which form part of negotiations made with a view to compromising a claim to be made by one party against the other, whether or not proceedings between the parties have commenced. Where a "without prejudice" qualification has been introduced into correspondence it will not be removed automatically by the absence of such qualification from any or all subsequent letters until such time as the correspondence is either expressly made open again,[43] or this interpretation of events can be made by necessary implication.[44] In the ordinary course of events, it is, prima facie, for the party who initiated the use of the qualification to waive it. The contents of an agreement reached in "without prejudice" correspondence are admissible.[45] Finally, as a general rule of practice the court will usually be entitled to see the documents and decide on the issue of admissibility itself wherever a dispute arises.[46]

"Without prejudice" documents

Evidence

This is discussed above at pages 11–13.[46a]

---

[40] Clearly, if one party (or the court) requires the original (or its copy) to have an exhibit number then this practice will not be necessary.

[41] See *Cutts* v. *Head* [1984] Ch. 290 where the Court of Appeal endorsed the *Calderbank* type of reservation as to costs, in the event of settlement proposals not being agreed, in "without prejudice" correspondence in a non-matrimonial civil action. See also C.C.R. Ord. 12, r. 10 for formal written offers "without prejudice save as to costs" introduced by the County Court (Amendment) Rules 1986 (S.I. 1986 No. 636) and Practice Note 22/1/6. In effect, the settlement offer is made "without prejudice" but subject to an express reservation of the right to refer to the letter on the issue of costs should the action proceed to judgment (*Calderbank* v. *Calderbank* is reported in [1976] Fam. 93).

[42] See *South Shropshire District Council* v. *Amos* [1986] 1 W.L.R. 1271 disapproving *Norwich Union Life Insurance Society* v. *Tony Waller Ltd.* (1984) 128 S.J. 300.

[43] *e.g.* by the words "open letter."

[44] See *Sherbrooke* v. *Dipple* (1980) 124 S.J. 345 and *Cohen* v. *Nessdale Ltd.* [1982] 2 All E.R. 97 (cases concerning "subject to contract" correspondence where a break had occurred in negotiations).

[45] See *Tomlin* v. *Standard Telephones & Cables* [1969] 1 W.L.R. 1378, following *Walker* v. *Wilshire* (1889) 23 Q.B.D. 335.

[46] See also *South Shropshire D.C.* v. *Amos* above.

[46a] See also R.S.C. Ord. 38, r. 2A for exchange of witnesses statements, at present, in any cause or matter proceeding in the Chancery Division, the Commercial Court, the Admiralty Court or on Official Referees' Business. For content and form of statements see Practice Notes 38/2A/7 and 38/2A/8. The right of cross-examination is preserved under R.S.C. Ord. 38, r. 1. See also Practice Note 38/2A/11 for direction of trial judge as to presentation of such evidence in chief.

Judgments and orders

Records

In the High Court, whilst an official transcript[47] of the judgment as recorded by the shorthand writer or the mechanical recording department can be obtained, it is the successful party who draws up the order.[48] In the county court the opposite applies.[49] The parties must record the judgment but the order will be drawn up by the court.

Settlements

By contrast with matrimonial cases, where the court has overriding powers to review[50] the terms of any settlement, an ordinary civil court will not interfere with any agreement reached between the parties unless it is manifestly clear that what is proposed is outside the jurisdiction of the court; for it follows that if the parties wish to have such an agreement made in the form of a court order, which is usually to be preferred for reasons of enforcement, the terms must be capable of implementation. Any draft order should be signed and dated by the parties' counsel or solicitors and/or (if appropriate) by the parties themselves. Additional terms or matters falling outside the ambit of the order itself are usually and more appropriately dealt with in

Memorandum

a separate memorandum, frequently endorsed on counsel's backsheets. In order to avoid later misunderstanding as to interpretation, it is advisable not only to have photocopies taken of any draft order, but also of such memorandum if it is of any significant length. The court office will usually provide such a service on this occasion if on no other.

Appeal

The following time limits apply for the issuing of the notice of appeal.

High Court

Master to judge in chambers   Five days under R.S.C. Ord. 58, r. 1(3) with two days' notice prior to the hearing.

District registrar to judge in chambers   Seven days under R.S.C. Ord. 58, r. 3(1) with three days' notice prior to the hearing.

Judge in chambers (or at trial) to Court of Appeal   Four weeks under R.S.C. Ord. 59, r. 4(1).[51]

---

[47] See R.S.C. Ord. 68.

[48] See R.S.C. Ord. 42, r. 5a (Q.B.D.) and Ord. 42, r. 6 (Ch.D.) (Orders).

[49] See County Courts Act 1984, s.80. The prior consent of the judge should be sought if a shorthand note is taken of the evidence (see *Neil* v. *Harland and Wolff Ltd.* (1949) 82 Ll.L.Rep. 515), and the judgment in *Bruen* v. *Bruce* [1959] 2 All E.R. 375.

[50] See, *e.g.* s.33A(1) of the Matrimonial Causes Act 1973.

[51] Under s.18(1)(*f*) of the Supreme Court Act 1981 leave is required for appeals on the question of costs only or from interlocutory judgments or orders (except injunctions) see Practice Note 59/1/12.

County court

Registrar to judge   Five days for an interlocutory order under C.C.R. Ord. 13, r. 11.[52] Fourteen days for a final order or judgment under C.C.R. Ord. 37, r. 6(2).

Judge to Court of Appeal   Four weeks under R.S.C. Ord. 59, r. 4(1).[53]

---

[52] The hearing on this occasion is *de novo*.
[53] See generally s.77 of the County Courts Act 1984. Leave is required where the claim (or counter-claim if larger) is for an amount not exceeding one-half of the County Court monetary limits (see above) or where the judge has been acting in appellate capacity or costs (see County Courts Appeals Order 1981 and Supreme Court Act 1981, s.18).

APPENDIX: PRECEDENTS

High Court

HC1: General indorsement on writ claiming declaration of title, injunctions and damages [High Court]

IN THE HIGH COURT OF JUSTICE   19 _____ B No. _____

[CHANCERY *or* QUEEN'S BENCH] DIVISION

[_____ DISTRICT REGISTRY]

BETWEEN:

AB

and

BB   *Plaintiffs*

—and—

CD & COMPANY

LIMITED   *Defendants*

The Plaintiffs' claim is for:

(1) A declaration that the Plaintiffs are the freehold owners of the strip of land lying between the Plaintiffs' dwelling-house situated and known as [address] and the Defendants' factory premises situated at [address];

(2) An injunction to restrain the Defendants, whether by themselves or by their directors, officers, servants or agents [or contractors] or otherwise howsoever from trespassing on the said strip of land by passing over and along it and by building upon it;

(3) An order that the Defendants do forthwith pull down, demolish and/or remove so much of the concrete roadway and wire fence [recently erected] [in the course of construction] on the said strip of land;

(4) Damages;

(5) Interest thereon pursuant to Section 35A of the Supreme Court Act 1981.

HC2: Statement of claim against local authority, as adjoining owner, in tree roots case [High Court]

IN THE HIGH COURT OF JUSTICE   19 _____ C No. _____

QUEEN'S BENCH DIVISION

(Writ issued the _____ day of _____ 19____)

BETWEEN:

	BC	*Plaintiffs*
	CC	
	and	
	XYZ DISTRICT COUNCIL	*Defendant*

STATEMENT OF CLAIM

1. The Plaintiffs are and were at all material times the owners and occupiers of a house and land situated and known as [address].
2. The Defendant is and was, at all material times, the local highway authority in whom the said road has been vested for the purposes of the Highways Act 1980.
3. On the verge of the said road at a distance of between 11 feet and 30 feet from the boundary of the Plaintiffs' land have grown three plane trees, the roots of which have extended and still extend under the Plaintiff's said land and house.
4. Since about the month of   19 , at which time the Plaintiffs first discovered the presence of the said roots, the foundations of the Plaintiffs' said house have been undermined by the said roots and/or the action of the said roots has led to the withdrawal of moisture from soil under the said foundations.
5. By reason of the matters aforesaid the Plaintiffs' house has been damaged in consequence of which the Plaintiffs have suffered loss and damage.

Particulars of Special Damage

(i) Underpinning and structural repair   £_____
(ii) Works of redecoration   £_____
(iii) Trial excavation   £_____
(iv) Consultants Fees   £_____
_____ (inclusive of VAT)

Particulars of Trouble and Inconvenience
[Please State]

6. By reason of the foregoing the said roots constitute a nuisance caused or permitted by the Defendant.
7. Further or in the alternative and by reason of the foregoing the Defendant is in breach of its statutory duty under section 96(6) of the Highways Act 1980 in that they have allowed the said trees to remain in such a situation as to be a nuisance or injurious to the Plaintiffs as the owners or occupiers of the premises adjacent to the highway.
8. In the yet further alternative the Defendant has been negligent by failing to take any or any adequate steps to remove the said trees and/or to retard their growth when it knew or ought to have known that the said trees were likely to cause damage to the Plaintiffs' property.

9. By a letter dated   19   ,the Plaintiffs, by the solicitors acting on their behalf, have requested the Defendant to cut down the said trees or otherwise prevent them continuing the damage to the Plaintiffs' house but the Defendant has refused so to do and intend to continue the said nuisance.

10. Pursuant to Section 35A of the Supreme Court Act 1981 the Plaintiffs are entitled to, and claim herein, interest on the amount found to be due at such rates and for such period as the Court may think fit.

AND the Plaintiff claims:

(i) An injunction to restrain the Defendants from allowing the roots from any of the said trees within the curtilage of the said highway known as   so to encroach on to the Plaintiff's said land as to cause a nuisance;

(ii) Damages;

(iii) The said interest thereon pursuant to section 35A of the Supreme Court Act 1981.

SERVED, etc.

HC3: Intended affidavit for *ex parte* injunction before issue of writ [High Court]

IN THE HIGH COURT OF JUSTICE   19 _____ B. No. _____

QUEEN'S BENCH DIVISION

[_____ DISTRICT REGISTRY]

IN THE MATTER OF SECTION 37 OF THE SUPREME COURT ACT 1981

AND IN THE MATTER OF ORDER 29, RULE 1 OF THE RULES OF THE SUPREME COURT

AND IN THE MATTER OF AN INTENDED ACTION

BETWEEN:

AB	*Intended Plaintiff*
and	
(1) CD	*Intended*
(2) EF	*Defendants*

I, GH, a Solicitor of the Supreme Court, of
[and a partner in the firm of   of the same address] MAKE OATH and SAY as follows:

1. I have the conduct of this matter on behalf of the intended Plaintiff and I am duly authorised to make this affidavit on his behalf in support of the application herein for an injunction from continuing the works of construction of which complaint is made in paragraphs 4 and 5 below.

2. The intended Plaintiff AB intends to commence an action

by issuing a writ out of this Honourable Court against the intended Defendants for a declaration, injunction and damages arising out of the construction of an extension to the dwelling-house of the Intended First Defendant by the Intended Second Defendant over an area of land within the freehold ownership of the Intended Plaintiff, as appears from the draft writ of summons, a copy of which is now shown to me, marked "GH/1."

3. [Set out the facts giving rise to the intended action].
4. [Set out the facts giving rise to the claim for an interlocutory injunction].
5. [Set out the facts justifying the application for an *ex parte* order].
6. [State whether any notice has been given to the Intended Defendant of the proposed application and exhibiting any relevant correspondence].
7. [State, if relevant, the Intended Defendant's counter-assertions and emphasise the merits of the case of the Intended Plaintiff].
8. [Set out the precise relief sought by exhibiting a copy of the draft minute].

Sworn by the said G.H.
at
this   day of   19
Before me,

A Solicitor empowered to Administer Oaths

This Affidavit is filed on behalf of AB, the Intended Plaintiff.

HC4: Draft minute of order for *ex parte* injunction before issue of writ [High Court]

[Title of Action]

Before The Honourable Mr. Justice _____ in Chambers on _____ day, the _____ day of _____,
19 _____
Upon hearing [Mr. _____], Counsel for the Intended Plaintiff

And upon reading the [draft] affidavit [proposed to be] sworn by GH and the exhibits thereto [and the draft writ of summons in the intended action] and the draft minute of order sought
And upon the said Intended Plaintiff, by his counsel, undertaking:

(1) To abide by an order that the Court may make as to damages in case the Court shall hereafter be of the opinion that the Intended Defendant shall have sustained any by reason of this order which the Plaintiff ought to pay;
(2) To issue a writ of summons [in the form of the said draft writ of summons] [forthwith] [as soon as practicable] [by noon]/4.00 p.m. on   day, the
day of   19   ];
(3) [To procure the said GH to [swear] [make and file] an affi-

davit] [in or substantially in the terms of the said draft affi-
davit(s)] [deposing to the facts stated/alleged by counsel
for the intended plaintiff];

(4) To inform the Intended Defendant forthwith of the terms
of this order [by telemessage or telex] and to serve upon
him as soon as practicable a copy of the exhibits thereto
together with a copy of this order;

(5) To notify the Intended Defendant [and any person upon
whom notice of this order is served] at the time of service
of his right, if so advised, to apply [on notice] to discharge
or vary the order.

IT IS ORDERED AND DIRECTED:

1. That the Defendant be restrained and an injunction is
hereby granted restraining him, whether by himself or by
his servants or agents or otherwise, from excavating or
removing any soil or other material howsoever from the
foundations of the Plaintiff's dwelling-house or from the
strip of land adjoining adjacent thereto [until after
the hearing of a summons to continue this injunction
returnable on   , the   day of
19   ] [until the   day of   19   ] or
until further order.

2. That there be liberty to apply to discharge or vary this
order on [24/48] hours' notice in the meantime.

3. That the costs of this application be reserved.

DATED the   day of   19

HC5: Summons to continue *ex parte* injunction [High Court]

[Title]

LET ALL PARTIES concerned attend the Judge in Chambers
[at Room No.   , Royal Courts of Justice, Strand, London,
WC2A 2LL] [sitting at The Law Courts,   , in the
County of   ] on   day, the
day of   19   at   o'clock on the hearing of an application on the part of the Plaintiff for an order that
the injunction granted herein by the Honourable Mr. Justice
          on the   day of   ,
19   restraining the Defendant by himself, his servants or agents
or otherwise from trespassing on the Plaintiff's land at [address]
whether in exercise of an alleged right of way or otherwise be continued until after the trial of this action or until further order, and
that the costs of this application and of the application made by
the Plaintiff on the   day of   19   be
[costs in the cause] [the Plaintiff's in any event].

DATED the   day of   , 19

This Summons was taken out by LM & Co. of   ,
Solicitors for the Plaintiff.
To the Defendant and NP & Co. of   his Solici-
tors.

HC6: Summons for interlocutory injunction [High Court

[Title]

LET ALL PARTIES, etc. on the hearing of an application by the Plaintiff for an order that the Defendants, whether by themselves, or by their directors, officers, servants or agents howsoever be restrained and that an injunction be granted restraining them from using or permitting to be used in or upon a site at [address] pneumatic drills, mechanical concrete mixers, mechanical excavators and dumper trucks so as to cause a nuisance by noise to the Plaintiff save between the following hours, namely,

(1) 7.30 a.m. and 12.30 p.m., 2.00 p.m. and 6.00 p.m. on Mondays to Fridays;
(2) 8.00 a.m. and 1.00 p.m. on Saturdays
until after the trial of this action, or until further order, and that the costs of this application be costs in the cause.

DATED, etc.

HC7: Order for interlocutory injunction [High Court]

[Title, etc.]

Upon hearing Counsel for the Plaintiff and the Defendants, and upon reading the affidavits of   and filed herein
And the Plaintiff by his Counsel undertaking to abide by any order the Court may make as to damages, in case the Court shall hereafter be of the opinion that the Defendants shall have sustained any by reason of this order which the Plaintiff ought to pay.

IT IS ORDERED AND DIRECTED that the Defendants and each of them, whether by themselves or by either [or any] of them or by their or his [her] servants or agents or otherwise howsoever be restrained from [playing or permitting to be played any gramophone records or tape recordings on the Defendants' premises at   ] [causing or permitting any noise to emanate from the Defendants' premises at   , or within the curtilage thereof whether by radio, record player, tape recorder, or television between the hours of 10 p.m. until 8.00 a.m. each day] so as to cause a nuisance to the Plaintiff or any other occupier of the Plaintiff's house until after the trial of this action or until further order.

AND IT IS ORDERED [set out any other directions given by the Judge, *e.g.* service of pleadings, a certificate for a speedy trial] and that the costs of the application be [costs in the cause] [reserved to the Judge at the trial].

DATED, etc.

HC8: Order for speedy trial where injunction not granted [High Court]

[Title, etc.]

Upon hearing, etc.
And upon reading, etc.
And upon the Plaintiff's application for an order that the Defendant do forthwith execute the temporary repairs to the boundary wall separating the Plaintiff's property at   from the Defendant's property at   specified in the report of   dated   within   weeks from the date hereof pending the trial of this action or until further order.
NO order is made on the said application save that there be a certificate for speedy trial.

AND IT IS ORDERED [set out the directions given by the Judge as to pleadings or as to the affidavits which are to stand as pleadings, discovery and inspection, place and mode of trial, estimated duration, listing category, and setting down] and that application to fix the date of trial be made to the Clerk of the Lists within seven days of setting down.

And that the costs of this application be costs in the cause.

DATED, etc.

HC9: Penal notice for indorsement on a judgment or order requiring a party to abstain from doing some specified act [High Court]

If you, the within-named RS disobey this [judgment] [order] you will be liable to process of execution for the purpose of compelling you to obey the same.

HC10: Penal notice for indorsement on a judgment or order requiring a party to do a specified act [High Court]

If you, the within-named TW, neglect to obey this [judgment] [order] within the time specified therein, you will be liable to process of execution for the purpose of compelling you to obey the same.

HC11: Notice of motion for an order committal [High Court]

[Title]

And In The Matter of An Application of behalf of XX against YZ for an Order of Committal.

TAKE NOTICE that the Court will be moved before [one of the Judges of the High Court] [the Honourable Mr. Justice   ] sitting at   on   day, the   day of 19   at   o'clock in the   noon [or so soon thereafter as counsel can be heard] by counsel on behalf of the Plaintiff XX for an Order:

1. That the Defendant herein, YZ, be committed to Her Majesty's Prison for his contempt of Court in continuing to be and remain upon the Plaintiff's land in breach of the injunction made by the order of the Honourable Mr. Justice   dated   day of   , 19   ;

2. That the Defendant do pay to the Plaintiff the costs of and incidental to this application and the order to be made thereon;

3. That such further or other order may be made as the Court shall deem proper.

AND FURTHER TAKE NOTICE that the applicant herein, the Plaintiff XX, intends to read and use in support of this application the affidavits of AB sworn [filed herein] the day of   19   and of CD sworn [filed herein] the   day of   19   , and the exhibits thereto respectively, true copies of which affidavits and exhibits are served herewith together with this notice of motion.

DATED, etc.

HC12: Order of committal to prison [High Court]

[Title, etc.]

Upon motion this day made to this Court by Counsel for the Plaintiff

And upon reading the affidavit of XX filed the   day of   19   and the affidavit of EF filed the   day of   19   of service on the Defendant YZ of a copy of the Order of the Court dated the   day of   19   and of notice of this motion

AND IT APPEARING to the satisfaction of the Court that the Defendant YZ has been guilty of contempt of Court in that between   day, the   day of

19   and   day,   the   day   of
          19   he remained on the Plaintiff's land in breach
of the Order of the Honourable Mr. Justice
dated the   day of   19

IT IS ORDERED that for his said contempt the Defendant do
stand committed to Her Majesty's Prison at   to
be there imprisoned for a period of   [days/weeks/
months] from the date hereof.

IT IS FURTHER ORDERED that this Order shall not be
executed if the Defendant YZ complies with the following terms,
namely,

DATED, etc.

HC13: Order for payment of a fine [High Court]

[Title, etc.]

Upon motion, etc.
And it appearing to the satisfaction of the Court that the Defendant GG has been guilty of contempt of court in that

IT IS ORDERED that for his said contempt the Defendant do
[forthwith] [within   days of this date] pay into court
a fine in the sum of £

DATED, etc.

HC14: Notice of application for leave to serve interrogatories in Queens Bench Division [High Court]

[Title]

TAKE NOTICE, etc. on the hearing of an application on the part
of the Plaintiff that the Plaintiff be at liberty to serve on the
Defendant interrogatories in writing, a copy of which is served
herewith, and that the Defendant [by its secretary or other proper
officer] do within [14] days answer the said interrogatories in writing by affidavit [by letter] and that the costs of and relating to this
application be costs in the cause.

DATED, etc.

HC15: General form of interrogatories

[Title]

INTERROGATORIES

On behalf of the above-named Plaintiff for the examination of the above-named Defendant pursuant to the Order herein dated the
      day of   , 19

   1. Look at Document No. 52 (all documents referred to in these interrogatories are those exhibited to the Defendant's Affidavit dated   in answer to the Plaintiff's application for specific discovery);
      (a) Have you or your agents had any correspondence since   19   with the   District Council or its employees other than the correspondence so far disclosed, relating to the development and/or use of the premises?
      (b) If so, what correspondence?
   2. (a) Have you or your agents had any discussions with the   District Council or its employees relating to the aforesaid development and/or use?
      (b) If so, do you or your agents have any notes or memoranda of such discussions?
      (c) If the answer to the last Interrogatory be yes, what notes or memoranda?
   3. (a) What has happened to the drawings referred to in Document No. 14?
      (b) Why have they not been disclosed?

SERVED, etc.

HC16: General form of answer to interrogatories

[Title]

ANSWER

Of the above-named Defendant, AB, for his examination by the above-named Plaintiff pursuant to the Order herein dated the
      day of   19

In answer to the said Interrogatories I, AB, the above-named Defendant, MAKE OATH and say as follows:
   1. In answer to the First Interrogatory, namely:

   "1. (a) Did you write the letter dated   19   referred to in paragraph 3 of the Statement of Claim.

    (b) If the answer is yes,
        (i) when did you write it?
        (ii) where was it written?
        (iii) by whom was it delivered?
    (c) If the answer is no,
        (i) who wrote the letter?
        (ii) was it written (a) with your authority and/or (b) at your direction?
    If the answer to Interrogatories 1(a) and 1(c) is no,
        (i) when did you become aware that the letter had been written?
        (ii) when did you become aware of its contents?"

Answer:

  (a) Yes.
  (b)(i) the   day of   19 ;
    (ii) at my home;
    (iii) my gardener, Adam Saltheath.

  2. In answer to the Second Interrogatory, namely:

"2. Do you or your agents have any drafts, notes or memoranda relating to the proposals referred to in Document No. 37?"

Answer:

    No, nothing beyond that already disclosed.

  3. In answer to the Third Interrogatory, namely:

"3. (i) What correspondence (other than that so far disclosed) have you or your agents had with,
      (a) The Home and Colonial Insurance Company Limited;
      (b) Their loss adjusters;
  (ii) Please produce copies of all such correspondence if the answer is yes.
  (iii) What other personal knowledge do you have of the progress of the claim?"

Answer:

I object to answering this Interrogatory on the following grounds:

  (i) That the further documents now sought by the Plaintiff are privileged, being information procured by my solicitors and their agents and received by me from them since this action was begun for the purposes of assisting me in the defence of it;
  (ii) That all information I have received in respect of the said insurance claim after   19 has been derived by me from information obtained by my solicitors and their agents in consequence of which I have no personal knowledge of the matters now inquired about.

Sworn, etc.

CC1: Particulars of claim claiming declaration of title, prescriptive rights, injunction and damages [county court]

IN THE _____ COUNTY COURT

Case No.

BETWEEN:

AB   *Plaintiff*

—and—

(1) CD
(2) ED (his wife)
(3) EG
(4) HJ
(5) KJ   *Defendants*

PARTICULARS OF CLAIM

1. At all material times the Plaintiff and her predecessors in title have been seised in fee simple of certain land and a house situate and known as Little Puddlemarsh, Upper Gurney, in the County of Wessex ("The blue land" hereafter) coloured blue on the map annexed hereto, access to which has been gained by a right of way over the roadway marked in brown on the said map ("the roadway") hereafter).

2. The First and Second Defendants are the current owners of a house and certain lands known as Gurney Manor, Upper Gurney, aforesaid, which land is edged in red where the same is crossed by the roadway ("the red section" hereafter) between the points marked A and B and B and C on the said map.

3. The Third Defendant is the current owner of the area of land edged in green where the same is crossed by the roadway ("the green section" hereafter) between the points marked C and D and D and E on the said map.

4. The Fourth and Fifth Defendants have at all material times also asserted rights of ownership over the green section in their capacity as adjoining land owners to the blue land, the full nature and extent of which is unknown to the Plaintiff at present and are also owners of the area of land cross-hatched in green on the said map.

5. The Plaintiff and her predecessors in title, whose estate the Plaintiff now has in the blue land, have continuously from time immemorial enjoyed openly and as of right a way of foot and with animals, wagons, carts, carriages and all other vehicles from the Plaintiff's land over the Defendants' respective lands to the public highway at Upper Gurney, coloured yellow on the said map, and at all times of the year for the more convenient occupation of the blue land and as appurtenant thereto.

6. Further, or alternatively, for a long time, namely for 20 years and upwards before this action, the Plaintiff and her predecessors in title of the blue land have by virtue of a deed and/or deeds of grant made unto them by the pre-

decessors in title of the Defendants who were seised in fee simple of the lands, the estate of which each of the Defendants now has (but which deed and/or deeds have since been lost or destroyed by accident) enjoyed the following rights in and over the Defendants' said lands, namely a right of way on foot and with animals, wagons, carts, carriages and all other vehicles to the said public highway at Upper Gurney at all times of the year for the more convenient occupation of the blue land and as appurtenant thereto.

7. Further, or alternatively, and in respect of the red section the Plaintiff will rely at trial upon an express grant of a right of way over the roadway through the lands numbered 707, 708 and 745 on the said map to pass and repass with or without horses, carts, wagons and carriages as contained in a Conveyance dated 22nd December 1929 made between (1) Charles James Mucklow and (2) George Carter and Henry Carter.

8. Further, or alternatively, the Plaintiff and her predecessors in title of the blue land and the several occupiers of the said lands thereof have for the full periods of 20 and 40 years respectively next preceding the commencement of this action enjoyed as of right and without interruption the said right of way referred to in paragraphs 1 and 5 hereof.

9. From time to time since in or about 1985 the Fourth and Fifth Defendants have caused and permitted their livestock to trespass on to the Plaintiff's said lands and to graze thereon without her permission and have caused damage thereby.

PARTICULARS

These will be supplied in Schedule form [in due course] OR [as soon as they can be fully quantified] OR [upon discovery].

10. The net annual value of the blue land for rating purposes is less than £1,000.

And the Plaintiff claims:
As against the First and Second Defendants

(i) A declaration that the Plaintiff is entitled to a right of way along the roadway between the points marked A and B and B and C on the said map and coloured brown thereon for herself, her servants and licensees on foot and with or without horses or other animals, wagons, carts, carriages and all other vehicles (including motor vehicles, tractors, and other conveyances) at all times and for all purposes; and/or

(ii) A declaration that the Plaintiff is entitled to use the said right as a legal right under section 2 of the Prescription Act 1832 and as appertaining to the said house and land known as Little Puddlemarsh, Upper Gurney, aforesaid; alternatively

(iii) A declaration that the Plaintiff is entitled to use the said right as having been enjoyed by her and the possessors of the said lands for the time being through which she claims from time immemorial and by virtue of a grant by deed made by all necessary parties which has been accidentally lost or destroyed.

As Against the Third Defendant and/or the Fourth and Fifth Defendants

(iv) A declaration that the Plaintiff is entitled to a right of way along the roadway between the points marked C and D on the said map and coloured brown thereon for herself, her servants and licensees on foot and with or without horses or other animals, wagons, carts, carriages, and all other vehicles (including motor vehicles, tractors and other conveyances) at all times and for all purposes; and/or

(v) A declaration that the Plaintiff is entitled to use the said right as a legal right under Section 2 of the Prescription Act 1832 and as appertaining to the said house and land known as Little Puddlemarsh aforesaid; alternatively

(vi) A declaration that the Plaintiff is entitled to use the said right as having been enjoyed by her and the possessors of the said lands for the time being through which she claims from time immemorial and by virtue of a grant by deed made by all necessary parties which has been accidentally lost or destroyed.

As against the Fourth and Fifth Defendants only

(vii) An injunction restraining them, by themselves, their servants, or agents or otherwise from causing or permitting livestock to trespass into and upon the Plaintiff's land known as Little Puddlemarsh, aforesaid;

(viii) Damages limited to £5,000;

(ix) Interest thereon pursuant to section 69 of the County Courts Act 1984 at such rate and for such period as the Court thinks fit.

DATED, etc.

CC2: Notice of application for interlocutory injunction [county court]

[Title of Action]

TAKE NOTICE that the Plaintiffs intend to apply to the Judge sitting at   on   day, the   day of   19   at   o'clock for an injunction [to restrain the Defendant until judgment in this action or further order from doing, whether by himself or by his servants or agents or otherwise howsoever, the following act, namely, trespassing on the Plaintiff's land at   by erecting or continuing to erect thereon a garden shed or other building] OR [in the terms of the draft Order annexed hereto].

The grounds for this application are set out in the attached affidavit.

DATED this _____ day of _____ 19____

....
KL & Co. of _____
Solicitors for the Plaintiff

To the Registrar of the Court
And to the Defendant

CC3: Affidavit supporting application for interlocutory injunction [county court]

Party : Plaintiffs
Deponent : N— M—
Affidavit : 1st
Sworn :

[Title]

I, NM, of   , MAKE OATH and say as follows:

1. I have been employed by the Plaintiffs and their predecessors in title   Limited for some
        years and currently as their Property Manager
   for East Anglia.
2. I am duly authorised to make this affidavit in support of
   the Plaintiffs' application for an injunction against the
   Defendant. Where the matters deposed to below are not
   within my own personal knowledge I have drawn the
   necessary information from the Plaintiffs' files.
3. I refer the Court to the Particulars of Claim in this action
   for a brief history of this matter. Where applicable I have
   adopted the same terminology for ease of reference.
4. A copy of the registered title of the Property is now shown
   to me, marked "NM/1," indicating the extent of the Plaintiffs' ownership of the premises in question.
5. The Defendant is a local jobbing builder in this part of
   Suffolk. He lives in a flat close by and, in addition, owns
   what is colloquially known as a "flying freehold" of the
   Upper Area together with such parts of the Flank Areas as
   immediately surround it.
6. Although I was personally aware from   in
   correspondence that the Defendant had plans to reinstate
   the Upper Area it was not until around
   when matters were drawn to my attention by Mr. OP, the
   new tenant of the Property, that the Defendant had vir-
   tually abandoned all work on the Upper Area that I visited
   the property on   . At this time the Defendant
   still had scaffolding erected in the courtyard which was
   becoming an increasing source of inconvenience for Mr.
   OP. A tarpaulin had been used to cover part of the roof
   carcass but no further attempts had been made to make
   the Upper Area wind and watertight.
7. There is now shown to me marked "NM/2" a bundle
   incorporating my initial letter of complaint dated
              and subsequent letters from the Plaintiffs'

solicitors, Messrs. LG & Co., to the Defendant. The court will note that all such correspondence has been one way. The Defendant has to date consistently ignored any attempts to resolve this matter on a practical basis, in consequence of which the Plaintiffs are left with no alternative but to commence these proceedings in view of the escalating damage to the Property.

8. I therefore ask this Honourable Court to grant the relief sought in the notice of application herein and to give directions for an early trial of the action.

Sworn, etc.

This Affidavit is filed on behalf of the Plaintiffs

CC4: Order for interlocutory injunction [county court]

[Title, etc.]

UPON HEARING Counsel for the Plaintiffs and the Solicitor for the Defendants

AND THE PLAINTIFFS undertaking by their Counsel to abide by any Order this Court may make as to damages, in case this Court shall hereafter be of the opinion that the Defendants shall have sustained any by reason of this Order, which the Plaintiffs ought to pay

NOW, THEREFORE, TQ and RS, the Defendants in this Action, by themselves, their servants, agents or otherwise howsoever are hereby strictly enjoined and restrained from carrying on the following acts, namely,

(i) Placing building materials, plant and equipment upon the land marked green, and upon and over the pavement area of the land marked yellow and brown on the plan annexed hereto;

(ii) Causing and/or permitting motor cars, vans and delivery vehicles to be parked on the land marked yellow and brown on the said plan save for the purpose of delivering building materials, plant and equipment to the land marked red on the said plan, such deliveries to take place only at dates and times of which the Defendants shall have given prior written notification not less than one hour before the said delivery at 105 Acacia Avenue, Norbiton, Surrey;

(iii) Causing and/or permitting cement mortar or any other form of building matter, other than dust in the ordinary course of building work, to be deposited upon any vehicle parked upon the land marked green on the said plan;

(iv) Erecting and/or continuing to erect the cavity wall, or any part thereof, adjoining and abutting the land marked green on the said plan;

[until the day after the day upon which this Action shall be heard or until further order]

DATED this _____ day of _____ 19_____

....

Judge

To TQ of _____ and RS of _____

TAKE NOTICE that unless you obey the directions contained in this Order, you will be guilty of contempt of Court and will be liable to be committed to prison.

[DATED this _____ day of _____ 19_____]

....

[Registrar]

CC5: Order for interlocutory injunction compromised on basis of an undertaking [county court]

[Title, etc.]

UPON HEARING, etc.
AND UPON the Defendant undertaking on behalf of himself, his servants or agents or otherwise not to permit his lime and poplar trees planted close to the boundary line between the properties of the Plaintiff and the Defendant, as identified in the Particulars of Claim, so to overhang the boundary line as to cause damage to the Plaintiff's garage and to his motor car or causing or permitting the roots of the said trees to encroach on to the Plaintiff's property so as to cause a nuisance to the Plaintiff's property

AND BY CONSENT
IT IS ORDERED:

1. That the Plaintiff's application for injunctions be adjourned generally with liberty to restore;
2. That there be no order as to costs save Legal Aid Taxation of the costs of the Plaintiff pursuant to the Second Schedule of the Legal Aid Act 1974;
3. Certificate for Counsel.

CC6: Committal—notice to show cause [county court]

[Title]

TO WX,
TAKE NOTICE that the Plaintiffs will apply to this Court sitting at   on the   day of
        19   at   o'clock for an order for your committal to prison for having disobeyed the order of this Court made on the   day of   19
restraining you, by yourself, your servants, agents or otherwise from obstructing the Plaintiffs' right of way over the pathway

known as Dingley Dell, Baker's Lane, Stratton, in the County of Wessex on divers occasions during the month of April 19 including the 3rd April 19   between 6.45 and 7 o'clock in the evening and on the 7th April 19   at 8.50 o'clock in the morning.

AND FURTHER TAKE NOTICE that you are required to attend the Court on the first mentioned day to show cause why an order for your committal should not be made.

DATED the   day of   19

Order 7, Rule 2(a)

Case No.

I certify that the notice of which this is a true copy, was served by me on the   day of   19 , on the Defendant personally, [in accordance with an order for substituted service].

Bailiff/Officer of the Court

NOTICE OF NON-SERVICE

I Certify that this notice has not been served for the following reasons:—

Bailiff/Officer of the Court

CC7: Request for issue of notice to show cause [county court]

[Title]

As solicitors for the Plaintiffs we hereby apply for issue of a notice requiring the Defendant to attend Court to show cause why he should not be committed to prison for his contempt in not having obeyed the order of this Court made on the   day of   19   restraining him by himself, his servants, agents or otherwise from obstructing the Plaintiffs' right of way over the pathway known as Dingley Dell, Baker's Lane, Stratton, in the County of Wessex.

DATED the _____ day of _____ 19____

....

Messrs. YZ & Co. of _____
Solicitors for the Plaintiffs

To the Registrar of the Court

CC8: Further and better particulars of the defence [county court]

[Title]

Under Paragraph 2
Of: "In or about July 1987 the Plaintiffs agreed with the Defendant . . ."

1. *REQUEST*:
   Identify all facts and matters upon which reliance will be

placed at trial in support of the assertion that there was a concluded contract between the parties by which the line of the said boundary was so varied and, in particular,

(i) when and where it was so made;
(ii) the name of the party acting or purporting to act, on behalf of the Plaintiffs;
(iii) the form of the said contract:—
    (a) if orally, the words used to form the same;
    (b) if in writing, the document and/or documents constituting it;
(iv) the terms of the said contract.

ANSWER:

(i) During the early evening of 15th July 1987 in the living room of the Defendant's home.
(ii) The First Plaintiff.
(iii) &
(iv) (a) [The Defendant will rely at trial on the following statements the gist of which is as follows:
Defendant: "Isn't it about time that we agreed where the new fence should run?"
First Plaintiff: "Yes"
Defendant: "Do you agree the line of my pegs?"
First Plaintiff: "Yes"] OR

[The Defendant cannot recall the exact words used by the parties but will say at trial that he proposed to the First Plaintiff that they should agree the position of the new fence along the line of pegs laid out by the Defendant. The First Plaintiff agreed with this course of action without reservation]

    (b) None.

Under Paragraph 6
Of " . . . it is admitted that a fire took place on the 28th July 1986 and as a result of the acts of the Defendant's servant or agent . . . "

2. *REQUEST*:
State precisely:
(i) how the fire was allegedly started and by whom
(ii) the distance of the fire initially from the said fence
(iii) the matter of substances being burnt;
(iv) the acts of the Defendant's servant or agent which resulted in the fire; and
(v) whether the Defendant's servant or agent or another supervised the said fire and for what period(s).

ANSWER:
The Defendant contends that this is, in the main, a request for evidence. However he gives the following voluntary particulars:
(i) The fire was started as a bonfire by one AB, the Defendant's gardener.
(ii) It was several feet away from the fence in the usual position in the Defendant's garden at which he normally had bonfires.
(iii) Garden refuse and wood.
(iv) Not entitled.

(v) Not entitled.

Under Paragraph 8
Of: the whole

3. *REQUEST*:
   State precisely all the facts and matters upon which reliance will be placed at trial to maintain:
   (i) that the said fire did not damage the Plaintiffs' property as specified in paragraph 9 of the Defence and Counter-claim.
   (ii) that the Defendant did not allow the said fire to escape thereby causing damage to the Defendant.
   ANSWER:
   Not entitled.

DATED, etc.

CC9: Reply and defence to counterclaim [county court]

[Title]
REPLY

1. The Plaintiff joins issue with the Defendant upon his Defence save in so far as the same consists of express admission and save for the matters hereinafter set out.
2. As to Paragraph 1 and subject to formal proof of title the Plaintiffs admit that the Defendant and the said CC are the joint freehold owners of [address].
3. In the premises the Plaintiff will apply to join the said CC as the Second Defendant in this action.
4. As to paragraph 2 [*etc.*,]
5. Paragraph 4 is denied and the Defendant is put strictly to proof of all matters contained therein.

DEFENCE TO COUNTERCLAIM

6. The Plaintiffs repeat paragraphs 1, 4 and 5 of the Reply.
7. No admissions are made as to Paragraph 8.
8. It is further denied that the Defendant is entitled to the relief sought or any relief.

DATED, etc.

INDEX